IMPERIAL BODIES

IMPERIAL BODIES

Empire and Death in Alexandria, Egypt

SHANA MINKIN

To Brandon— with so much love! Shana Jan 2020

P.S. the book is done— lets all go back to Charleston :)

STANFORD UNIVERSITY PRESS
STANFORD, CALIFORNIA

Stanford University Press
Stanford, California

© 2020 by the Board of Trustees of the Leland Stanford Junior University.
All rights reserved.

No part of this book may be reproduced or transmitted in any form or by any
means, electronic or mechanical, including photocopying and recording, or in any
information storage or retrieval system without the prior written permission of
Stanford University Press.

Printed in the United States of America on acid-free, archival-quality paper

Library of Congress Cataloging-in-Publication Data is available upon request.
ISBN 978-1-5036-0892-4 (cloth)
ISBN 978-1-5036-1050-7 (electronic)

Cover design: Angela Moody
Cover photo: Foreign cemetery, Alexandria. Levantine Heritage Foundation.
Typeset by Motto Publishing Services in 10/14 Minion Pro

For Heiko and Harry

CONTENTS

ACKNOWLEDGMENTS

Writing this book has been a long process. That it is now in print is exhilarating, and I have many, many people to thank in helping me get here. Some of you could fit into many categories, and some of you should be thanked on every page of this book, but I have tried my best to mention you only once in the interest of brevity. Please know that all of you are close to my heart, and for all of you, I am grateful.

I begin with a heartfelt thank you to Kate Wahl and the staff at Stanford University Press. Your generosity with and excitement for this project have kept me working on it even when it felt overwhelming. Thank you for believing in this book. And to the two anonymous reviewers, thank you. Your suggestions have been tremendously helpful and sharpened this book immensely.

The research for this book began during my time in Cairo with the Center for Arabic Studies Abroad, funded by CASA I and II fellowships and a Foreign Language Area Studies yearlong fellowship. The American Center for Research in Egypt funded me for another year in the archives; subsequent research fellowships from the History Department and the Middle Eastern and Islamic Studies Department of New York University, Research Fellowships from Swarthmore College and the University of the South, and funding from the Barclay Ward Fund and the Melon Globalization Forum enabled me to travel to archives in Egypt, France, and Great Britain multiple times. A fellowship at the Center for Women and Work at the University of Massachusetts, Lowell, as well as a sabbatical from the University of the South, proved to be crucial to the writing process.

This has not been an easy story to tell. When I was in Cairo for what was more than a year of research, in 2004–2006, the powers-that-were limited my access to archives, restricting my ability to follow up on certain threads of this story. Multiple attempts over a six-year period to get into the Alexandria municipality archive failed—and ended when I was told, in June 2011, that the archive was within the governorate building that burned down earlier that year. I was rejected that same year when I tried to renew my archival pass to Dar al-watha'iq. With these setbacks, I was forced to be inventive in the paths of research, and multiple archival trips to London and Nantes, combined with what I had already found in the Egyptian archives, have helped me round out this story. The result is, I hope, a unique take on the end of the nineteenth century, reflective of the creativity historians must use to tell our inevitably incomplete histories. To all the archivists who helped me get here, thank you, *merci*, and *shukran*. Your willingness to work with me and share your knowledge was to my great benefit. With all of the generous help I have received along the way, from the many archivists and my generous colleagues, all remaining mistakes in this book are mine and mine alone.

Thank you to the Edinburgh University Press for allowing me to use parts of my chapter "Documenting Death: Inquests and Foreign Belonging in Post-1882 Egypt," published in *The Long 1890s in Egypt: Colonial Quiescence, Subterranean Resistance*, in Chapter 4 of this book. Each chapter of *Imperial Bodies* has been improved greatly from the various conferences, workshops, and junior faculty writing groups at which I presented, and I thank the organizers of each for encouraging my work.

I have been lucky enough to work in three supportive departments. The History Department at Swarthmore College welcomed me when I was an academic naïf, and their commitment to creative teaching and research was the inspiration I needed to morph this work into a book of death studies. I am grateful to all of them, especially to Bruce Dorsey and Bob Weinberg. The History Department of UMass Lowell was another source of inspiration for me, and I am thankful to all of my colleagues there, and especially to Chad Montrie and my all-around mentor and friend Christoph Strobel. Outside my departments, Deina Abdelkader, Brahim el Guabli, Farha Ghannam, Ayse Kaya, and Gwynn Kessler all helped me work through ideas in this book.

In 2015, we made the brilliant decision to move south, and I joined the International and Global Studies faculty at the University of the South. Emmanuel Aseidu-Acquah, Donna Murdock, Nicholas Roberts, Donald Rung, and Ruth Sanchez have been the core of our IGS department since my arrival and are a thoughtful, compassionate team. Everyone in academia should be as fortunate as I have been in finding an academic home. Beyond my department, special thanks go to my Sewanee friends and colleagues Julie Berebitsky, Manuel Chinchilla, Abby Colbert, David Colbert, Leigh Anne Couch,

Mila Dragojevic, Aaron Elrod, Derek Ettensohn, Sandy Glacet, Benjamin King, Andrea Mansker, Jessica Mecellem, Terry Papillon, Tam Parker, Laurie Ramsey, Woody Register, Betsy Sandlin, Elizabeth Skomp, Kelly Whitmer, and Jessica Wohl for engaging with my ideas, answering my many questions, and becoming a personal and professional support system over our years here.

Friends and colleagues outside my institutional homes also patiently answered queries, kept me strictly bound to writing days, listened to me think through tough questions as I worked, challenged me to consider new paths, and helped me locate materials. Some of you are dear friends, and some of you I know only through your work, but all of you have taken the time to help me fine-tune this book in one way or another. Zachary Lockman was my first mentor in this research project, and he remains an intellectual inspiration. Fred Cooper, Khaled Fahmy, Michael Gilsenan, and Lisa Pollard helped nurture this project through its opening stages, as did Emad Abu Ghazi. Lucia Carmanati, Omar Cheta, Brock Cutler, Lerna Ekmecioglu, Dina el Khawaga, Matthew Ellis, Rabab El Mahdi, Aaron Jakes, Hussein Omar, Joshua Schreier, Sarah Stein, and David Todd pointed me to archives, answered detailed questions, helped me with translations, and read sections of this book. Conversations with Charles Anderson, Haytham Bahoora, Orit Bashkin, Zvi Ben Dor, Marni Davis, Jennifer Derr, Sasha Disko, Sarah Dwider, Israel Gershoni, Pascale Ghazaleh, Adam Guerin, Noah Haiduc-Dale, Will Hanley, Jens Hannsen, Martha Hodes, Lauren Kaminsky, Eileen Kane, Hanan Kholoussy, Priya Lal, Tsolin Nalbantian, Dina Ramadan, Naomi Schiller, Sherene Seikaly, Naghmeh Sohrabi, Franny Sullivan, and Jamie Whidden helped me sharpen my arguments or took the work in new directions. Allison Brown and Pamela Haag provided much-needed editorial interventions at different points. Amil Khan housed me more than once in London, as did the inimitable Klara Banaszak, who also volunteered to find missing documents for me at the National Archives. Hossam Bahgat, Rabab El Mahdi, and Sahar Nassar make Cairo one of my homes. Julian Voss and Stefan Zammit provided space and library access for me to work in Germany.

A few colleagues and friends have continually provided above-and-beyond help and support. I am eternally grateful to Liesl Allingham for our walks in the woods dedicated to my thinking through ideas, for our writing days, and for her careful reading of sections of the book. Dharitri Bhattacharjee encourages and inspires me daily. Carmen Gitre and Jennifer Pruitt are my adored Skype-writing group, avid readers of my work, and dear friends. Simon Jackson has been a friend and interlocutor through every stage of this project—in Egypt, in England, in France, and in the United States. It is his influence that led me to consider French Empire in Egypt, opening up my research and improving this project immensely. Sara Nimis helped ignite a passion for Egypt more than fifteen years ago and remains a key presence in my academic and personal success. And thank you to Shira Robinson for reaching out to me years ago, offering to be my book mentor, and becoming my cherished friend.

No friend or colleague has been more engaged with my work than Lisa Pollard and Nicholas Roberts. Thank you to both of them for reading every word I've written, often more than once, and spending countless hours talking through each idea with me. Lisa has been with me on this journey since my early days in the Egyptian archives in 2005; I was lucky enough to join Nick at Sewanee after meeting him in graduate school. Their input has shaped the book profoundly, and it is a significantly better history—and I am a significantly better scholar—because of them.

A heartfelt thank you as well to my students, who have challenged me to refine my thinking and ideas in our classroom in so many ways—work that kept me on my intellectual toes as it forced me to keep reading, thinking, and learning. Bret Windhauser deserves special notice here for his outstanding work with me, and I thank the many students at Swarthmore College and the University of the South who also helped me with various aspects of document translations.

Many other friends kept me (relatively) sane and (relatively) happy, enabling me to complete this project. Thank you to Jalaa' Abdelwahab, Laurie Bernstein, Katy Berry, Lilian Busse, Raquel Flatow Haas, Farris Ralston, and Jill Bernie Yormak. A thank you to my beloved *Stammtisch* as well: April Berends, Kelli Camp, Julie Elrod, Mary Heath, Leyla King, Cassie Meyer, Leigh Preston, and Megan Roberts. Nicoline Good helped me with child care when I needed it most. Moving close to Gloria and Paul Sternberg has proven to be one of the most fortuitous decisions of our lives. Stacey and Mayur Malde are extraordinary neighbors. So many others have helped me in countless ways; it is impossible to name everyone here. If I have forgotten to mention you here, please forgive me. And to all of you, thank you.

And, finally, my family. My family has long wondered if I would ever finish this book—surprise! I did. My extended in-laws in Germany have welcomed me with great joy into their family, and I am happy to be one of theirs. *Vielen Dank*. My extended family in the United States—Jon Eldan and Trent

Gegax, nieces, cousins, aunts, and uncles—has been supportive and loving since long before this project began. Thank you. My sister Samara Minkin has kept me organized in so many facets of my life—I'd be lost without her. Sarah Anne Minkin is my intellectual partner, whose wisdom I rely on both personally and professionally. My mother, Glenda Minkin, challenged me to finish before she turned ninety—and I have beaten her challenge with nearly two decades to spare, thanks to her willingness to help me thrive along the way. My father, David Minkin, has long asked me to recommend books, read everything I've written, and taken a keen interest in my intellectual life. I'm beyond thrilled that the next book I recommend can be my own. And to my husband, Heiko Reinhard—thank you. It's been over a decade, and I'm still glad we chose each other. Here's to our lives together, always. And to our son, Harry, we love you higher than the sky and deeper than the ocean. This book is finally in print—want to go outside and play some soccer?

NOTE ON TRANSLITERATIONS, NAMES, AND ARCHIVAL DOCUMENTS

This book is written with an eye to accessibility for specialists and nonspecialists alike. When the Arabic word for something or someone has a common English spelling (e.g., *waqf* or Khedive Isma'il), I have used that spelling. For places, I have used the most common current English spellings (e.g., Alexandria). With Arabic words that I have transliterated, I have chosen to use a simplified version of IJMES, indicating only the (') for the hamza and the (') for 'ayn and forgoing other diacritical markings.

I do not transliterate the Arabic names of imperial citizens and subjects whose deaths placed them in the British or French archives; instead, I have preserved the spelling of these names as I found them in French and/or English, enabling future researchers to find my archival documents more easily. This is especially important in Chapter 4, which is full of North African names rendered into French. I have left the names as they were written more than one hundred years ago.

And on the topic of multiple spellings of names, I am known as both Shana and Shane. I have published this book under Shana Minkin, but please note that articles, chapters, and my dissertation are published under Shane Minkin. I know it is confusing. You may take up the issue with my parents, who named me Shane yet called me Shana.

Finally, please note that the research done for this book in Dar al-Watha'iq al-Qawmiyya was completed before the digitalization of the archives. I have given all information I have about the documents in order to facilitate future researchers' work, but it does not correspond to the current system.

IMPERIAL BODIES

INTRODUCTION

The Imperial Bodies of Alexandria

"ON THE 10TH OF MAY LAST, Mr. John Engell, a German subject, reported that Miss Gertrude Beasley Woodward, a British subject, had that day died of typhoid fever in lodgings in Alexandria," wrote Alexandrian British consul Edward Gould to Lord Cromer, British consul general of Egypt, in June 1899. Gould continued: "This was the first that anyone at the consulate had heard of the case. Arrangements were at once made for the funeral[,] which took place on the same day at the European cemetery."[1]

Alexandria of the late nineteenth and early twentieth centuries was home to thousands of British, French, and other European imperial subjects. Wealthy and destitute, permanent and temporary residents, they lived far from their homelands. And when they died, consulates sprang into action, accounting for, burying, and documenting the imperial dead.

And so it was with Gertrude Beasley Woodward. The flurry of activity surrounding the burial and processing of Woodward's death revolved around the consulate. Consular employees arranged for a religious funeral, purchased a plot in a communal cemetery, and paid for her death registration.[2] They located the doctor who cared for her to ascertain that not only had she died of typhoid as reported but that the doctor and others who cared for Woodward treated her with dignity in her final days. The consular employees pieced together the story of her Egyptian life, including her work as a barmaid; her German fiancé, Mr. Engell; her Greek landlord; and her Arab doctor.[3]

By centering on the imperial dead, this book takes the end of life as a purposeful, public foundation of political and social community.[4] Death is both a local phenomenon—people die *in* Alexandria and are buried in the city—and a transnational, transimperial one in that the imperial dead had roots elsewhere, including family, friends, and property across the ocean or across the desert. In managing death, consulates marshaled the social belonging of foreign nationals in Alexandria and put it to political use. In doing so, they also inscribed that belonging as empire's belonging in Egypt.

International treaties had guaranteed consulates jurisdiction over the bodies of foreign subjects in death as in life.[5] Yet consulates repeatedly relied on the Egyptian national government to do its job.[6] European consular officials regularly entreated the Egyptian government for land and financial resources for their hospitals and cemeteries and for control over the documenting of their dead. The protracted, and not always successful, negotiations they undertook to secure those resources and that control point to the imperial powers as beholden to the decisions of the Egyptian administration. Inquiring into this apparent beholdenness, *Imperial Bodies* uses British, Egyptian, and French archives to examine the unevenness of imperial power and apparent robustness of Egyptian governmental authority in matters of death and dying. The management of death among foreign nationals in Alexandria in the late nineteenth and early twentieth centuries revises our understanding of the relation both between imperial governments—here the British and the French—and with the Egyptian state. It reaffirms that the British were never the sole power in Egypt and that the French never fully relinquished their claim to imperial space in Egypt, despite lacking territorial control. Moreover, this book reveals the continued role of the Egyptian national government in vital decisions about the resources and land needed to care for the dead. This book thus demonstrates that in regard to the mundanity of the day to day, of protecting national and imperial subjects in Egypt, imperial power asserted itself not through unilateral assertions of the colonial state but through the local consulate's attenuated claims of belonging. In this peculiar reversal, empire, rather than claim the colonized state as belonging to it, presents itself as belonging to the colonized state.

UNEVEN POWER IN THE VEILED PROTECTORATE

Egypt went through a series of political, social, and infrastructural changes in the nineteenth century that consolidated state power in the hands of a hereditary ruling family. A province of the Ottoman Empire, Egypt became a semiautonomous land under Mehmed 'Ali by the mid-1800s and continued to be ruled by his descendants until 1952.

Over the course of the first half of the nineteenth century, Mehmed 'Ali restructured the state via broad infrastructure projects. These included the Mahmudiyya canal, which connected the Mediterranean to the Nile, along with an extensive system of new agricultural irrigation canals, a new medical system inspired by French medical practices, a revamped education system that was also reorganized along French practices, and the overhaul of the Egyptian army, including the institution of a draft that fundamentally altered the relationship of state to individual.[7] This last project precipitated several successful military campaigns, such as those in Greece, Sudan, and Syria, both for the Ottoman state and to challenge it.

Mehmed 'Ali's reign saw tremendous growth for Alexandria as well. The Mahmudiyya canal, while built at immense cost to human life, eventually revitalized the port city entirely; it grew from a tiny hamlet of approximately 5,000 people at the turn of the nineteenth century to more than 104,000 inhabitants around the time of Mehmed 'Ali's death at the end of the 1840s.[8] With the growth of the city came the development of its economy, and with the new monetary opportunities, a small, but steadily growing, foreign-national population emerged, numbering nearly 5,000 in 1848.[9] Foreign consulates also sprang up throughout the city during the first half of the century, formalizing diplomatic relations and international presence. These consulates honed their power through the expansion of trade protection to both national subjects and those who succeeded in gaining diplomatic shelter and legal backing through the Capitulations, a series of primarily trade agreements between the Ottoman Empire and the European powers dating back to the sixteenth century.

By the time Khedive Isma'il ascended to rule in 1863, Egypt was embroiled in growing infrastructure and growing debts. Isma'il's sixteen-year reign would be marked by ever-increasing attempts at "Europeanization" in municipal planning and government structure, excessive spending, and eventual bankruptcy. The opening of the Suez Canal in 1869 came at great financial and political cost to Egypt, even as it created enormous trade and economic opportunities.[10] The massive overhaul of the state left the government bound to European creditors. Their increasing demands, spearheaded by the British and the French, led to the establishment of European financial oversight through the Caisse de la Dette Publique in the 1870s.[11] Additional compromises included the installation of one British and one French overseer in charge of ensuring the repayment of debts through revenues collected from the Alexandria Port, among other places.[12] Eventually, European creditors, backed by their governments, forced Khedive Isma'il to abdicate his rule in favor of his son, Tawfiq (1879–1892). Important to our story in this short overview is the dominance of European imperial powers in Egypt before the onslaught of British colonization in the 1880s. Indeed, Alexandria's foreign-national population had grown to almost 43,000 people by 1878, out of a population of approximately 220,000.[13] Foreign nationals now accounted for nearly 20 percent of the population. Informal empire permeated the country long before the 1882 British occupation; Egypt was already under the influence of multiple European empires, with Britain and France together at the helm.[14] It is within this time frame, beginning with the rise of the khedive in the early 1860s, that this book begins.

The 'Urabi rebellion precipitated direct British occupation of Egypt. Led by Ahmed 'Urabi, a colonel in the Egyptian army, the rebellion marked the first organized effort within the Egyptian army to challenge the Ottoman/Egyptian hierarchy and the Europeans who supported it. 'Urabi's installation as war minister, after a skirmish with the sitting Egyptian government, as well as his subsequent dismissal after the maneuverings of European powers, occasioned both a growing popular movement and outbursts of violence.[15] Rioting in the summer of 1882 killed approximately fifty foreign nationals and up to three thousand Ottoman/Egyptians.

While both the British and the French were alarmed by the 'Urabi movement, the British alone bombarded Alexandria in July 1882, moving from being one of the financial imperial powers to the sole governing colonial power of Egypt.[16] Following the riots and bombardment, the foreign-national population of Alexandria spent years trying to recoup losses; the imperial archives are full of files marking claims of monetary and property damage.[17] While the 'Urabi revolt and subsequent British occupation were undoubtedly a time of great fear and turmoil for the population of Egypt—both foreign national and Ottoman/Egyptian—it did not represent a transformation in the day-to-day governance of Alexandria.[18]

Over the next several decades, the British remained in Egypt, taking over most facets of the government. It has long been accepted historical knowledge that the British were the rulers of Egypt after the occupation and that the

Egyptian national government had minimal powers without independent authority in governance.[19] Yet Egypt remained a "veiled protectorate," wherein the facade of Ottoman imperial governance was key for maintaining the balance of international relations with the Ottomans and within Europe.

That the British were colonial rulers of Egypt, even under a veiled protectorate, was complicated by the ongoing diplomatic relationship between the British and Ottoman Empires. Recent scholarship argues that the British never had any intention of cutting Ottoman ties to Egypt; rather, the original plan for the British occupation was to maintain Ottoman territorial sovereignty while limiting Ottoman governmental access.[20] At the same time, the British believed that they would be in Egypt for a short stay, revamping the government structure and leaving as quickly as possible.[21] It is this continuing relationship between the British and the Ottomans, as well as the lack of immediate commitment to a long-term project by the British, that accounts for the structure of British colonial rule in Egypt. Lord Cromer was agent and consul general of Egypt, marking him as subordinate to the British ambassador in Istanbul.

Despite the diplomatic power hierarchy, Lord Cromer rarely appears in the British consular records or communications with the Egyptian and French governments consulted for this book; the sultan and Ottoman government in Istanbul are missing as well.[22] The day-to-day work of empire was done at the consular level and in negotiation with the Egyptian national government.

While the British may have hoped to leave Egypt quickly, they were soon entrenched as quasi-colonial rulers. The unofficial incorporation of Egypt into the British Empire had international as well as domestic ramifications. It allowed Britain more control of the route to and from India via the Suez Canal.[23] Pilgrims to Mecca also flowed through Egypt; British control of the state was a key to control of the empire's Muslim population.[24] Egypt served as a space for financial experimentation, where the British government could flex its economic muscles in an increasingly global capitalist market under large-scale projects marked as "public utility."[25] The boundaries of Egypt were negotiated and settled under British control, as the "Egyptian West" was brought under government jurisdiction through a series of complicated judicial and legal negotiations with local tribes and other regional actors.[26] Years of British rule and the emerging nationalist movement wrought new forms of social and political organization, gender stratification, cultural cognizance, educational priorities, public health, and more.[27] Egypt under Cromer saw an explosion of public works projects and other efforts to advance infrastructure and the economy. Yet it was also a country of strikes and increasing public agitation by Egyptians and lower-class migrants and a country ruled by colonial discrimination and outbursts of violence.[28] In short, Egypt was a country in flux.

Although it was the only governing colonial power, British rule was never British alone. Continental European powers could and did limit what the British could do, and other foreign governments tussled for relevance and power throughout the end of the nineteenth century and start of the twentieth. However, it was France, Britain's greatest imperial competitor in the European scramble for overseas influence, that was firmly ensconced as a cultural influencer and as the key country involved in the industry, legal reforms, and finance of Egypt.[29] Long after the defeat of Napoleon's army in Egypt in 1803, a French developer spearheaded construction of the Suez Canal, completed in 1869; a French diplomat worked with Lord Cromer on saving Egypt's finances; French law formed a crux of the Mixed Court system in 1876; and French diplomats at all levels continued to challenge British rule in Egypt.[30] This book, concerned as it is with the building and maintenance of imperial power, places the British and French Empires and related Protestant and Catholic institutions at the center of the story.

Alexandria as a site for inquiry reveals the interweaving of these European empires, as well as the multiplicity of other communities, and the myriad and overlapping affiliations and forms of governance that were at play in Egypt and elsewhere at the end of the nineteenth century.[31] The city grew as migrants arrived from all over Egypt and the world, migrants both of upper and lower economic classes, and continued to grow through the first decades of the twentieth century.

Within a few years of the start of the British occupation, a khedival decree created the new Alexandria municipality, replacing an ineffective system in which the national government appointed administrators and committees to govern the city.[32] The municipality was specifically designed to incorporate multiple nationalities; no more than three men of the same nationality could serve on the early municipal council at once, ensuring that there would always be at least five different, unspecified nationalities represented within the governing body. The municipality was more concerned with European neighborhoods and economic growth than with the indigenous and poor populations.[33]

Egypt remained an autonomous province of the Ottoman Empire until 1914, under British control, until the British declared a formal protectorate over Egypt at the start of World War I. This book ends its exploration of death and empire in Egypt at the end of the veiled protectorate, right before World War I brought not only a different colonial governing system but also an overflow of wartime refugees to Alexandria.

TRANSIMPERIAL, MULTIEMPIRE ALEXANDRIA

Rich and poor, Muslim, Jewish, and Christian, connected to colonial rule and lost to the archives, European imperial subjects and citizens traipsed through Alexandria throughout the late nineteenth and early twentieth centuries. Many of these foreign nationals were permanent residents, representing generations in the city, never living or dreaming of elsewhere.[34] Others were passing through, temporary workers or travelers. Some were intimately engaged with the political, economic, and social needs of both Alexandria and their national or religious communities, while others existed seemingly beyond the reach of the municipality, the imperial consulates, and the colonial state. But all of them benefited from being affiliated with imperial rule. Their ability to travel, to settle in the city, to get jobs, and find opportunities were all linked to this era when the European scramble for global supremacy included dominance over the Ottoman Empire and the nascent Egyptian nationalist state.

This era is commonly known as the age of "cosmopolitan" Alexandria (ca. 1860–1960). A multitude of scholars celebrate the city's European population and orientation as "the paradigm case of Middle Eastern cosmopolitanism . . . the stuff of subsequent nostalgia."[35] The framing of Alexandria as cosmopolitan saturates writings of the city: memoirs, literature, nostalgic monographs, and academic studies abound.[36] Many of them pointedly posit cosmopolitanism to mean a city that was more European than Egyptian, resulting in something lost when the era of colonization ended harshly in the 1950s, marking the city's grandeur as inherently incompatible with Egyptian national rule.[37] Others look at the cosmopolitan era as a time that produced a boom in infrastructure and governance development.[38] These versions of cosmopolitanism in Alexandria are almost always synonymous with the elite, and the lower classes and Ottoman/Egyptian natives are largely ignored.[39]

Not all writing on nineteenth- and early twentieth-century Alexandria relies on the framework of an elite-driven cosmopolitan city. Highlighting the lower socioeconomic classes or insisting on the lens of the indigenous Egyptian Muslim population shifts the narrative of the city, but often does so while maintaining engagement with the framework of cosmopolitanism, "vulgar" or otherwise delineated.[40] Other scholars are increasingly embracing the messiness and subtleties of the broad range of imperial affiliations before legal codification of nationalities, when empire allowed people to move through actual and "jurisdictional" borders with relative ease.[41]

The migratory possibilities of empire that resulted in so many foreign dead in Alexandria were largely and unsurprisingly limited to Europeans and those with European protection.[42] That these imperial migrants often lived far beyond their consulates, associating with them when it was of benefit and keeping distance otherwise, is also not surprising; indeed, this was common practice in Alexandria and elsewhere.[43] It is impossible—and would be irresponsible—to write a history of the city, of the building of empire within Alexandria, without acknowledging the power dynamic that privileged these European imperial citizens and subjects. Yet it is equally impossible—and equally irresponsible—to assume that they were necessarily foreigners to the city, any more or less a vital part of Alexandria's story than the Ottoman/ Egyptian Muslim native who may have been from anywhere in Egypt.[44] To write these others—here meaning both foreign-national citizens and subjects as well as religious minorities—as more or less of Alexandria or Egypt than any other category of people is to impose a teleological story on the city, ending in either Egyptian nationalist rule or ruin with the end of empire.[45]

Like other places touched by the mobility and movement of Europe across the globe in the nineteenth century, Alexandria was a transimperial, multiempire port. Whereas I use "multiempire" to signify the various imperial powers that had interests in Alexandria, I use "transimperial" to signify the imperial subjects of Alexandria, who were simultaneously constructing and constructed by the categories of imperial governance.[46] Rather than try to capture them within the framework of "cosmopolitan," "transimperial" allows me to probe the networks of mobility they represented, even when firmly ensconced for generations in Alexandria. These networks were inherently uneven and unequal; class, gender, and religion mattered, as did access to colonial governance and resources.[47] Imperial networks spanned the western desert of Egypt across North Africa, sailed the Mediterranean and the English Channel into continental Europe and Great Britain, and passed through the

Suez Canal to reach India quickly. Imperial networks were equally grounded in Alexandria, within a decidedly local community of imperial and native subjects. Their diversity and specificity are part and parcel of empire, which was always created as much by local permutations as by international agreements or decisions made in European metropoles.

People crossed borders with relative ease throughout the nineteenth- and early twentieth-century Middle East and beyond. Empire facilitated the mobility of populations and goods, providing for protection and legal coverage across oceans and deserts. The ambiguity of the time, when legal categories had specific benefits but lacked definitive boundaries, led travelers, businesspeople, religious pilgrims, missionaries, and others to travel across boundaries or to settle abroad. Local indigenous populations, often the religious minorities, used the protections laid out in diplomatic agreements to request affiliation with foreign consulates. Needing to differentiate among the peoples under its control or asking for its protection, empire was a system of divisiveness, of creating, fostering, exacerbating, reproducing, and enforcing difference in its reach and benefits.[48] These empires were based on differentiation, both from without, in their concern with who was *not* an imperial subject, and from within, in their focus on subject versus citizen. They functioned by aligning themselves with religion, even as empires might work to distinguish between those in a country such as Egypt to proselytize and those who were there for economic or other reasons. Empire in this sense was a struggle for the classification of peoples and control over governance and resources. That control occurred both within and between empires. Empire, while built from above in military and diplomatic victories, was insinuated, made a part of the daily life, on the ground. The social implications of this reached far beyond simply a territorial phenomenon or an economic endeavor.[49]

In this way, each imperial space was a unique representation of the people and goods that migrated there, combined with the specificity of the local space. Empire, then, did not mean the same thing in any two places; it was always a locally constituted experience.[50] It was a product of the web of networks and connections that predated it and were created and manipulated by it. Shaped by the local and the metropole, empires were equally engaged with and formed by interactions with each other. People cajoled and manipulated categories created to control and classify them and, in the process, claimed local resources and places to establish a foothold in both physical and imaginative space. Institutions such as local consulates, which worked both with imperial power from imperial metropoles and within the constraints of their local setting, demonstrate the ways in which empire was both implemented and developed in the immediate surroundings.

The multiple foreign consulates and powerful, long-established foreign communities in Alexandria were integrated as local players in the city under both Ottoman and British rule. They are the heart of the overlapping layers of governance that resulted in this transimperial, multiempire city. This interplay of consulates is key to understanding not only the history of the Egyptian state but also the various conditions under which different empires were formed, both from above, such as through high-level negotiations and international agreements, and on the ground, such as through the mourning, documenting, and burial of bodies.

In Alexandria, the British and French used the power of the consulate in the creation and manipulation of categories of the population. This enabled them to engage in governance in Egypt, as an overseas empire and as a nonterritorial empire, respectively. Consulates were the implementation both of empire and of active, vital local resources.

THE PEOPLE OF ALEXANDRIA

The population of Alexandria was divided along both religious and national lines. These lines were regularly blurred, as we saw when Gertrude Beasley Woodward was buried in what was most likely the Protestant cemetery yet was called a European cemetery by the British Consulate in the archival records. Jewish, Muslim, Catholic, Orthodox, and Protestant communities coexisted. These broad religious categories, used both in communal and governmental archives, masked differences within the denominations, such as splits within the Jewish community, or between the Coptic Orthodox and Coptic Catholic Churches, or among the Maronites and other sects of Christianity.[51]

The 1897 census provides an overview of Alexandria in the middle of the time period considered here. The city was always majority Muslim, with 250,000 of 320,000 residents claiming Islam as their religion.[52] Nearly ten thousand Jewish residents, alongside more than fifty-five thousand Christians (approximately twenty-six thousand each Orthodox and Catholics and four thousand Protestant) rounded out the total. By nationality, the census recorded more than fifteen thousand Greeks, nearly twelve thousand Italians, more than eight thousand English, just over five thousand French, and five thousand "others" among the population of Alexandria.[53] Scholars have established that the taxonomies of the national census must be questioned, as the census was not a neutral exercise.[54] I am not concerned here with the taxonomies at play in this Egyptian governmental practice; instead, I am using these census numbers to set, in broad strokes, the scene of the city. Exact numbers of British and French imperial subjects are not as important to this story as the ways in which the empire used the bodies of the subjects, materially and performatively, to claim imperial power and space.

Lumped together as foreign both by choice and by the Egyptian national government, these communities were different from one another. The Greek community was the oldest of these foreign-national Egyptian communities, with some tracing its history to the founding of the city under Alexander the Great. During Ismaʿil's reign (1863–1879) there were nearly twenty-one thousand Greeks in Alexandria, making it by far the largest of the foreign-national communities.[55] The origins of the Italian community were mythologized to have begun during the Middle Ages; almost nine thousand Italians were settled in Alexandria by the mid-nineteenth century.[56] In comparison to these long-standing communities, the French and British communities, which stood at approximately eighty-four hundred and twenty-two hundred in 1878 respectively, were much more closely tied to imperial projects, as the presence of French and British subjects and citizens in Alexandria was linked to nineteenth-century European colonial expansion. The British community was disproportionately made up of Maltese, under British rule at the beginning of the nineteenth century.[57] The French community was largely linked to French North Africa.

The grouping of the population was loosely divided into communities and colonies. The term "community," or *communauté* in French, related to the millet system in the Ottoman Empire.[58] In 1880 there were eleven recognized communities in Egypt, and by 1907 the list had grown to fourteen.[59] "Colony," however, was used mainly to connote national affiliation. The distinctions were not definitive, and over time many communities subdivided by national identity and affiliated with consulates, causing the differentiation between community and colony to blur.[60] Neither "community" nor "colony" is adequate to describe the various overlapping configurations of alliances and groups working toward managing the dead. Consulates and religious communities worked in tandem, combining religious and national affiliation in the organization of funerals, death registration, and hospital and cemetery committees. I have chosen to use the terminology "community" rather than "colony" throughout this book, emphasizing that colonies and communities in Alexandria were often working together, not clearly separated in presence or goals, and often made up of the same people.

The Egyptian government did not challenge the legitimacy of constructions of communities as they appeared in the archives used for this book. Institutions and individuals represented themselves as members of overlapping, and at times divergent, communities simultaneously. Consulates embraced and produced both religious and national community formation, working sometimes at the forefront and sometimes in the background.

The imperial bodies discussed in this book were divided into citizens, subjects, and protégés. Those called "citizens" were most often citizens of a European country, with the primary exception being Algerian Jews, as discussed further in Chapter 4. "Subject" was the terminology used for imperial subjects, such as the Maltese for the British. "Protégés" encompassed those who had some form of consular protection under the Capitulations system. While "protégé" was a protected status peculiar to the Ottoman Empire, it was often used interchangeably with "subject" in everyday practice for the British and French and in regard to death and burial processes. In some sense, these broad definitions of who might fall under consular control in life mirrored how consulates collected their dead. The consulates used protection in life and in death to claim people, as it were, and expand their imperial reach, which was, of course, significantly bolstered by the inclusion of protected persons.[61]

The archives of death show that the imperial residents of Alexandria were simultaneously local and foreign, of Alexandria and of empire. However, rather than engage in debates about the best way to characterize this heterogeneous population that was divided in some ways but fluid in others, I am interested here in what happened when this fluid population died. In death, subjects needed their consulates. Bodies needed to be recognized and protected, and consulates, in turn, needed those corpses to show that they could provide for their living. In a world where people often seemed to exist beyond the reach of the imperial state, they were nonetheless claimed by it in the end. In death, these imperial subjects could be put to use for empire. Their bodies were imperial tools, and their lives were now, after death, categorizable, controlled, contained, and commemorated by one national consulate in the name of religion, geography, and politics. Their lives were flattened into categories. This act was not centered around depriving an individual of complexity, and indeed this complexity was saved within these same processes, but nonetheless this flattening demonstrated the way a diverse imperial population could be rendered uniform and put into service for empire. Legal nationality may not have been fixed, but death was. People who did not live in categories died in them.

GOVERNING THE DEAD

Throughout the late nineteenth and early twentieth centuries, recognized foreign communities, defined by both national and religious affiliation, processed and buried their dead. These communities controlled the issuance of death certificates, the inquests, burials, and estate distribution.[62] There was no cemetery for the poor, and the Alexandrian municipal and Egyptian national governments were seen as the last resort for help in burying a body, available only if an untended body became a public health issue.[63] Management of the foreign dead was a private, communal process tended to by individual foreign communities but under Egyptian governmental oversight.[64] Foreign consulates reported back to the Egyptian state about their dead; thus, the state outsourced the management of the population living within its borders. In the negotiations for land and resources, foreign consulates pushed back at the Egyptian government in an attempt to hold on to sovereignty over their subjects, but they could not demand results. Empire had to contend with local government and governance.

Thus, despite the mammoth effect of the British on the Egyptian state and the indigenous populations, there was little change in the institutions, bureaucracies, and rituals surrounding the dead from before the occupation in 1882 through the decades following it. Instead, the evidence shows that the foreign hospital committees and foreign cemetery committees—and their associated consulates—maintained stable relationships with the Egyptian national government. When administrators from the British consulate tried to help with the expansion of the cemeteries or with new hospital space, they spoke with the Egyptian ministers (Majlis al-Wuzara', or the Council of Ministers, the government cabinet that served the khedive), not with a British colonial official. Egyptian officials, not British colonial administrators, determined whether a hospital would be funded or whether land would be granted for a cemetery; indeed, the archival record suggests that, beyond the consulate, the British colonial state played almost no role in managing illness and death within its own national community in Alexandria. The ability to decide on land and resource use in these situations was not a shared power with the colonial state or the international consulates, nor was it something a charity or benevolent society could organize; the power to dole out land and resources rested with the Egyptian national government alone.[65] The high politics of British colonial rule on an international and political scale versus the gritty day-to-day drudge of managing bodies reveals the power of the Egyptian national government, alongside that of the individual consulates, as key to the building of European empire under British colonial rule.

In this moment, various forms of governance—city, national, imperial— were constantly getting pushed and pulled together in ways that were both intimate and personal and in the realm of the abstract political negotiations and relations of the time. At this moment of concentric governance, imperial powers were determined to assign categories to claim bodies and, with that, to claim and redefine belonging. Belonging here was not only that of the individual corpse to the consulate but of the empire to the colonized state. For this reason, death matters, and this is the moment when we see stories of the imperial bodies of Alexandria, of the Egyptian state, and of international imperialism rub up against one another.

Death, then, became a determining ritualistic and bureaucratic process by which empire asserted power in Egyptian land. Because a body could not be flown home, as one might do today, those who died in nineteenth-century Alexandria were buried there. Death required presence and, with that, a connection to the place in which one died. It forced foreign communities and foreign consulates, which were overlapping but not mutually exclusive entities, into action; they were necessary and essential actors in the process. The handling of the imperial dead reveals empire because one *had* to bury the dead; it was an inescapable necessity in everyday life.

Death showed the moments when these differences mattered, such as in regard to the different death registries, and where they did not, such as who could be a patient at which hospital. Death showcases empire in the macro, demonstrated by the international struggles and agreements, and in the micro, as consulates worked to count bodies. In doing so, death reveals the priorities of building empire in Egyptian land. Empire, at the end of the nineteenth century, was still going strong despite nationalist murmurings. If those living in Egypt did not know empire was to end, then it was empire that claimed primary space in the imaginative and physical life of Alexandria through death.

Thus, this book, by centering on death, presents a history of Egypt, highlighting a different view of the state in the late nineteenth century. This is not a book about an emerging national consciousness, even as it demonstrates Egyptian governmental strength. Instead, it consciously places itself in the lived experience of empire. It accepts as a starting point that the end game of nationalism was not yet known, that the imperial subjects moving in and through Alexandria and Egypt did not yet understand that this land would soon be a nation-state. They could not have known. Rather than locate nationalism, this book keeps its eye dead set on empire and, through empire, makes an argument for the agency of Egyptian national governance.

CHAPTER OVERVIEW

The organization of this book mimics the movement of the dead from dying to documentation. It primarily uses sources from Dar al-Watha'iq al-Qawmiyya (the Egyptian National Archives) in Cairo, the National Archives in London, and Centre des Archives Diplomatiques (the French Diplomatic Archives) in Nantes to highlight the various events and moments wherein a consulate or community acted to claim the body as its own. As with all sources, the stories told here are incomplete and possibly somewhat inaccurate at times, but instructive nevertheless. French was frequently the language of communication between governments and peoples, such as correspondence between the French and the British or from the hospital and cemetery committees to the Egyptian government. Within the governments, the language of the country dominated. Egyptian governmental departments filed their reports in Arabic, French in French, British in English. Regularly, Arabic, Italian, and other languages made their way into estate files, inquest reports, and other consular documentation in both French and British archives. The linguistic mishmash of the documents used for this book reflects the transimperial, multiempire nature of Alexandria at the time.

We follow the imagined path of the dying, from the hospital to the funeral, from the grave to death registration. Chapter 1 begins at the foreign-national, non-Muslim hospitals. This chapter demonstrates that in the work of caring for the sick and dying, foreign communities and consulates consciously and purposefully served the city at large. These foreign hospitals were sites of belonging, of inclusion, and of local need. They were the result of negotiations between the Egyptian national government and the various foreign communities, as these hospitals were physical structures using city land and resources and designed to serve the public health of the city.

Chapter 2 addresses funerals. Decent, proper funerals, with coffins, religious officials, and mourners, were signs of a good death. The funeral service occupied public space and public imagination in pulling together an ephemeral community of mourners in a public performance of burial and belonging, while many of the details and payment were often negotiated through imperial consulates. Focusing on the very public funeral of Latin Archbishop Bonfigli in 1904, this chapter asks how these performances could be used to claim imperial space in Alexandria.

Chapter 3 uses the non-Muslim cemeteries to cycle back to questions of land use and resources. In the building of cemeteries, consulates and communities turned again to the Egyptian national government, only with different goals. In contrast to the welcoming institutions that were the hospitals, cemeteries were open only to specific communities, creating exclusive, closed, permanent physical space for imperial bodies in the city.

Chapter 4 brings the journey of the imperial body to a close, through the writing and documentation about the dead. Looking at whose deaths get counted by whom, this chapter shows that the bureaucrats of the imperial consulates served not only their home countries but also the Egyptian state. Documenting the dead of empire archived the living of Egypt.

This book concludes by thinking about the specificity of death as a historical actor for and of empire. Death forces us to rethink the building of empire, showing its unevenness, between the high politics of legal, political arrangements and the gritty day to day of bodies. Death insists on questions of governance, whether in the form of imperial consulates, the Egyptian national government, or cemetery or hospital committees. At the same time, death requires us to think about space—in the form of land, in the physical manifestation of registries and court cases in writing death, in institutions, in churches and cemeteries, in the corpse itself.

Thus, in counting bodies, in processing and burying the dead, the imperial consulates and communities were not only competing with each other but also negotiating with the Egyptian state, often from a position of neediness. The Egyptian state could bequeath resources to help bury the foreign dead, and, in turn, the resources bestowed on a community would underline the presence and importance of that community to the Egyptian state. That these imperial communities were awarded state resources showed both that they were valued in their local presence and in their commitment to the social and health needs of Alexandria and that the Egyptian state had persistent agency in making these resource allocations. Indeed, this was very much the case in regard to the foreign national hospitals, to which we now turn.

1 FOREIGN HOSPITALS, LOCAL INSTITUTIONS

LISETTE BOHREN, a native of Bern, Switzerland, arrived in Egypt sometime before 1897. By the time of her death, she had lived and worked as a cook in Alexandria for at least eleven years.[1] We do not know why Bohren came to live in the city, although the presence of single European women was not uncommon at the turn of the twentieth century.[2] We do know that the last two years of Bohren's life were marred by illness; she was a patient at the Deaconess Hospital for three weeks in December 1906 and at the European Hospital for most of February 1907. She died during a return trip to the Deaconess after a three-day stay, on March 1, 1908. Her official cause of death was "pseudoleukemia," a viral infection that mimics cancer.

In death, we learn much more about Lisette Bohren. Soon after she died, the French Consulate of Alexandria began an accounting of her estate to settle her bills. A paper trail ensued, making up what would later become part of an archival record of Europeans' lived (and dying) experiences in Egypt. Bohren's medical and hospital bills allow us a brief glimpse both into her life and into the world of the patients who made their way through Alexandria's foreign-built and foreign-run hospital system (hereafter foreign hospitals) in the late nineteenth and early twentieth centuries. As both a foreigner to and a resident of Alexandria for more than a decade, Bohren was much like the foreign hospital system that provided her with care throughout her slow demise: stranger and Alexandrian all at once.

Alexandria's collection of foreign health-care institutions reflected the diversity of the city. Although lay committees, consulates, and missionaries created a system along national and sectarian lines, they also organized hospitals and outpatient clinics under the common principle of open doors to all who sought treatment, turning their institutions into key city infrastructure.[3] The most influential of these establishments were the foreign hospitals, which offered services to all of the city's residents, regardless of creed or country of origin. In exchange, hospital administrators expected that municipal and national governments would grant their requests for land and subventions. Foreign hospitals were institutions created both for and by the city they served.

The foreign hospitals came to play a primary role in Alexandria in the late nineteenth and early twentieth centuries. They were quasi-governmental institutions for the city at large, collecting information that would be sent to the Egyptian national and Alexandrian municipal governments, enabling those governments to focus on citywide improvements in public health and hygiene.[4] Through the hospitals, foreign communities served Alexandria as local players, and foreign consulates enmeshed themselves in questions of city planning and population management. The hospitals were also a place where European consulates could bolster the international influence of their nation, using the sick and dying as a means to create and claim space in Ottoman and British Egypt.

Foreign hospitals were thus key agents in the facilitation of belonging in Alexandria. The hospitals were affiliated with specific foreign consulates and communities, and each community used its own categories for classifying the Alexandrians whose health needs they served. At the same time, however, the hospitals defied categorical limitations by welcoming all those in need of medical care, whether paying patients or charity cases. This dual role of dividing the population while simultaneously serving it as a whole reflects the complexities of empire and belonging concerning both institutions and people in Alexandria circa 1900.

This duality similarly played out as hospital administrators regularly negotiated with the Egyptian national and municipal governments for land to build and expand on and submitted requests for annual subventions. These hospitals relied on these government subventions to function as charitable institutions for the population of Alexandria as a whole. By maintaining the power to determine which land would be used for hospitals, the Egyptian national government remained the final arbiter of the built environment for the dead and the dying in the city. In this sense, the foreign hospitals presented themselves to the Egyptian government as municipal rather than colonial or missionary spaces. Their existence in Alexandria reflected neither a simple civilizing mission nor the colonization of Egyptian public health by outside powers, but rather the complexity of negotiations of power between the colonizing and colonized.

Understanding the foreign hospitals as local centers of public health stands in contrast to established scholarly narratives on the origins of the modern Egyptian medical system, which tend to discredit the role of the foreign medical system. As a result, these hospitals are usually written out of the city's story.[5] When such hospitals do figure into histories of the city, they have been represented as tools for controlling the foreign population, not as institutions charged to serve the indigenous.[6] Neither approach adequately accounts for the key role that foreign hospitals play in what we think of as the Egyptian bureaucracy. Foreign hospitals cared for their subjects on a very local level, while at the same time using that care to claim imperial space within the Ottoman and later British Empires.[7] Hospitals were sites of imperial influence, where competing European powers struggled for dominance and missionaries worked to heal bodies and save souls. Yet many of those involved in Alexandria's foreign hospital system were not simple agents of colonial interests. Foreign missionaries and consular employees worked alongside lay hospital leadership from long-established Alexandrian families.

To explore these institutions and their spheres of influence, this chapter examines the three primary foreign hospitals in Alexandria: the European Hospital, the Deaconess Hospital, and the Greek Hospital. It illustrates how the categorization of inpatients, the distribution of free days, the payment of fees, and the negotiations between the hospital committees and the Egyptian national government all brought the hospitals into the city's social-service infrastructure. The data on patients challenge the notion that these hospitals were solely spaces of segregation or that the indigenous population avoided them. Rather, the hospitals were zones of inclusion, unbound by national or religious requirements in their treatment of the ill.

MODERN MEDICINE IN EGYPT

Mehmed 'Ali, ruler of Egypt during the first half of the nineteenth century, enacted broad-reaching reforms that changed the physical, legal, and social makeup of the Egyptian state. Within these, he revitalized the government's medical system, facilitating the building of Egypt's first "modern" hospitals in Cairo and Alexandria in the 1820s.[8] During the same time period, the Europeans (many nationalities grouped as one) and Greeks of Alexandria also built their first modern hospitals in the city, with the original purpose of serving their own populations, though they soon began to serve many more.[9]

Foreign communities by and large did not participate in the government health-care system; of the dozens of British inquests I consulted, British bodies ended up in the government hospital only in the case of mistaken identity.[10] While some of the death registers of the French Consulate mention the European, Deaconess, or Greek Hospitals, none of the hundreds of entries I read mentioned the government hospital. Rather, the population at large— foreign national and indigenous—used the foreign hospital systems. Egyptians, or those who would later be categorized as such, made up a large percentage of the patients at each of the foreign communal hospitals.

Patients of the foreign hospitals consisted disproportionately of the urban poor. Similarly, in nineteenth-century Europe, hospitals were widely regarded as places where the poor went to die, while the rich preferred to die at home.[11] Government or municipal hospitals were usually almshouses, established for those living in extreme poverty.[12] The voluntary or private hospitals built soon thereafter served the working poor.[13] In many cases a person's admission to the hospital was dependent on recommendations from respected members of the community, a practice that also spanned both Europe and the United States.[14] Patients consisted primarily of those stuck in the lower economic strata, without family or resources that might enable them to be cared for at home.[15]

The makeup of the hospital population in nineteenth-century Egypt was not significantly different from that of the United States and Europe. Some Egyptians fought against going to hospitals, seeing them as another institution through which the government could interfere in their personal lives.[16] Others quickly took to the new medical system, using it "fearlessly."[17] The government hospitals were filthy and broken down, and those who used them were often already extremely ill.[18] Petitions from the foreign hospitals likewise suggest that the maintenance of their facilities was a constant worry.[19] Ample evidence of the various foreign hospitals selling and building new "modern" spaces also attests to the struggle to keep hospitals up to date.[20]

In Alexandria, which in 1878 was home to forty-two thousand "Europeans" out of a population of more than two hundred thousand, the foreign medical establishment prospered alongside the government-run institutions.[21] Historians of Alexandria have alternately claimed that these foreign hospitals served as a means to control foreign populations and that they lay outside the reach of the urban poor.[22] However, every year thousands of indigenous Egyptians checked into the foreign clinics, and hundreds more entered the foreign hospitals. Europeans were patients at any and all of the foreign hospitals, not simply the hospitals associated with their national colony. Lisette Bohren was a patient at both the European and Deaconess Hospitals, which were primarily affiliated with the French, Austro-Hungarian, and Italian Consulates and the British, Swiss, and German Consulates, respectively. The interplay of the various groups in the hospitals, such as administrators, staff, and patients, reveals that foreign hospitals are not classifiable as entirely colonial structures or entirely local Egyptian institutions. Instead, they serve as a space in which the complexities of imperial European power and everyday lived experience intertwined to serve the people of Alexandria.

THE FOREIGN HOSPITALS OF ALEXANDRIA

'Ali Mubarak was an Egyptian governmental official and prolific writer whose twenty-volume work, *al-Khitat*, painstakingly details government and society in late nineteenth-century Egypt. His volume on Alexandria records six hospitals in the late nineteenth century, and he describes four of them: the government hospital, and three foreign hospitals: the European Hospital, the Deaconess Hospital, and the Greek Hospital.[23] In 1870, writes Mubarak, the European Hospital served 1,366 patients; the Greek Hospital, 773; and the Deaconess Hospital, 304.[24] A Department of Public Census survey commissioned by the Egyptian government in 1911, more than forty years after Mubarak's observations, registers a flourishing and far-reaching medical establishment in Alexandria. Institutions included a general clinic; a clinic run by Islamic charitable endowment (*waqf*); and numerous specialty clinics both government and foreign owned, such as the eye clinic associated with the European Hospital and aimed at the indigenous Egyptian population, alongside the foreign hospitals.[25]

The original government hospital in Alexandria, built to be a naval hospital, was established by Mehmed 'Ali in 1827 and later transformed by the Egyptian government into a civilian hospital called the Mahmudiyya.[26] It was the only hospital paid for entirely by the Egyptian national government, and it served the urban poor. A closer look at the Greek, European, and Deaconess Hospitals shows that they, too, were hospitals for the urban poor.[27]

The Catholic European Hospital, the oldest foreign hospital, was built near the neighborhood of Attarine in the center of the city close to the sea.[28] The French, Austro-Hungarian, and Italian Consulates sponsored the hospital, alternating leadership roles and providing the bulk of subventions for its costs. Other European countries, such as Belgium, Portugal, and Sweden, played smaller roles in its affairs.[29] The Daughters of Charity (Filles de la Charité) were in charge of its day-to-day operations, making sure that patients followed their medical treatments and did not smoke, spit, or otherwise "morally or materially" challenge the integrity of the hospital.[30]

The German, British, and Swiss governments worked together to build the Protestant Deaconess Hospital, established in 1857.[31] Originally, the hospital was a rented house with thirty beds. In 1870, the hospital committee built a new hospital in the southeastern part of the city on land that the Egyptian government donated in Muharram Bey.[32] The hospital committee later took "advantage of the financial boom," sold the Muharram Bey facility, and built a new hospital that had "no equal in spaciousness and completeness" in the early 1900s.[33] The hospital's governing board was made up of one Swiss, three German, and three British men, and the hospital relied on the women of the Kaiserwerth Sisterhood, which was affiliated with the German Deaconess (Christian Protestant) movement, to provide nursing services.[34] The Greek Hospital was built in the first half of the nineteenth century in the northeastern part of the city near the eastern port.[35]

These hospitals had deep connections to the elite of the city through advisory boards and subscriptions, leading one historian to argue that the hospitals represented elite control of their colonies.[36] Yet the hospital patients do not demonstrate the type of communal loyalty that such control would presumably entail. Instead of each hospital serving none but its own community, it attended to patients regardless of religion and nationality, creating ample opportunity for people to use hospitals outside their own communal affiliations. These hospitals thus should not be seen, as another historian has argued, as exclusive symbols of foreign protection and detachment from the rest of the city, nor were they exclusive to those who could pay for their services.[37] Indeed, the hospitals also functioned as charitable establishments where patients of all ethnicities, religions, and nationalities could, and did, get treatment for free. The foreign hospitals were central public health providers for the city at large.[38]

PATIENT CLASSIFICATION
AND IMPERIAL COMPETITION

Of the 5,800 patients admitted to Alexandria's hospitals in 1870, the European Hospital cared for 1,366 of them, or almost 24 percent, placing it as the primary hospital among the foreign institutions.[39] The Greek Hospital was the next largest, serving 773 patients that year, 13 percent of the total patients.[40] The Deaconess was significantly smaller, serving only 304 patients, or just 5 percent. Together, these three hospitals accounted for 42 percent of the inpatients of Alexandria. Their numbers grew significantly after the turn of the century, with the Greek Hospital serving 3,055 patients, the Deaconess serving 2,451, and the European serving 1,791 patients in 1911.[41] The European and the Deaconess Hospitals documented the sex of their patients, and male patients used the hospitals much more frequently than women.[42] Well over 50 percent of the patients were men, with the remaining divided into categories of both women and children (boys as well as girls).[43]

In addition to keeping track of the sex of its patients, each of these hospitals recorded its patients by nationality and, in some cases, religion or ethnicity. A hospital's statistics were then used to account for its activities and budget in its annual report, to attract donors, to show its strength in comparison to other foreign hospitals, and to provide leverage in negotiations with the Egyptian government for subventions and land. "We are appealing to your zeal for all things, sirs, to contribute to the prosperity of the European Hospital," French consul and European Hospital president Paul Verchère de Reffye wrote in the hospital's 1909 annual report, which was then sent to all donors. He continued, "To maintain our work at the level of our recent progress in the sciences and at the head of the hospitals of Alexandria, we would need greater financial resources each year."[44]

The Deaconess, European, and Greek Hospitals used different categories to track inpatients, suggesting that there was not yet universal classifications of people of Alexandria. Instead, hospital administrators could choose to accept or disregard a category—or, perhaps, to limit the categories offered—in registering patients. While some of the categories in play had legal definitions, others were socially defined. For example, while there would not be a legally defined Egyptian nationality until 1926,[45] both the Deaconess and the

European Hospitals regularly employed the category "Egyptian" in their reports during the end of the nineteenth century.[46] The Greek Hospital did not.

Records reveal how porous and arbitrary hospital categories could be and suggest that the categories could be utilized to bolster consular claims of imperial strength. The European Hospital's 1911 annual report, for example, documented 656 Arab inpatients, the single largest group. Another 82 inpatients were classified as Egyptians. We have no way of knowing exactly who these Arabs were and if or why they were different from Egyptians, presumably indigenous Muslims, in the eyes of the hospital. They could very well have been Bedouin, as there was a distinct increase in the numbers of peoples registered as Bedouin in the Egyptian census by the end of the nineteenth century.[47] Still, eight times as many Bedouin than other indigenous Muslims seems dubious. It is also highly unlikely that North Africans in Alexandria would be called Arabs, yet there is no other category in any of the hospitals that might account for the French North African population. It is likewise implausible, if not impossible, that North Africans would be classified as French nationals. We cannot know who these patients were.

In contrast, the category "Arab" is not used at all by the Deaconess Hospital, which employed only the category "Egyptian," presumably to cover the indigenous Arabic speakers, marking 524 of 1,112 patients as such in 1890. These Egyptians were by far the largest percentage of patients in the Deaconess statistics, most likely comprising those marked as both Arab and Egyptian in the European Hospital annual reports.[48] The Deaconess and European Hospitals each had separate categories for Syrians, Armenians, and Turks, and neither utilized the classification "Ottoman."

While we do not and cannot know why or if the hospitals chose the categories used, we can suppose how the categories served imperial powers in their claims to space and resources in Egypt. For the European Hospital, which was affiliated with European countries that were not the dominant imperial powers of Egypt, it is quite possible that the division of both indigenous and foreign-born Muslim patients into Arabs and Egyptians was a means by which to challenge British rule of Egypt. Note that Copt, or native Egyptian Christian, was often listed as yet another separate "nationality."[49] That is, by diminishing the category "Egyptian" numerically and using the more generic category "Arab," the French and Italian Consulates, in their leadership role in the European Hospital, could conceivably claim their own colonial subjects, Maghribi and, after 1912, Libyan, respectively, as a part of the population of

Alexandria and therefore underscore the importance of the French and Italian presence in the city.[50] And even if these patients were Bedouin, then the separation of Arab from Egyptian once again minimized the number of those who would be considered indigenous under British rule. That is, this category suggests that the European Hospital is serving a population specifically *not* covered by the British colonial rule, which is focused on Egyptians. The British consular employees acknowledged the European Hospital as a site of French influence, regularly referring to it as "the French Hospital."[51] And although the German Consulate officially controlled the Deaconess, the British held equal power on the hospital's governing board.[52] Arguably, then, the Deaconess Hospital could well have lumped all "natives" into the category "Egyptian" so that the British colonial government could more easily make the case for its impact on public health.[53]

Additionally, it is most likely no accident that the category "Ottoman" is missing from both the Deaconess and European Hospital annual reports. The various European countries involved would have reason to note that the Ottoman Empire consisted of multiple ethnic and national groups and was therefore not one nation; indeed, this assertion was a key component of European colonialism in the region. By dividing people into different ethnic categories, the European countries stated that the Ottoman Empire was not a unified entity, and therefore a takeover of part of it was not a challenge to all of it. Thus were the British and French able to justify seizing control of Mount Lebanon, Egypt, and North Africa, all without declaring war on the Ottoman Empire as a whole.[54]

Whereas both the Deaconess and European Hospitals grouped Arabic-speaking Muslims into broad categories, they maintained very detailed national divisions in regard to their European patients. In the 1890 Deaconess Hospital annual report, European categories include "German," "English," "British Empire" (*Sujets des Possessions Anglaises*), "French," "Spanish," "Swiss," "Dutch," "Austrians," "subjects of the Danube states," "Italians," "Russians," "Scandinavians," and "Greeks." The specificity of category for the European states, in comparison with the lack thereof for indigenous Muslims, mirrors a narrative that places nationality within the realm of Europe, slowly making its way to the Middle East and, in this case, Egypt.[55] It underscores that in the late nineteenth and early twentieth centuries, categories of nationality were in the service of empire. "Scottish," "Irish," and "Welsh," for example, are not their own European categories within the Deaconess report, despite appearing as separate national categories elsewhere in British consular records.[56]

English, British Empire, German, and Swiss together account for 221 patients at the Deaconess in 1890, just under 20 percent of its total patients. That the British subjects, English and other, were by no means the majority of patients there was reinforced in a letter written by the British consular surgeon, Dr. Morrison, over two decades later: "Of the motley crew of 2127 as many as 279 were British subjects," wording that makes it obvious that 279, or just over 13 percent, was considered a significant number of British patients.[57]

Unlike the Deaconess, the European Hospital across this time period had a much larger percentage of patients from its affiliated consular nationalities. In 1909, more than 45 percent of its patients were from France, Italy, and the Austro-Hungarian Empire.[58] In 1911, when the hospital's administrative council included the consuls of France, Italy, and Austro-Hungry, 129 patients either identified as or were identified as French, 502 as Italian, and 30 as Austrian, which altogether represented approximately 37 percent of the patients. Another 3 were German, 5 were British, and 34 were Greek. Armenians and Syrians together made up nearly 175 patients, alongside 155 Maltese. Crete, Russia, Switzerland, Belgium, the Ottoman Empire, Turkey, Bulgaria, Montenegro, and Spain were also represented within the rainbow of patients. Categories used in other years look much the same, with a few exceptions: the 1909 annual report included categories for "Copts," "Chaldeans," and "Syriacs," along with "Egyptians" and "Syrians."[59] These were the only religious categories detailed in the European Hospital reports; Jews, Muslims, Catholics, and Protestants went unnoted. The majority of European Hospital annual reports divide the patients only by nationality, and not by race, religion, or other affiliations; this singularity of categorization was in contrast to the Greek and Deaconess Hospitals, both of which had separate accountings of patients' religions or ethnicities.

The Statutes of the European Hospital, first published in 1861, declare that the mission of the hospital was to serve all *Europeans*, regardless of nationality or religion; that it would privilege no single country or person; and that it would be run by no single person: "It is irrevocably established that the European Hospital was founded for indigent European patients of every nation and religion . . . and will never be given to any country or person."[60] Yet the consuls involved in the leadership of the hospital all came from majority-Catholic countries on the continent.[61] Interestingly, the Deaconess Hospital was already in existence when the statutes were published; perhaps the European Hospital was created to be a specifically separate medical system for these *Catholic* Europeans, or perhaps these statutes were a response to this Protestant-affiliated competition. The annual reports also regularly referred to the hospital as an international charitable organization, stating that "these considerations of human solidarity, without any distinction of race or of religion," marked it as a hospital worthy of promotion and protection.[62]

The European Hospital of Alexandria may have been founded as a hospital for Europeans, but it in fact served people from all over the world, most of whom appear to have been neither European nor Catholic.[63] As its mission grew from European to Alexandrian, the hospital's supporters, which included the Egyptian government, British, and several other European consulates as well as local businesses and individuals, became equally diverse.[64] In the hospital's 1911 annual report, de Reffye describes the European Hospital as a fundamentally Alexandrian institution increasingly valued by the municipal government, a participant in the lively world of science, a part of the economy of the city, and most important, a dedicated service for the entirety of the population.[65]

Similarly, the majority of patients at the Protestant Deaconess Hospital were not Protestant, though its governing board largely was.[66] Although the British population was the largest Protestant community, even it was not majority Catholic; most British subjects were Catholic Maltese.[67] That is, the overall Protestant population pool from which the Deaconess might find patients was relatively tiny. It would not have been able to survive if it were limited to the Protestant community. The hospital administration kept tallies of its patients' religions and nationalities. Thus, we know that in 1890, 484 Muslims sought treatment at the hospital, nearly 44 percent of the 1,112 patients seen. A quarter of the patients were either Roman or Greek Catholics. Only 16 percent (180) of those who sought treatment at the hospital were Protestants. Medical staff also extended services to Copts, Jews, Armenians, and Maronites.[68] As in the case of the European Hospital, categories both mattered and did not matter: administrators made note of the faith and nationality of their patients but treated them regardless.

Unlike its counterparts, the Greek Hospital served mostly Greeks, whether self-defined or institutionally identified as such.[69] In 1879, 83 percent of those who sought treatment at the hospital listed their nationality as Greek; in 1882, slightly more than 57 percent would claim the same national affiliation.[70] The

Greek Hospital administration had less interest in national categorization than the Deaconess and European administrations: "European," "Greek," and "indigenous" are the only national categories used in the hospital's records. Likewise, the secretary of the Hellenic-Egyptian community, who sent the statistics to the Egyptian government, marked only three possible subject categories when dividing patients: "Hellenic," "Ottoman," and "diverse."[71]

In the data provided by the Hellenic-Egyptian community, those classified as "Greek" or "indigenous" in the nationality section and "Hellenic" or "Ottoman" in the subject section are the clear focus. "European" and "diverse" stand in as catchall categories for those who are less important in each statistical grouping, respectively. But it is not only the Europeans who are placed in a megacategory. Ottoman subjects are all one category; only Hellenics are unique. Since Greece was not a European imperial player in Egypt in the way that the British and French were, the Greek Hospital had less at stake in managing the classifications of European and indigenous bodies and in accepting or defining the peoples of the Ottoman Empire.

That the Greek Hospital was unconcerned with other European communities is evident in the presentation of its statistics, which are included matter-of-factly as an addendum to a letter the patriarch of Alexandria wrote in February 1884 to Nubar Pasha, president of the Council of Ministers, requesting Egyptian governmental subvention of the hospital.[72] In the letter, the patriarch emphasizes the high number of indigenous patients served: "The hospital provides great service not only to the members of the Greek colony but also to *other* European colonies and more specifically to the local subjects."[73] Here, the patriarch positioned the Greeks as Europeans, against the "local." The Greek Hospital thus positioned itself as serving a separate community, "the Greek colony," and being a vital Alexandrian institution at the same time.

HOSPITALS AS CHARITABLE INSTITUTIONS

The hospitals were local institutions, but they were also missionary and colonial spaces serving a primarily civilian population. Within the European Hospital, although the members of the administrative council and the consul who was serving as president held the final power, the nuns made the hospitals function. The sister superior was the final voice, responsible for the staff, the treasury, and the receiving and registering of patients.[74] She collected fees, which made up the majority of the budget. In 1908, for example, the European

Hospital claimed 99,079.90 francs in ordinary receipts or fees and 10,534.50 in subscriptions and allocations, which were diverse donations and municipal subventions. The sister superior was also responsible for spending funds as necessary, such as for nurses' private space and lives,[75] and sent monthly reports to the hospital's treasurer and president. Extraordinary expenses had to be approved by the hospital's Special Council of the Administration.[76]

Missionaries were associated with charity, and the hospitals were, at their core, charitable organizations. However, often it was not the hospitals themselves that covered all the medical expenses of the poor. The consulates and national relief societies also stepped in. The Swiss Relief Society, for example, paid for the hospitalization of Lisette Bohren; she was one of many whose medical needs were paid for by strangers. Examples of the consulates helping their medically distressed subjects abound in hospital records and consular correspondence.[77] Foreign hospitals may have opened themselves to patients of all religions and nationalities, but they were able to do so because it was often the responsibility of religious and national groups to pay for their own poor. Some consulates paid directly for the medical needs of their citizens; others employed relief societies to keep track of their sick and dead. The British consulate paid 5,593 francs in 1909 to cover the costs of fifty-four sick and seven dead at the European Hospital. Similarly, the French Relief Society paid 2,921 francs for forty-four sick and two dead.[78] The hospitals' annual reports provide evidence of the many consulates and relief societies involved in making the hospitals solvent.

The British Consulate struggled with the overwhelming health needs of the British expatriate poor long before the inception of official British colonial rule in 1882. In 1866, G. E. Stanley, British consul of Alexandria, wrote to his foreign secretary: "There is no hospital here [in Alexandria] where pauper patients are taken in gratis, the consulate on which such pauper depends undertaking to pay his expenses in hospital."[79] While by the 1860s the government hospital as well as a number of foreign hospitals had open-door policies, Stanley's language suggests that the system of "free" patients was more complicated: the patient still remained the responsibility of his or her national or ethnic community, even though the individual might have sought medical care at another foreign community's hospital.

Why, then, were there times when the consulate or relief society did not pay for these patients?[80] What made one patient able to tap into the consular/relief society network and another unable to do so? Are the discrepancies the product of negotiations between consulates or relief societies and hospitals over discounted fees? The blurry boundary between Stanley's imperial subject dependent on consulates and the charitable cases delineated by the hospitals themselves suggests the ambiguity of categories, as the patient was both British (or French, Greek, Italian, etc.) and a local impoverished person in need of cost-free medical care.

Even when the consulates paid for their subjects' hospitalization, they tried to recoup the costs, as in the case of Lisette Bohren. Despite each government's efforts, however, the loans and assistance offered by consulates were not always returned. The case of Margaret Hughes is instructive. Hughes was an English woman who worked as a servant in Alexandria. In 1872, she was deemed "insane," and the British Consulate paid for her return trip to England, as there was no "acceptable" hospital for insane Europeans in Alexandria. The consulate made numerous attempts to get the money spent on her return fare to England from Hughes's employer, to no avail. The Foreign Office in London objected to the consulate's expense: "If people choose to have European servants in foreign countries, they are hardly entitled to get rid of them at public expense."[81] Acting Consul General Henry Calvert both acknowledged the Foreign Office objections and overruled them. He argued that the consulate often had no choice in cases of extreme illness or need.

This exchange between Calvert and the Foreign Office hints at the limits and function of charity. His Majesty's government was available as a last resort, but only for the very sick and the very poor. Family, friends, and employers were expected to pay first, as tending to the sick was not a strictly governmental affair. Moreover, while the consulate may have stepped in when necessary, it lacked the ability to force others to pay.[82]

Free patients continued to make up a substantial percentage of those who used Alexandria's foreign hospitals throughout the decades under study in this book. In 1876, 20 percent (203 of 1,000) of the patients treated at the Greek Hospital were indigenous, and 183 (90 percent) of those indigenous patients could not pay. These numbers were not unique to one year of statistics but represented the norm at the Greek Hospital, year after year. Decades later, the 1913 Department of Public Census statistics show that in 1911, the last year for which the 1913 report had numbers, the four hospitals listed as foreign (European, Greek, Jewish, and Deaconess) served a total of 6,769 inpatients, of whom 1,028, or approximately 15 percent, were free patients. Fewer than 3 percent of people treated at the European Hospital, which had vastly more beds for third- and fourth-class patients than for first- and second-class, were free patients, according to the Department of Public Census. However, statistics provided by the European Hospital itself reveal that the institution provided 1,661 days of free care that same year.[83] That number translates into free care provided to more than 4.5 patients a day. Also in 1911, the Greek Hospital treated nearly 50 percent of its patients for free, and the Jewish Hospital treated more than 90 percent for free. It is impossible to know from these statistics if consulates or benevolent societies paid for these free patients. Nonetheless, it is clear that the hospitals were a fundamental part of a broader social services network in Alexandria. These medical establishments were part of the city's charitable infrastructure, serving alongside the government hospital and clinics, and it was to these institutions that the poor turned for medical care.

HOSPITAL GOVERNANCE AND IMPERIAL PRESENCE

The list of donors to the foreign hospitals of Alexandria shows the overlap of the Ottoman, British, and French Empires in Egypt; the position of the various imperial powers that vied for dominance in the region; and a complex web of local governmental and civil power relations. Donating to the hospitals gave businesses, consulates, and individuals the chance to vote on hospital policy. Relief societies, organized by national affiliation, donated to the hospitals that served their patients. For the Deaconess, money came from a number of sources. The hospital received contributions and fees paid by patients of the hospital and affiliated clinics. In addition, the hospital received large (*extraordinaires*) and small charitable gifts. Other monies came from consulates and relief societies. The hospitals collected monies both in private donations and in public collections.

Private donations were not always made directly to the hospitals: societies and associations often raised funds for hospital care and other medical services. The Italian Benevolent Aid Society organized ambulances to bring patients to hospitals during the 1883 cholera outbreak.[84] The First Aid Society of Alexandria rushed the victims of an explosion at the port to a nearby hospital in 1909.[85] The Association of Charitable Ladies of Alexandria received a donation from a dying woman at the European Hospital in appreciation for all their good works.[86] Likewise, the German Society of Alexandria received a private donation to pay for the "recreation of convalescents" at the Deaconess

Hospital.[87] Additionally, the hospital collected monies through a variety of other financial tools. While the vast majority of the money for the European and Deaconess Hospitals, as well as nearly 50 percent of the money needed to run the Greek Hospital, came from inpatients, the hospitals were nonetheless dependent on the society in which they were embedded to fund their institutions.[88]

Yet donating to "national" hospitals in turn-of-the-twentieth-century Egypt was anything but straightforward. One might assume that the primary donors to the European Hospital, for example, would be the French, Italian, or Austro-Hungarian Consulates. However, the British Consulate contributed 938 francs to the European Hospital in 1909, despite the low numbers of patients identified as English (5). Even if we were to add Maltese patients (129), the British still donated disproportionately more than their French counterparts, who doled out only 106 francs, or the Austro-Hungarian Consulate, which donated a mere 62. It is worth noting as well that the British donated through their consulate, whereas the French donated through a beneficence society. This pattern repeated itself in other years. Clearly, the various national communities recognized that the hospitals would not and could not be medical institutions solely for specific nationalities. The hospitals, indeed, were reliant on the inclusion of all sorts of foreign institutions and organizations in their definition of community.

Hospital boards and councils also sold subscriptions to raise funds. For the European Hospital, one subscription cost four talaris, equal to approximately twenty francs.[89] Purchasing a subscription gave the buyer the right to vote on hospital policy and procedures at the general assembly or during annual meetings. Individuals, consulates, and businesses could purchase more than one subscription, but no more than fifteen in a year; therefore, no one individual, consulate, or business could have more than fifteen votes.[90] While each hospital also boasted a list of individual subscribers, only five subscribers, aside from banks and consulates, bought subscriptions to both the Deaconess and European Hospitals.[91] One notable dual subscriber was Barker and Company, a shipping company linked to a British family that had been in the region since the mid-eighteenth century and in Alexandria since the time of Mehmed ʿAli.[92] The Barkers were patriotically British, although they were committed to living in Alexandria. The family regularly donated to both the Deaconess and the European Hospitals, very purposefully *not* limiting themselves to the hospital officially affiliated with the British community.[93]

An administrative council consisting of a president, vice president, treasurer, and twelve delegates from among its subscribers formed the hospital committee of the European Hospital. The president was always the consul of one of the main European countries involved.[94] It was the council's task to approve of all new subscribers, which allowed it to maintain control over who influenced the overseeing of the hospital; consulates were generally the largest hospital shareholders.[95] The Italian, French, Austrian, Portuguese, Belgian, and Swedish Consulates all bought subscriptions in 1894.[96] The French and Austrian/Austro-Hungarian Consulates held the most power, buying the maximum allowance of voting rights, with the Italian and Belgian next, and Swedish and Portuguese Consulates the least influential.[97] By 1911, only Italy, Austro-Hungary, and France bought subscriptions, each holding equal—and the maximum allowed—shares in the hospital.[98] While sharing power in the hospitals, the consulates vied for influence: hospital bylaws insisted that the hospital would not "belong" to any one country, but the countries involved nonetheless jockeyed for leadership using whatever means necessary.[99]

Local business interests also competed for leadership roles in the hospitals. In 1894 the Anglo-Egyptian Bank, the Bank of Egypt, the Imperial Ottoman Bank, Credit Lyonnais Bank, and the Gas Company of E. Lebon and Company all held more voting power within the European Hospital committee than any other entity but the French and Austrian Consulates. The Credit Lyonnais and E. Lebon and Company held the same amount of shares as the French and Austrian representatives. The banks and utility company—the economic backbone of Alexandria—understood the vital role that hospitals played in the functioning of the city. Four years earlier, the same four banks had also been among the largest donors to the Deaconess Hospital.

WHOSE MONEY? EGYPTIAN GOVERNMENTAL SUBVENTIONS AND FOREIGN HOSPITALS

The Egyptian government was not absent from the lists of hospital donors. The government funded the hospitals as part of its provision of public services to the city. Its subvention to the Deaconess Hospital, where a majority of the patients were categorized as "Egyptian," made up the single largest portion of the hospital's donated monies. (The British, who understood the hospital to be theirs, were the second-largest donors.)[100] The Greek Hospital used its service to the indigenous as a reason to receive money from the government. The European Hospital made similar claims.[101] These medical institutions not only requested money from the Egyptian government but also utilized their requests for government assistance to demonstrate that they were part of the municipal fabric, even during times of political turmoil. The Egyptian government, however, did not get the same return for investing in the hospitals as the European consulates did; it was not offered voting rights in return for subventions, for example. Whereas European consulates were involved in hospital governance as functionaries of the hospitals and not as representatives of the city or state, the Egyptian government was involved because it was the final arbiter of space and public utility. This key difference explains why the Egyptian government neither received nor asked for voting rights in the hospitals, despite its financial and real estate contributions to them.

The Egyptian government had previously relied on the foreign hospitals in times of upheaval. In the late 1870s, when the bankrupt Egyptian government was forced by European governments to reassess its spending and cut subventions to the foreign hospitals, these hospitals continued to attend to the people of Alexandria, regardless of nationality or religion, supplementing Egyptian governmental funding with monies from their budget.[102]

Although the colonial occupation of 1882 exacerbated the differences between the so-called foreigner and local, the foreign hospital committees maintained stable relationships with the Egyptian government. And although the Egyptian government was to report to the British as the new colonial rulers, it was not to the British but to the Egyptian national government that hospital committees directed their requests for subventions to help with operating expenses or acquisition of new land. The Egyptian government maintained the right to refuse these requests, even those of the Deaconess Hospital, despite its affiliation with the British community.

After the financial crisis of 1876, and especially after the British occupation of 1882, the hospital committees made concerted efforts to maintain their hospitals as public institutions. A request from the Greek community to the Egyptian government in 1884 provides evidence of the extent to which foreigners saw their future tied to that of Egypt. That year, the Greek Orthodox patriarch of Alexandria wrote to Nubar Pasha, president of the Council of Ministers, to ask for help with funds for the Greek Hospital: "Indeed, Your Excellence cannot ignore the deplorable state of the Hellenic-Egyptian community's finances. Their revenues had already decreased and had become insufficient for their needs before the insurrection ['Urabi revolt], and following this event, they have reduced to levels that threaten the very existence of all institutions of the community, including, most important, the hospital."[103] In this rendering of the sad state of the Greek colony and the service of the Greek Hospital, the patriarch links the community's fate to that of Egypt at large: they, too, have suffered since the British invasion. This strategy, taken up not only by the Greeks, to position hospitals as serving Alexandria reaffirmed the hospital's belonging and commitment to the city and the country at large.[104]

A closer look at additional petitions to the Egyptian government for subventions reveals the ambiguous status of the foreign hospitals within the city after the financial crisis and then the revolt and occupation. Like its counterparts, the European Hospital received, and then lost, subventions from the Egyptian government during the financial crisis in the late 1870s. In January 1880, the French consul general and interim president of the European Hospital, Alphonse Dobigne, submitted the first of several requests asking that the Egyptian government return to its practice of providing an annual subvention of ten thousand francs.[105] Dobigne's petitions repeatedly pointed out that the hospital continued to serve all Alexandrians, without discrimination, at its own expense when required. Dobigne requested that the government help the hospital board preserve this practice. He presented the work of the hospital's board and its employees as that of stalwart participants in the battle for the public health of Alexandria, painting a picture of a hospital staff dutifully attending to all Alexandria's peoples at a time when the Egyptian government was unable to help its own population.

These hospitals were thus serving as functionaries of the Egyptian government, as spaces of colonial influence, and as local institutions. These multiple roles were underscored in a letter written to Riyad Pasha, president of the Council of Ministers and minister of finance, in 1880 from twelve members of the Committee for the European Hospital (alternately called the Administrative Council). The signers stated that

> the European hospital of Alexandria is the oldest establishment of its kind in Egypt and has never stopped serving the population of this city, irrespective of nationality or religion, providing all the services that it had. . . .
>
> When the Egyptian government hit on bad times, it stopped paying the subvention as of 1877. . . . Today, however, in V. E.'s [the khedive's] efforts to reorganize the country and the government it is time to give money back to the organizations that work for the public good. . . .

The government recognizes the true interests of the country and the public assistance that is necessary.[106]

This letter positions the committee as allies of the people of Alexandria. They present the hospital as part of the city, and in service to it. The letter writers additionally mark themselves as having done more for Alexandria than the Egyptian government had, noting that the government had stopped paying subventions during its financial crisis, thereby abandoning the public health needs of the city, yet the hospital "never stopped serving" the public. By stating that the government "recognizes the true interests of the country," the European Hospital placed itself as an institution acting not for religious beliefs or for imperial political goals but for the state of Egypt, for the "public good." If we remember that the European Hospital, according to its own bylaws, was always under the direct tutelage of a European consul, it is remarkable that it is asking for money from the Egyptian national government as a purveyor of Egyptian public health. By doing so, the hospital exposes that the Egyptian national government, weak though it may have been in the face of European encroachment, had the ability to define the public good, to encourage institutions to help their people, and to welcome European institutions to its shores.

The correspondence about the European Hospital's subventions shows the complicated layers of Egyptian governmental bureaucracy. Letters between the Council of Ministers and the Alexandria Municipality reveal that the municipality had previously paid the ten thousand francs to the European Hospital, using earmarked khedival funds (al-da'ira al-khassa).[107] However, since the national government stopped providing money to the municipality, the municipality could not and would not cover the expense.[108]

In support of the European Hospital's request for subventions, the governor of Alexandria wrote the Council of Ministers in the summer of 1880. He reminded them that the hospital was very important to the European community, pointing specifically to the French, Italians, and Germans.[109] In encouraging the Egyptian government to fund a foreign-owned and -operated hospital because of its importance to several foreign communities, the governor signaled that these groups were not outside the boundaries of the city's population. Indeed, in later annual reports, the president of the European Hospital would go out of his way to thank the municipality of Alexandria for help securing funds.[110]

Within two days of receiving the letter from the governor of Alexandria, the Council of Ministers decided to reinstate a subvention to the European

Hospital in the amount of five thousand francs.[111] For the next two years, the European Hospital continued to agitate for the return to the earlier amount of ten thousand francs.[112] Consul Alexander Ritter von Suzzara of Austria-Hungary, also the president of the European Hospital, wrote to Riyad Pasha: "While we are very appreciative, we think that perhaps you did not realize how important our need for money is, and we are now asking for the other five thousand francs."[113] The willingness of the hospital committee to continue to press for money and land indicates a conception of their hospital as a vital civil service and of themselves as fully deserving partners in the city's public health infrastructure. In other words, by choosing to challenge the national government repeatedly, the members of the European Hospital committee continually reasserted themselves as specifically local entities, and their hospital as a local institution, in Alexandria.[114] Their pleas were successful: as of October 1886, the European Hospital received the largest single annual subvention from the Egyptian government.[115]

In the early 1880s, the Deaconess Hospital also agitated for the Egyptian government to resume the subventions it had given to the hospital between 1858, soon after the hospital's founding, and 1876.[116] The consul general of Germany contacted the governor of Alexandria for help. The Deaconess had been accustomed to receiving money from the municipality of Alexandria, also taken from earmarked khedival funds. The municipality had petitioned the national government on behalf of the hospital in both 1876 and 1877, and in both years the hospital received monies from the khedival emergency fund,[117] which typically had been used for necessary public works such as expansions and roads. In this case, funds were given to a foreign hospital, which indicates the extent to which these hospitals were seen as vital parts of the Egyptian infrastructure and necessary to the success and well-being of the country.

FOREIGN HOSPITALS, THE EGYPTIAN GOVERNMENT, AND THE QUEST FOR LAND

Alexandria's foreign communities regularly built, expanded, renovated, and rebuilt their hospitals. The physical building and maintenance of the hospitals further linked these communities with the municipal and national governments, which were focused on public health and hygiene during this time period.[118] This kind of exchange recommitted the foreign communities to Alexandria and at the same time obligated the city, as represented by the national and municipal governments, to them. Throughout the late nineteenth and early twentieth centuries, the European, Deaconess, and Greek Hospital committees all asked the municipality for help in building or expanding their hospitals, in addition to the subventions for covering operating expenses.[119] As was the case when hospitals requested subventions, administrative committees interacted directly with the Egyptian government both before and after British occupation. In their petitions, the hospitals positioned themselves as deserving of national land and resources. More than simple requests to construct a space for communal health concerns, these petitions expressed a desire to build and tangibly add to the structural and service-oriented infrastructure of the city of Alexandria. The hospital petitions also reveal the extent to which foreign consulates were both imperial representatives and key local players. Foreign requests for Egyptian land therefore represent multiple goals.

The Alexandria Municipal Authority held the power to maintain and expand the infrastructure, manage the private land market, and control and monitor vacant lots.[120] Nevertheless, the municipal powers did not take the lead in negotiations for hospital (or cemetery) space. Instead, the Egyptian national government was the primary decision maker about which public institutions could build where, and the municipal authorities served as facilitators for communication between the national government and the hospital lay boards.[121] In choosing to enable or obstruct the foreign communities in the building of their hospitals, the national government determined what the built environment of public health would look like in Alexandria. Thus, when European consulates and hospital committees requested land from the Egyptian government, they participated in the governmental process of the creation and maintenance of local space—this was specifically beyond private land sales. In this way, foreign nationals were part of the building of the everyday city, of the decisions about what to do with public land, to be used by all of its inhabitants regardless of their origin. By asking for a government donation of and/or subvention of land instead of purchasing land through the private market, hospital administrations positioned their institutions as Egyptian establishments for the public good. This relationship between hospital committees and the Egyptian government is evidence of the Egyptian government's ability to maintain and meticulously control on-the-ground governance, even in the face of imperial powers and colonial institutions.

There was, however, a power struggle over dominance in the city, as can be seen in the details of the negotiations between the hospitals and the Egyptian government. For example, when the European Hospital requested a subvention of ten thousand francs in the early 1880s, it also submitted a separate petition asking for land to enlarge its outpatient eye clinic and to build a garden for convalescents. Over the next two years, the hospital alternated between requests for land and requests for monies, each time reiterating how the European Hospital, specifically the eye clinic, which served primarily the indigenous population, was essential to the city as a whole.[122]

In 1882, the Egyptian government approved of land for the European Hospital so that it could build a new facility, but the hospital committee sought help with more than just land acquisition.[123] A section of the property had formerly been a foundry, and a large piece of equipment remained on the land.[124] The hospital, together with the Catholic monastery abutting it, asked for government aid in getting rid of the equipment and readying the land for building. As it pressed for more help, the hospital committee pointed to its ability and willingness to work within the Egyptian bureaucracy.

During the two years (1880–1882) of wrangling with the government for land and subventions hospital leadership changed, with Consul Suzzara of Austria-Hungary replacing Alphonse Dobigne of France as hospital president. While the leadership represented the pan-European nature of the hospital, this change in personnel also illustrates another point: the hospital outlasted the comings and goings of individual Europeans in Alexandria. The building itself was evidence of the permanence of the multinational foreign community as a whole and of its commitment to the city. In other words, while the individual might be a temporary foreigner, the hospital was very much a permanent local.[125]

After the Deaconess Hospital secured the reinstatement of Egyptian government subventions in the late 1880s, its committee likewise sought to build a new hospital, which would replace the one built on land donated by the Egyptian government in 1870.[126] The Deaconess Hospital's petition for land reveals how hospital committees learned to navigate local bureaucracies, concretizing their institutions within the local landscape. In 1899, Consul Hartmann of Germany, president of the Deaconess Hospital, wrote to the Council of Ministers on behalf of the hospital committee to renew a request from the German consul general in Cairo to the khedive. Hartmann asked for land on the edge of Alexandria, in the suburb of Ibrahimiyya, on which to build a new hospital; the hospital committee offered to pay for the land. The old hospital was crumbling and could not uphold the standards of modern hygiene.[127] Moreover, the new property would allow a garden to be built for sick people, providing open air and sunshine. In a definitive tone, Consul Hartmann explained that the new land was not only a request but also fundamental to the upkeep of public health in Alexandria:

> Due to the expansion of the city of Alexandria, the Deaconess Hospital is currently surrounded by people and noise, and the small garden no longer offers tranquility or the necessary clean air to the sick. . . . Modern hygienic necessities require us to extend [or move] our hospital; the current situation is impossible. . . . As the city of Alexandria does not have a big garden and a place for sick people and convalescents to relax, we ask for this space.[128]

In phrasing the request in terms of modern hygiene, Hartmann used the logic of empire that suggested that health and political progress were synonymous.[129] The wording of this request reaffirms the European-sponsored hospital as a part of an international public health effort to civilize the colonized countries, just as it orients the hospital to the specific needs of the city.

The Egyptian government, however, rejected the request, citing the land's proximity to Muslim and military cemeteries. The government concern was twofold: The proposed hospital land was too close to dead bodies for public health regulations, and it was reserved to meet cemetery expansion needs. In other words, the Egyptian government reclaimed the mantle of public health from the imperial hospital. The Europeans in Alexandria did not have an exclusive claim to authority on this subject. Rather, Europeans had to negotiate with the Egyptian government and ultimately defer to its judgment. The Deaconess Hospital committee responded by pointing out that the land in question was actually far enough away from the cemeteries by law and that these cemeteries were already marked for transfer to the neighborhood of al-Maks.[130]

More important, the committee argued that the government had already allowed an indigenous hospital and an English school to be built on land that was closer to the cemeteries than the plot currently requested. In making this argument, the committee insisted that they, too, were equally in need and deserved equal consideration. By charging that the indigenous or government hospitals could build closer to the cemeteries in question, the Deaconess Hospital moved the question from one of public health to one of political favoritism. By denying this land and using an excuse the hospital claimed to be untrue, the Egyptian government was denying the Deaconess Hospital's importance in the local infrastructure. Moreover, in their push for the proposed cemetery land, the Deaconess Hospital committee argued that living Alexandrians and those who worked on the behalf of living Alexandrians were as important as, if not more important than, those buried in the surrounding cemeteries. The committee members affirmed, "The land would be used not just for worship or for the sick people but for the public interest, with no regard of nationality or religious affiliation."[131] Despite increasing pressure from Hartmann and others, a letter sent from the finance minister to the president of the Council of Ministers on June 27, 1899, pointed out that the land was not available either to the hospital or to others who had requested expansion. In the end the Egyptian government refused the request.[132]

The Deaconess Hospital finally opened in a new location in May 1909.[133] It is unclear if the government reversed its decision about the cemetery or if the hospital was built on a different plot. In either case, moving the hospital did not come completely without cost. The Egyptian government granted the property to the hospital at half price, which limited the financing possibilities of the hospital building. The status of the hospital land as a donation meant that the hospital committee would be unable to sell the building in the future and could therefore not obtain the necessary mortgage for the remaining cost. The members of the hospital committee were forced to privately finance the debt. Interestingly, the purchase of the new building was possible, in part, because the hospital committee "had the good fortune to sell the old hospital at a high price."[134] Because we know that the government donated the land for the previous hospital, this case suggests that the government changed its rules regarding the private sale of charitable land grants, perhaps as a result of the financial crisis under Khedive Isma'il. Whatever the case, government involvement required foreign communities to understand government bureaucracy and be willing to work within its confines. And the Egyptian government waited ten full years to fulfill the request of land to build a new hospital that the hospital administration deemed essential to modern hygiene.

Years before the European and Deaconess Hospitals' requests, when the Greek Hospital began to crumble, its hospital committee, too, turned to the Egyptian government for help.[135] The Greek community was in a bind. Like the Deaconess, the hospital was not able to keep up with modern hygienic standards. Even more pressing, the old building was collapsing. Unable to purchase additional land, in 1878 the community asked the khedive to donate or subsidize land close to the military hospital.[136] The khedive offered the hospital land in Muharram Bey, but the land was not available.[137] C. M. Salvagos, vice president of the Committee to Build a New Greek Hospital and the primary donor of its eye clinic, wrote to Zaki Pasha, governor of Alexandria, asking for help.[138] Salvagos explained that the land offered by the khedive was divided into four sections; of these, the first belonged to a private resident, who had bought it in order to build a summer home. The second section was free, and the third and fourth belonged to an agricultural society.[139] The hospital attempted to buy the land from the agricultural society but could manage to pay only one-fourth of the asking price.[140] The Greek community asked the government to pay the remaining sixteen thousand francs before the existing hospital fell into ruins.

By January 1879 the Greek Hospital committee, frustrated by the government's inaction and by the agricultural society's counterclaims, managed to find a new plot of land that was close to the military hospital and petitioned the government for permission to build on it.[141] Known as the "Cemetery of the Jews," the land was part of the larger Bab Sharqi Fort, and the War Ministry therefore considered it strategic military land, too close to the sea, cannons, and other fortifications to be appropriate for a foreign hospital.[142] Moreover, the ministry pointed out that it had already rejected a number of other requests for building on the land, which was a *waqf* and, as the gift of a family to the city, was not available for sale.[143] The request of the Greek community was therefore rejected.[144]

In a follow-up letter to Sharif Pasha, president of the Council of Ministers, Salvagos asked that the government find other land as quickly as possible for the Greek Hospital if the Cemetery of the Jews was not acceptable, as the hospital was close to collapse.[145] Consul General Dragounis of Greece supported Salvagos in his request, although the patriarch, who had intervened on behalf of the Greek Hospital in its previous request for subventions, was missing from this conversation. Nonetheless, the hospital committee's ability to call on the heads of Greek national and religious institutions demonstrates the importance of the Greek Hospital to its founding community. With Dragounis's request, the Egyptian government moved to reconsider, but it did not change its decision.[146] Not until 1905 did it finally approve a piece of land—in the neighborhood of Shatbi, most likely in the aforementioned fortifications and in the general area of the foreign cemeteries—to be sold at a reduced price to the Greek community for the construction of a new hospital.[147] If these archives tell the complete story, it took the Greek Hospital at least twenty-seven years to find a new home at the hands of the Egyptian government.

In each of these case studies, the local hospital committees needed the Egyptian national government in order to build and help the hospitals function. These are not stories in which the so-called natives are left to be acted on by outside powers. Rather, they are complicated stories of intertwined institutions of governance wherein the population of Alexandria could and would be served by a multiplicity of actors. Power was dispersed among these diverse players, not simply imposed by the European communities on the Egyptian government. Stories about the interactions between foreign communities and the Egyptian government are tales of the complexity of this imperial moment when Alexandria was an Egyptian city, an Ottoman city, and, after 1882, a British imperial city. The number of years required to secure a new home for the hospitals suggests both a bogged-down bureaucracy and a deliberate approach to the building of infrastructure. Delays in granting land suggest that foreign hospitals were institutions tied to the local processes of building and were not exempt from Egyptian laws. That the Greek Hospital asked for space for twenty-seven years while the Deaconess waited only ten might be a sign of the extra influence of the British, who were at the time the colonial rulers of the land, or it might highlight the lack of funds in the Greek community. It might simply be a matter of which lands were available at the moment when the various hospitals negotiated. No matter the reason, each example is further illustration that these various European hospitals were not colonial institutions that could unilaterally impose their will on Alexandria, separate from the Egyptian government. The Egyptian government could—and did—alternately block and help them. The hospitals epitomized complex, local institutions.

The foreign hospitals embodied the complexity of the categories "foreign" and "local" in late nineteenth- and early twentieth-century Alexandria. They were open spaces in which people from all walks of Alexandrian life could—and did—find medical care. From Lisette Bohren's sojourn in the Deaconess and the European Hospitals to the nameless indigenous patients of the Greek Hospital, these institutions served the people of Alexandria as a whole. In a time of financial crisis, growing nativist challenges, and burgeoning colonial rule, hospital administrations and lay committees positioned these hospitals as charitable local organizations and the communities they represented and served as belonging to Alexandria. These hospitals were simultaneously public and private institutions, at once separating and integrating Alexandria's diverse communities on national, religious, ethnic, and socioeconomic levels. Contrary to what prevailing scholarship on Alexandria suggests, these hospitals served the urban poor and functioned as mixing grounds for the population. By connecting the public health concerns of the foreign communities to those of the city as a whole, and by providing space for Alexandrians to provide for one another, the foreign hospitals became local institutions.

From the healing spaces of hospitals we now move to the funerals of the dead. In death, the individual Alexandrian could no longer enjoy the flexibility of movement between communities that had defined Alexandrian life. In death, consulates and communities that prided themselves on openness in their hospitals closed ranks. The openness and flexibility with which Alexandrians lived life had a firm deadline.

2 MOURNING THE DEAD, CONNECTING THE LIVING

ROSE NORTHCOTE WAS BORN in 1878 in Kent, England. By the early twentieth century, she found herself in Alexandria, where she worked as a private nurse. On April 26, 1904, she fell ill with typhoid fever and was admitted to the Deaconess Hospital. Doctors were unable to cure her, and Rose Northcote died at 5:30 p.m. on May 9, 1904.[1]

When she became ill and entered the hospital with a communicable disease, Rose Northcote simultaneously entered the bureaucratic system that would intertwine her fate with the British Consulate and the city of Alexandria, marking her as both a foreign national and a local resident. And when she died, an expansive religious, economic, national, and social network sprang into action to bury her body, inform her family, document her death, and wrap up the loose ends of her life. She was given a funeral, the rituals of which illustrate the complexities of being Alexandrian, as they were at once local and imperial. Her funeral, like that of the many other foreign-born residents of Alexandria, was an ephemeral moment of public performance, a "constitutive ritual act,"[2] wherein a cross section of Alexandrian society came together as a community of mourners, bound together only by death. Like Northcote herself, those who participated in the rituals surrounding her death were emblematic of the everyday in this transimperial, multi-empire city.

Death in Alexandria was also a bureaucratic moment. When Northcote and others like her died, imperial nation-states, in the form of consulates,

claimed bodies and lives as their own.[3] By claiming the dead, consular officials and the countries they represented used bodies to bolster the political
and social power of European empire and colonialism in Alexandria. So, on
May 9, the British Consulate received notice of Northcote's death. Sister Dora
Brooke, the sister superior of the Deaconess Hospital, wrote the death notice
and informed the consul general that a clergyman from the Church of England had visited with Northcote before her death.[4] Should the consul general want that particular clergyman to officiate Northcote's funeral, he would
have to wait, as the vicar was not available until late the next day. Sister Dora
left all further arrangements for the funeral in the consulate's hands.

In addition to initiating the funeral arrangements, Sister Dora's letter informed the consulate which British and Alexandrian social and financial networks to access to sort out payment for Northcote's funeral and settle her estate. Her sister in Kent knew of her illness, Sister Dora wrote, but her mother's
whereabouts were unknown. Sister Dora also reported that Northcote's employer, Monsieur Goar, had given the hospital one British pound to cover her
expenses but had declined all further responsibility. One unopened trunk,
belonging to Northcote, was at the hospital along with some cash; Sister Dora
arranged for both to be delivered to the consulate.

The British Consulate went to work arranging a "decent funeral," the
mounting of which would be primarily its task.[5] Consular officials contacted
undertakers, who arranged for a hearse with two horses, a coffin, and two
cars. Those services were provided not by the British but by the Society of
Funeral Parlors (Société des Pompes Funèbres [SdPF]).[6] The consulate reserved a grave at the British Protestant cemetery and engaged the services of
a carver to make a gravestone and a plaque for the cemetery walls.[7] Payment
for Northcote's funeral services fell to the British alone: in addition to funeral
costs, the consulate paid for the official registration of her death; her hospital
bill, which included her fifteen-day stay; transport of her goods to the consulate; and a half bottle of champagne.[8]

Employees of the consulate also set about figuring out (re)payment for services surrounding Northcote's death. Staffers were given a few weeks to sort
out her belongings, find any related debts, and report back to Constable James
Whitfield. Accordingly, those employees tracked down Northcote's monetary deposits, solicited money from her friends and acquaintances in Alexandria to pay for her funeral, held an auction to sell her material possessions,
made sure that all her outstanding bills were covered, and then sent her re-

maining goods and money to her sister in Kent.[9] To accomplish all of this, consular employees navigated at least three different currencies and multiple languages to work with the many people who made up the Alexandrian community that buried Rose Northcote.

While she was alive, Rose Northcote was seemingly unknown to the British Consulate. It was only in death that consular officials learned of her job, her family connections, her sickness, and her demise. Nevertheless, the consulate became the guarantors of her burial and estate. Sister Dora charged the consulate with planning her funeral. The consulate became the stand-in for Northcote's family and friends and her community—the facilitators of a respectable, good death.[10] The complexities of imperial life in Alexandria, where one could associate, live, and be hospitalized among people of all nationalities and religions, were reduced to one consulate. It was necessary, on a basic level, for these bodies to have a consulate in death, and consulates took on the task of burial because someone *had* to.

This chapter examines the funeral, the most public of rituals attendant to the processing of the dead. People with roots all over the world died in Alexandria. In death those people came into contact with consular officials, neighbors, nurses, doctors, funeral parlor employees, gravediggers, gravestone carvers, and family and friends in Alexandria, in Europe, and elsewhere. The ritual of the funeral was a momentary act of symbolic community creation. Yet funerals were the product of financial, bureaucratic, and often political transactions, regularly negotiated through consulates.

The different roles the funeral played highlight the place death had in publicly declaring a body both imperial and local. In death, Northcote and many other Alexandrian residents like her were transformed into imperial bodies, whether British or French. The funeral was therefore an instant of physical closure, of marking an individual's final resting place, and a ritual through which the dead were claimed within national and religious frameworks on Alexandrian soil. Still, death and its attendant practices sat peculiarly at the juncture of politics, commerce, and culture. Funerals constituted a bureaucratic process, a financial transaction, and a sacred observance. Thus, death and its rituals in Alexandria reveal much that is otherwise hidden about how imperial communities were created and connected on the ground. A study of Alexandrian funerals at the turn of the twentieth century illustrates how empire was maintained not only from the metropole but also in the quotidian doings in the colonies. At times, such daily events worked against the grain of the high-level treaties and diplomatic entanglements of empire. Consulates played a key role in the execution of funerals and estates, enabling the consulate to fill a geographically based need while at the same time representing imperial states. Within such a context, the consulates could and did use funerals—especially the funerals of public figures—to define and push back against other consulates' space in Egypt, much as they did with the hospitals.

Through private funerals this chapter explores how imperial bodies enabled consulates to show both their strength and their importance to Alexandria by fulfilling the very local need of processing the dead. Consular involvement with the dead predated European empire in Egypt but was fundamental to the creation and perpetuation of imperial power. Using British and French estate records, this chapter considers the ways that funeral rituals created their own communities, reflective of a diverse city, and often foiled assumptions about religious and national belonging even as death brought Alexandrian residents like Northcote decisively under the responsibility of specific consulates. Finally, this chapter uses the very public funeral in April 1904 of the Latin archbishop of Alexandria, Father Gaudenzio Bonfigli, a month before Rose Northcote's death, to reveal how the French Consulate's control of the ritual and memorial served to underscore its rivalry with the British and reconfirm the necessity of French presence in Alexandria. In each example, funerals serve to emphasize that Egypt was not simply Ottoman, British, or nationalist but rather a place where multiple empires shaped and challenged the lives of those who lived there.

BURYING IMPERIAL BODIES

On March 2, 1893, the police of Alexandria found the body of Said Basselm, an Indian national and British subject, in a hut behind the Deaconess Hospital.[11] He had been dead approximately three weeks. In an inquest report to Charles Cookson, the British consul general, Constable Whitfield explained that the body was too decomposed to make its transport to a mortuary possible. Instead, Whitfield returned to the hut with the consular surgeon, who certified the death and, according to Whitfield, "ordered the burial at once (after performing the rights [sic] according to the Mohammedan faith by their clergy)."[12]

Said Basselm died alone, without family, far away from his homeland. No one knew that he had died. Why, then, was it important for the British Consulate to organize a "Mohammedan" funeral for him? In the most tangible, bureaucratic dimension, burying Basselm was a health requirement: in the late nineteenth and early twentieth centuries, bodies had to be buried close to where the person had died and could not be exhumed for reburial without special permission of the Health Ministry.[13] In other words, everyone who died in Alexandria was buried—and most, if not all, of them were buried in Alexandria.

We know the stories of these dead Alexandrians because of the work of the consulates. Consulates were different from embassies or diplomatic missions. They did not have the status of the embassy and were assumed, on some level, to be separate from international politics and government relations; they were ostensibly local entities.[14] In the British Empire, consular employees lacked the professional training and social cachet of those in the Foreign Service, although consuls in the Levant were held to a slightly higher standard than others because their work was seen as potentially helping the empire.[15] Originally charged to address only matters of commerce, consulates also took care of their citizens and subjects in foreign lands, a task that was seen as integral to commercial needs. Consular responsibilities dated back to the Consular Act of 1825, which attempted to professionalize consular services and, with that, consular involvement in the building of hospitals and cemeteries abroad.[16] An 1858 report on the consular service to the British Parliament stated: "Should a tourist of his country die at a hotel, he [the consul] takes care of his property, conducts his funeral, and hunts out his next of kin. All these things in the regular way of business."[17] That the consulate worked with the dead is, therefore, not surprising.

The "British Order in Council, Regulating Her Majesty's Jurisdiction within the Dominions of the Ottoman Porte," signed August 8, 1899, reiterated the role of the consulate surrounding the bureaucratic processing of the dead.[18] Article 113 (1) states: "Each Consular officer shall endeavor to obtain, as early as may be, notice of the death of every British subject dying within the particular jurisdiction, whether resident or not, and all such information respecting his affairs as may serve to guide the Court with respect to the securing and administration of his property."[19] That the provisions begin with a reminder that the role of the consulate and the court is to protect property is also not surprising,[20] as consulates were founded in the protection of trade. Indeed, all of the articles relating to the dead speak of the processing of wills and what to do if someone dies intestate.[21] In fulfillment of this duty, however, consulates did much more than simply process the paperwork related to property.

Many of the fundamental services necessary to release a body for funeral services and to pay for, or to reimburse those who paid for, funeral costs originated in the consulates. They served not only as the site for reporting deaths but also as the bill payer and collector, the family therapist, and the institutional memory of a life.[22] Consulates, in essence, curated the funerals and deaths of their subjects, creating and then collecting imperial bodies. They marked the dead as theirs, and while collecting evidence to process the dead as their national subject, they labeled the dead as Alexandrian, for the details of that person's life would frequently show the individual to be someone who lived beyond the national category. By identifying the dead British and French as Alexandrians, consular officials claimed British and French presence in the city.

The consulate worked in a way that replicated the protective net of a family for British subjects in Alexandria and guaranteed them a modicum of protection in their deaths. Helping subjects and their families cope with death arrangements was an act of necessity and an act of kindness, as well as an example of how colonial communities kept track of their citizens and subjects. Consulate employees such as the chief constable, the consular surgeon, and the consul general himself were often the first to be notified when someone died. The chief constable played a central role in managing cases of death.[23] He would notify others at the the consulate and oversee all bureaucratic necessities such as paying hospital and burial bills, organizing estates, and contacting relatives. It was up to the consular officials to find the family, investigate the reasons for the death, document belongings, arrange for the funeral, gather bills for the funeral and estate, and process the estate if necessary. A consular undertaker offered services and coffins to the hospitals in town when needed.[24] In other words, it was up to the consulate to facilitate the performance of and payment for the funeral and burial. This does not mean that the consulate would always pay; as it was for the hospitals, this was preferably a last resort. Rather, the consulate was the guarantor of a decent burial; if family, friends, or employers did not or could not plan for and pay for the funeral, the consulate would arrange for the funeral to happen, as done for Said Basselm and others. As long as one had a consulate to claim or be claimed by, one could rest easily in life, assured of a decent funeral and therefore a good death.

When Massaoud Daoud Hayou died, the Alexandria rabbinate covered all costs.[25] This was not unusual: religious organizations often paid for funerals through burial societies or directly through the church or rabbinate. The rabbinate then petitioned the British Consulate to help recoup the money spent on Hayou's death and interment. Interestingly, while Hayou and his wife were British subjects, his two sisters were not. They held "local" nationality.[26] Nonetheless, the women had the British Consulate divide the estate.

When consulates collected bodies, they made themselves relevant in the colonial space of Alexandria. The consulates' claim of relevancy, like the consulates' use of autopsies and death certification and like the hospital's use of categories, allowed them to claim space in Alexandria. That is, the French imperial project was needed in Alexandria because Alexandrians of all sorts were French; the large numbers of dead bodies cared for by the British likewise demonstrated British presence and strength in the city. Claiming a body for France or Great Britain thus bolstered the number of people—both dead and alive—who needed French or British governmental aid and authority.

Funeral payment was connected to estate distributions, which were a consular responsibility. Imperial subjects and citizens in Alexandria at times chose to have consulates provide for funerals, leaving them free to request charitable donations as a part of their dying wishes, to be included when settling the estate alongside funeral costs. Thus, when Aurelia Gardner died in 1910, she asked the hospital to distribute her belongings to the poor.[27] Yet Gardner also had the British Consulate pay for her funeral costs. In other words, rather than sell her belongings to pay for her funeral, she chose charitable donations with the understanding that the consulate would pay for her. The arrangement was mutually beneficial; the execution of her funeral service would allow the consulate to claim her body as belonging to it, to count her death among its numbers. The consulate served as a given, a final arbiter of the good death.

While the occupation did not change the bureaucratic process through which consulates negotiated among family members, employers, and organizations to pay for funerals and administer estates, it did change the meaning of that work.[28] This shift in meaning was particularly pronounced for those working under the Egyptian flag. As the veiled British colonial state began to oversee the Egyptian state, an increasing number of British came to Egypt to work for Egyptian governmental institutions. These men were not officially working for the colonial state but for a foreign government. In the case

of William Beach, the peculiarities of the British-Ottoman-Egyptian governance highlighted the limits of consular protection of the individual Briton.

Beach worked as an engineer for the Egyptian Coast Guard on the SS *Nur
al-Bakr*. Beach was also a member of the Oddfellows Society, a British fraternal organization that pledged to support its members. When he died in 1889,
a "master mariner" who knew his family petitioned the British Consulate to
declare Beach as having reverted to a life "under the British flag" before his
death. Dying while working for the Egyptian government, it seemed, would
have made it the responsibility of the Oddfellows Society to take care of his
widow in England null and void. His friends argued that by entering a British hospital and leaving his job with the onset of his illness, Beach had indeed
stopped working for the Egyptian state, thus reverting to a life "under the
British flag." The consulate disagreed, and Beach's widow was presumably left
without the fraternal benefits of the Oddfellows Society.[29]

This delicate dance between the British and Egyptian government is of
particular interest: Beach was working with the Egyptian government specifically because the British were colonial rulers of the land. The Egyptian
national government was answerable to the British colonial ruling appara-
tus. By working for the Egyptian Coast Guard, Beach was arguably fulfilling the very need of the British state for British men willing to work in Egypt.
Yet when Beach died, even though the British Consulate guaranteed his funeral, his burial, his death documentation, and even the settling of his estate,
it would not mark him as under the British flag.

This seeming paradox might be explained by the nuances of British rule in
Egypt. That the British could not, and did not, declare Egypt as their colonial
possession until the start of World War I meant that British citizens working
for the Egyptian state were indeed working for a foreign power. Only those at
the very highest level of the British administration could be acknowledged as
working for the British Empire. That Beach would most likely not have been
in Egypt were it not for the British presence was not of concern to the consulates, as they protected all resident British subjects regardless. But they were
also political entities of colonial governance facing increasing pushback from
a rising nationalist native population, and helping British Empire would at
times trump helping individual British subjects.[30]

As the Beach case shows, the British Consulate in Egypt balanced the
Ottoman-British-Egyptian relationship that required some British subjects
working in Egypt to be private citizens and not colonial officials. Likewise,

the French balanced their role of protecting French subjects with international political pressures. In processing all imperial dead, whether colonial officials, private citizens, travelers, or imperial subjects, the consulates represented the people of Alexandria inside the city and their home governments in London or Paris. The consulates were therefore conduits, guarantors, negotiators, facilitators, resources, and banks. When the consulates stepped in to help their people in Alexandria, in the process they defined who their people were. By increasing the numbers and scope of people they helped, consulates and their officials highlighted the importance of their mission. Such increased importance, in turn, allowed the consulates to use dead bodies to make political claims.

In 1895, a train ran over Jacob Gherson, and his body was taken to the Egyptian government hospital. The British Consulate intervened to stop the burial of Gherson, who was poor and without family or identification, until the consulate could establish him as British.[31] His was not the only corpse the consulate investigated. Bodies were also dug up and reburied, even after inquest and funeral, if they were thought to have been wrongly buried as non-British. Such was the intensity of the need to have the British dead counted as British and for the British consulate to provide a decent funeral for its subjects. And while these exhumations of British Protestant men buried as Muslims and Jews may have demonstrated the obsession with "social foreignness" that would reclaim *individual* legal status, these exhumations also served the *communities* and posit the consulates as protectors of the dead, even more so than they are concerned with the individual.[32]

Likewise, in Gherson's case, it was the British government chasing down the body and family members before allowing for a funeral and burial; it set out to prove that Gherson was British.[33] Even here, at a moment when death might have been a dodged consular responsibility, the British pursued the recovery of a corpse to save it from burial by the Egyptian government. The dead lent meaning to the consulates, giving purpose to their accumulation of bodies, information, and power.

FUNERALS AS CREATION AND PERFORMANCE OF COMMUNITY

More than simply a bureaucratic affair, the funeral services of British and French nationals and subjects in Alexandria were performances that created a living community in Alexandria. The bodies of Said Basselm and others, once interred, became a physical, permanent part of Alexandria.[34] Funerals were experiences that played a vital role in shaping the social and symbolic fabric of the city. Funerals demonstrated that the person who died was a part of a public.[35] The promise of a decent funeral, a service that allowed the dead and their kin to avoid the embarrassment of a pauper's funeral, was vital to the work of the British and French Consulates of Alexandria and demonstrated that the dead person had, in life, been cared for and that he or she had had resources.[36]

Funerals were, and are, a performance of community. An examination, therefore, of who participates in funerals provides insight into how rituals for the dead knit the living into a community, or a network of belonging. Political, economic, or religious authority can be honored or challenged at funerals, signaling the strength or demise of a defined community.[37] Nineteenth-century funerals were infused with religion, modernity, kinship, class, and more.[38] A funeral is both a private, meaning individual, moment and a collective and public act of memory.[39]

In the Alexandria of our time period, there was no single template by which a funeral was organized. In cases such as Basselm's, in which the body of someone without family was found, the consulate stepped in immediately. In most other cases, someone else first organized the funeral. Employers, family, friends, benevolent societies, hospitals—everyone had a role to play. When family could not or would not pay for the funeral, employers and friends did. A hospital, as we have seen in the case of Rose Northcote, might well have suggested funeral arrangements to the consulate, making the preliminary introduction of the existence of the dead to their consular representatives.

The British Burial Ground helped bury British subjects in Egypt. It organized the funeral of Thomas Baldrock, a quarantine officer living in Alexandria who died in Suez in 1903. The Egyptian government paid for it, later seeking repayment from the British Consulate of Alexandria.[40] Baldrock's body would be laid to rest away from both his home in England and his chosen home of Alexandria. His burial in the Suez would not have been complete without a chaplain to conduct a funeral service. The Egyptian government honored the tradition and hired a chaplain to officiate. Like the British Consulate, the Egyptian government understood that burying someone went beyond just the physical and financial aspects but also involved a kind of spiritual guardianship. This kind of service was part and parcel of the burial process; the responsibility was not simply to bury but to provide for a decent funeral, which, in late nineteenth- and early twentieth-century Alexandria, meant a religious funeral.

As public events, funerals were opportunities for the living to connect with one another as mourners and as members of similar social, economic, religious, or political classes. When Jean Antoine Marius Autran, a French businessman, died in Egypt on June 15, 1909, his friends rushed to pull together a funeral notice. The black-bordered invitation featured the letter "M," for Marius, as Autran was known. Underneath, a scythe, a cross, and a blade of greenery overlapped, suggesting the intimate coexistence of life and death. The words below read "The friends of Mr. M. Autran have the honor and regret to tell you of his death, occurring this morning, 15th June, and you may follow the convoy today at 5 p.m. We will meet at 32 Boulevard de Ramleh. Alexandria, June 15, 1909."[41]

This invitation is a clue to the funeral process. The turnaround between funeral to burial was often quick when an autopsy or inquest was not needed or when the dead was not famous enough to warrant a delay in burial to allow political figures to arrive in the city. In the case of Autran, friends, not family, took charge of arranging the procession taking the mourners through the streets of Alexandria before arriving at the church or cemetery. The urgency of community participation was evident in the invitation: The friends of Autran clearly mobilized after news of his death. Printers were able to rush orders. Cemeteries, churches, and other businesses involved could and did respond immediately. Because Autran had been sick long enough to accumulate significant medical bills, perhaps his death was expected, and decisions had been made about his funeral before he died; we have no way of knowing.[42] Nonetheless, in less than a day, his friends printed and presumably distributed personalized funeral invitations, and people's schedules were flexible enough to create a convoy in just a few hours. Autran was part of a community large enough, and perhaps formal enough, to warrant written notices of his death,[43] and his death was important enough to dedicate public space to the mourners' procession. His funeral was a public event.

Funerals also created spontaneous, improvised communities. The affiliations of mourners with the dead, even if the mourners were strangers, created a group: a specifically local, Alexandrian group that would not necessarily have existed elsewhere. Of course, the fact that a funeral created a kind of temporary community is not unique to Alexandria.[44] What is unique to the

Alexandrian case is the complexity of inclusion and exclusion engendered by the multiplicity of empires involved at this particular moment.

The wide-ranging items considered part of funeral costs in estate cases provide further clues about what the public ritual of private funerals might have looked like for those who died in Alexandria. The quality and quantity of goods and services used at a funeral reflected the dead's social status.[45] Funeral expenses included a coffin, a grave, gravediggers, carvers to make a gravestone or a church plaque, crosses or other religious symbols, and greenery to plant at the gravesite.[46] Priests, chaplains, and masters of ceremony billed for their time as well.[47] Church rentals, car rentals for both the body and for those organizing the funeral, white sheets and gloves, and "sundry" or "small things" were all a part of funeral bills, as were printing charges for invitations and programs. At least one estate counted "testamentary" charges, or charges related to the execution of the will, as a funeral cost, although most kept such charges separate.[48] Additional "mourning costs," unspecified, were at times claimed against an estate.[49] At least one funeral charged nearly as much for two cakes as it did for three priests, listing the cakes as part of the death festivities.[50]

Many funeral costs were paid in one lump sum to the SdPF, the umbrella organization of funeral parlors. Most of those who used the SdPF's services opted for a package deal, and payment was calculated in British, French, and/or Ottoman/Egyptian currencies, and often in more than one for the same funeral. A receipt for services provided by the SdPF was the single common denominator in almost all estate cases, which suggests that the services of an undertaker and the basics of a funeral service were universal across nationality and religious denomination. Use of coffins was the norm, with just one Jewish man, Yehuda Nahom, buried without one; this was not the norm in Muslim funerals.[51] In addition to coffins, the SdPF charged for rented hearses and horses, with the number of horses ranging from the standard two to four in the case of certain "first-class" funerals.[52] Funerals also used anywhere from one to ten cars, most likely to carry people to the services.[53] Two to eleven men were typically employed to carry and bury the body and to dig and fill the grave. Charges also included tips given to the men who assisted at the cemetery. Medical personnel, drivers, artisans, printers, religious clergy, and others of diverse national, religious, and ethnic backgrounds all charged for their services in the death and burial of an individual. Together with the mourners, they formed the funereal community.

Funeral services in turn-of-the-twentieth-century Alexandria were al-most always religious, and close attention was paid to clergy and content. We saw that Sister Dora Brooke of the Deaconess Hospital worked hard to make sure that the "right" type of reverend would be available for the funeral ser-vices of those who died in her care.[54] Eugenia Phillips, who died in 1911, had three different priests as part of her funeral services.[55] However, while funer-als involved religious rites, Alexandria's dead often subverted assumptions about categories of belonging, which tended to meld religion and national-ity. John Papadopulo, a Greek Orthodox British man; Marguerite Lancon, a French Protestant who was buried by a German pastor in Alexandria; and Said Basselm, the British Indian Muslim whose decomposed body was found in a hut and who was also interred in Alexandria—each in death challenged prescriptive designations of the British as Protestant or the French as Cath-olic in nineteenth-century Egypt. Their stories illustrate the extent to which religion and nationality are more complicated as categories within which to understand turn-of-the-twentieth-century Alexandrians. Their stories also indicate the extent to which these residents of Alexandria were imperial sub-jects, beyond the categories of "religion" and "nationality" that were so vital in the functioning of the city.

The funeral plans and estate case of Sara Roca reflect a world of multiple languages, currencies, ethnicities, religions, and nationalities. At her death, Roca, a British Catholic woman who wrote a detailed will in Arabic and cal-culated her funeral costs in "dollars," was clearly a woman of some means. Her will arranged for her ownership of one and a half houses to be sold and added to her estate before her money could be distributed. It also included be-quests to two great-nephews, both of whom were priests, and Roca designated money to be used to hold masses to "pray for her soul" at Catholic churches in Jerusalem and at Maronite Greek Catholic churches in Alexandria.[56] Her individual beneficiaries included Ottoman, by which she meant indigenous Egyptian, subjects as well as French. The sick, poor, and orphans of the Cath-olic community of Alexandria were all additional beneficiaries of Roca's es-tate, as was the European Hospital of Alexandria. After these charitable do-nations, the remains of her estate were to be divided among five great-nieces, scattered between Alexandria and Jerusalem.[57]

Sara Roca's will noted that she wore several gold bracelets and stipulated that they be sold to pay for her funeral. Thus, her will dictates what would count as a funeral expense (mortuary, mass, alms, and death festivities), how much she was willing to pay for it (150 dollars, unclear if this means US dollars), and how costs were to be paid. She curated her own "decent death." Similarly, by involving so many different churches in her will, Sara Roca used it to create the community that would mourn for her, as did the funeral service itself. In death Roca created another community that crossed national boundaries. She delineated a group among the living that would be responsible for her in death and in so doing prioritized religion over nationality.

Indeed, Sara Roca may very well have been the only British subject in her family, aside from her husband, Girgis Roca, whose name suggests that he may have been an indigenous Copt. The fact that her will was written in Arabic and translated by the British Consulate only after her death suggests that she may not have spoken English. Yet to implement her various wishes, Sara Roca had to rely on a national consulate. That consulate did not necessarily reflect the nationalities of her living community or her group of mourners. Ironically, although Roca specifically requested the British Consulate to be the executor of her estate and pay for her funeral as she wished, the consulate rejected the request.[58] Instead, consular officials appointed a local (here meaning Ottoman/Egyptian) subject, the father of two women who received bequests from Roca. This case may point to the limits of consular involvement in that the consulate abrogated the request to be the executor of Roca's estate while managing, and thereby executing, the estate from afar. While not the executor, the consulate guaranteed that an executor would fulfill her wishes, thereby guaranteeing her decent death. Despite the consulate's rejection of its executor rights, in protecting the implementation of her wishes, the consulate ensured that Roca would become a British imperial body.

This flexibility of national categories often manifested itself in funerals in Alexandria. Moise Abeasis, a Jewish man with British protection, died in Alexandria in 1910. Abeasis's sisters, one in Portugal and one in Alexandria with Austrian protection, subsequently demanded to see his will. The sisters were upset with the money their brother's will had dedicated to his wife, Elvira Caruana, a much younger local whom he had married in the British Consulate some years earlier.[59] The legal wrangling that followed Abeasis's death revealed that Caruana had spent 1,500 piasters tarif on the funeral and another 1,180 on "mourning costs." She also spent a total of 1,706 piasters tarif for three months' rent. The funeral must therefore have been lavish, and the mourning must have been decidedly costly as well.

In this example, nationality has a malleable quality: Abeasis had a sister, also in Alexandria, who was Austrian, whereas he himself was British and married to a woman of local nationality, which suggests the lack of any other legal protection for Caruana before her marriage to Abeasis.[60] Having British nationality specifically meant access to legal protection as well as economic and bureaucratic advantages.[61] Not only was the British Consulate the site for what appears to have been a specifically civil and nonreligious marriage, but consular officials were also the central figures who implemented Abeasis's will and therefore worked on behalf of his wife after his death. In this sense, they guaranteed that Abeasis's death would bureaucratically mirror his life.

Maria Mondello was a Maltese woman who married an Italian. Her husband left her but did not divorce her, and she spent the last twenty-five years of her life living with Spiridione Camilleri, a Maltese man. When she died in 1892, Camilleri paid for her funeral, and the British Consulate stepped in to help him sort out the funeral bills and the estate.[62] Her case is particularly interesting, as she married the Italian man before the Naturalisation Act of 1870 mandated that all women married to foreigners became the nationality of their husbands; previously Britishness was understood to be "indelible" on the body of a person.[63] The British consular involvement in Maria Mondello's case highlights the ambiguities around the law and the determination of imperial bodies and consular control. The British consulate noted in her file that she might be an Italian subject. Nevertheless, they helped Camilleri work through the payment of her funeral; the consulate was ready to claim her as British.

Unnatural deaths and the deaths of the wealthy and powerful were often covered in detail by the press, facilitating a public record and an acknowledgment of the existence of Alexandria's ephemeral funereal communities. For example, an *Egyptian Gazette* article about the funeral of Samuel Fawcett, who was murdered in his home in April 1914, noted that "the floral tributes were numerous and very beautiful, among the senders being the general-manager and staff of the Khedivial Mail Line." The article continued to list the titles of several mourners, including the general manager of the Khedivial Mail Line and "representatives of the Ports and Lights, Customs, Post Office, and other Government Departments, mercantile and tourist agencies, captains of British ships now in harbor and many other personal friends."[64] The public mourning of Fawcett linked the Alexandria that was home to so many with the city that was an imperial hub on an international trade network. The momentary community created by Fawcett's funeral highlighted the layers of a multifaceted city in which everyday lives, here embodied by his personal friends, overlapped with imperial structures, here represented both within Egypt by the members of the government and in the broader British Empire by the captains of the ships.

In each of these cases, the funeral underlines the flexibility of national and religious categories as well as the complex ways in which they overlap. Funerals were moments of performance in which communities of mourners crossing national and religious boundaries were drawn together to participate in the event or to provide services for it. At the same time, the organization and payment of the funeral often passed through the consular offices, leaving a paper trail that marked people as belonging to certain categories and as part of the record of the British or the French of Alexandria. That is, funerals were momentary performances with implications of perpetuity; they were collections of the rituals through which a body was consecrated to Alexandria and to the living, imperial population. Through the actions of the bureaucracy and the consulates, funerals were the moment in which the British or French dead became bureaucratic cases in these imperial spaces. In death, the corpses of Alexandria's boundless citizens became imperial bodies, and these imperial bodies added both to the numbers and to the tangible responsibilities of national consulates.

DEATH OF THE ARCHBISHOP

In accounts of funerals of the famous, especially those of heads of state, death proves a powerful means of choreographing imperial or national rituals; this was neither unique to Alexandria nor limited to the nineteenth century.[65] Processions took over the streets of cities, public poetry and art defined national and imperial characteristics, and performative rituals demonstrated the importance of the person who died and thus the person's importance to nation or empire.[66] Funerals thus created and redefined the norms of governance by lauding those in power or warning of the chaos to come now that such a pillar of society was gone.[67]

The public funeral of the Latin archbishop of Alexandria, Father Gaudenzio Bonfigli, in April 1904, just five days after the signing of the Entente Cordiale—a negotiation that Paul Cambon, the French ambassador to London, described as "we give you Egypt in exchange for Morocco"[68]—illustrates how the liminal, transactional moment of the funeral gave the French Consulate a tangible, specifically Alexandrian means of challenging British control of Egypt. That is, at the same time that diplomats and high government officials in London and Paris were signing an agreement in which the French recognized Egypt as British space, French officials in Alexandria were using death as a means to show French power, emphasizing how empire is created, defined, manipulated, and re-created on the ground even as it is being prescribed from above. Far more than the celebration of an individual life, the funeral was an event that reaffirmed Egypt as a land with a multiplicity of European empires within it. It was an Alexandrian, a Catholic, and a French occasion all at once.

On March 29, 1904, "Father in God, His Grace Gaudenzio Bonfigli, of the Franciscan Order, Archbishop of Cabase, Apostolic Vicar of Egypt, and Delegate of the Holy See of the Oriental Rites of Egypt and Arabia, Grand Cordon of the Order of Medjidieh" had a stroke. His incapacitation made the news in Alexandria, marking Bonfigli as someone "all of Egypt cares about," someone important to the happiness and well-being of the city at large.[69] City notables, including prominent clergy and business leaders, rushed to his bedside. Bonfigli had at his service several doctors, all of whom hoped—to no avail—to witness a sign that the archbishop would recover. The resident French-language newspaper, La Réforme, reported that Bonfigli put his hand to his stomach in response to a question from French consul Pierre Girard, providing the only indication that he was still with the living.[70]

Bonfigli was an important person in Alexandria whose influence extended beyond religion and nationality to encompass Alexandria's financial market. La Réforme repeatedly emphasized the special relationship between the archbishop and the French Consulate, noting that Consul Girard was close enough to the archbishop to be at his bedside, trusted enough to be alone with him, and honored enough to be the only one who could get the archbishop to respond during his illness.[71]

Bonfigli did not linger long between life and death: he died at 1:00 a.m. on the morning of April 6. Newspapers treated his death as a major Alexandrian event, presenting a wealth of details about his life and death and information about his embalming and funeral. The archbishop was buried on April 9, following a grand spectacle of mourning. A large funeral cortege escorted the body from the archbishop's palace, where it had been on view for three days, to St. Catherine's Church. Music played, shops closed their doors, flags flew at half-mast, and gas lamps, wrapped in black crepe, lit the way. The French monitored, negotiated, and controlled each step of the mourning ritual: the body lying in state, the lineup of the procession, the seating arrangements and eulogy at the funeral, and the post-funeral receiving line.

Yet it was not a given that the French would bury Bonfigli. An Italian born in the town of Matelica in 1831, Bonfigli joined the Franciscan priesthood in 1853. The French held the right to act as "Protectors of the Catholics of the Orient," including all members of the Latin Catholic clergy; France would not relinquish its hold over Italian clergy until 1906.[72] But Bonfigli's case was not a simple one: Not only were the French acting in Ottoman territory that the French state was in the process of acknowledging as British, but within France and its empire the relationship between the state and Catholicism was up for debate.[73] Still, even as France passed a series of laws domestically to control the power of the Catholic Church, consuls and diplomats used Catholicism as a means of furthering the French Empire.[74] While this symbiosis was uneven at best, Catholicism remained a tool of empire in the Middle East, including in lands such as Egypt that were not under direct French governance.[75] That the French would use Catholicism to promote its empire in Egypt was expected, perhaps, but as the funeral of Bonfigli shows, it was not without pushback and contradiction.

For the French to claim Bonfigli, they first had to minimize his Italian roots. The eulogy and articles in the French press presented the archbishop as someone who transcended nationality. In the posthumous portrait painted of him, Bonfigli also emerged as a man with no blood family. Missing from the story of his life are parents, brothers, sisters, or cousins; instead, Bonfigli's eulogist and the press indicated that it was the children of the Middle East who sustained Bonfigli's life of service, and those children were marked as having been his closest kin. "His kindness to the Arabs of the city [Aleppo] was proverbial. The older children gladly played with the etymology of his name *Gaudenzio* and called him Father Happy, paying tribute to his untiring affability."[76] Such a portrait made him out to be fluent in multiple languages and able to move easily throughout the empire; in other words, he was the consummate Ottoman man.[77] By claiming Bonfigli as theirs, the French insinuated themselves as part of the Ottoman Empire, and Egypt, the land in which Bonfigli died, as Ottoman, not British, land.

At his funeral and in the press reports that surrounded it, Bonfigli was remembered as someone who brought peace and stability to the regions of the empire he touched. *La Réforme* reported:

During his six-year stay in Jerusalem, all fights seemed suspended, every ani-
mosity subsided, and good terms were reestablished. It is fair to say, however,
that if his kindness was connected to this marvelous result, it was no less connected to the diplomatic tact of the eminent consul general of France, whose
name will long remain valued and revered by all.[78]

According to the local French-language press, therefore, the archbishop was
successful in large part because he was connected to France. Thus, the archbishop of the French press accounts was also a European man who was a sta-
bilizing figure in a region of fragmented allegiances. He was an idealized
image of French presence and French imperial interest in Egypt. In its assess-
ment of Bonfigli's accomplishment, *La Réforme* mentioned several times that
the archbishop's appeal extended beyond the European Catholic community
in Alexandria: "Then he comes to Egypt, and everyone loves him, regardless
of religion or nationality."[79] In other words, Bonfigli was someone whose purpose in the Middle East transcended his office in Alexandria, transcended his
Catholic mission, and encompassed the region.

The British were starkly absent from both Bonfigli's eulogy and *La Réforme*'s coverage of the archbishop's death. There may be no reason to think
that one would find the British in a eulogy about a Catholic archbishop in
Alexandria. Even if there were more British Catholics than Protestants in
Egypt, it was the French that held the role, as noted, of the protectors of the
Catholics of the Orient. [80] And even if Egypt was a veiled British protectorate, it was still bound to the Ottoman Empire. Nevertheless, the British rule
of Egypt had been firmly established by 1904, and the death of a key religious
figure would therefore have been a governmental event that could, and in this
case did, involve British officials. Furthermore, the Entente Cordiale, signed
just one day before Bonfigli's funeral, could be read as a British victory, since
France had to accept British terms.[81] Yet the funeral would provide the French
with a very public moment to challenge the British (and other European competitors) less than twenty-four hours after the signing of an accord in which
France promised to stop questioning British rule in Egypt.

Despite the diplomatic advantages the French would ultimately grab in
the planning and execution of the public memorialization of Bonfigli, their li-
onization of the archbishop was not a given. Nor was it a given that holding
Bonfigli's funeral would be the French prerogative or would serve French imperial interests. Rather, the first telegrams between Consul Girard in Alex-

andria and the French diplomat in Cairo, Jules de la Boulinière, suggest that Bonfigli's death was not initially a concern. It was uncertain whether La Boulinière would make the trip to Alexandria for the funeral or even whether he would send personal condolences.[82]

In the meantime, in Alexandria, Girard was busy posturing not only with his own diplomat but also with the Italian Consulate, Vatican representatives, the municipality, and the British Consulate, as well as local gas companies.[83] Over the course of the three short days between Bonfigli's death and his funeral, Girard worked to ensure that the funeral was a grand public event, connected to all of Alexandria and surpassing the funerals of other public figures. Girard, in other words, worked to facilitate French imperial power in Alexandria. He contacted the Alexandria Municipality and the Health Ministry the day Bonfigli died. He asked for permission to display the corpse for three days in the archdiocese and subsequently to bury it in the grounds of the church rather than in the Catholic cemetery, as the health regulations typically required. Girard punctuated his letter by reminding the municipality that it had allowed the same for the Greek patriarch, who had died five years previously.[84] Rather than assume a positive response, or equal treatment among the various religious communities of the city, Girard preempted the municipality—an organization notably concerned with the city's European residents[85]—with a demand that this death be seen as on par with that of the Greek patriarch, the religious leader of the largest and oldest non-Muslim sect in Egypt. The municipality's Health Ministry agreed to Girard's requests immediately. Bonfigli's body was embalmed without delay, in preparation for its three-day viewing. The municipal doctor, as well as the delegate consul of France, attended the embalming, and an Italian sculptor created a mask of Bonfigli for his tombstone.[86] Photographers took photos of the process, donating them to the French consul to honor Bonfigli in death.[87]

Having successfully secured permission for a public mourning of several days and having helped organize the artists needed to make the physical remains satisfactory for viewing, Girard turned to planning the funeral procession from the archbishop's palace to St. Catherine's. Girard invited numerous prominent officials of the city to take part in the procession and service, including the head of the Municipal Commission, the director and assistant director of customs, the inspector of the Sanitary Council of Maritime and Quarantine, the commander of the garrison, the commandant of the police, the governor of Alexandria, the head of the Mixed Court of Appeals, the president of the Mixed Courts, the controller of ports and lighthouse, and various other consular officials from around the world.[88] Almost all accepted Girard's invitation to accompany Bonfigli to his resting place.[89]

France's consul general controlled not only who the public mourners would be but also how the mourners would dress. Girard insisted that the consular corps wear their uniforms in a sign of respect to Bonfigli and Alexandria's Latin Catholic Church. But the British would not appear in uniform: on April 8, less than a day before the funeral, Britain's consul Edward Gould wrote to Girard: "I am sorry but I cannot wear uniform tomorrow as we did not do so on the occasion of the funeral of the Greek Patriarch."[90] Girard took umbrage and insisted that no one had been asked to wear a uniform at the patriarch's funeral five years earlier; moreover, he insisted, the tardiness of Gould's response suggested that the British consul was purposefully playing politics. Girard may have been right, as Gould subsequently bowed out of participation in the funeral because of "such a very bad cold."[91]

Girard also managed the appearance of the procession route, intervening with the municipality and the gas company to provide somber mood lighting along the route.[92] Girard ensured that the lamps along the route would be lit during daylight and covered in black crepe, at no cost to either the municipality or those organizing the funeral. The lamps served to delineate a specific space for mourning. As was the case in Marius Autran's funeral, it was as if the city itself transformed into a space that mourned the archbishop.

With arrangements for a grand public event now finalized, Girard sent another telegram to La Boulinière in Cairo, informing him of the details and of the participation of representatives of the khedival government and the municipality. Recognizing the political largesse of the funeral, La Boulinière now sent word that he was on his way to Alexandria and would participate in the funeral.[93] Indeed, the French consul general had a position of honor.[94]

As the French worked to stamp the public spectacle of Bonfigli's funeral with their authority, they also worked behind the scenes to make themselves a player in the execution of his estate. Because Bonfigli was an Italian subject who died abroad, the Italian Consulate wanted to manage his estate. But there were complications. First, Bonfigli had no personal possessions. He lived in a house owned by the Holy See (Saint Siège) and had taken a vow of poverty.[95] Second, Father Amato of the Vatican objected to Italian consular intervention in the settling of Bonfigli's estate, as the Vatican claimed to want to work alone. It sought to bring Girard into alignment with its aim to sideline the Italian Consulate. The Italian consul had not approached Girard regarding Bonfigli. Accordingly, Girard's correspondence with La Boulinière reflects a tone of frustration: "It did not occur to [the Italian consul] that I could help him in this mission. Au Contraire!"[96] Girard found himself negotiating to help with the Vatican and thus reconfirming the French as "the Protectors of the Catholics of the Orient" and operating in direct conflict with his Italian colleague.

The moment called for diplomacy, as Girard navigated his country's religious and civil interests. The execution of an estate was a civil event, to be handled by a civil authority, as Girard reconfirmed in his report to La Boulinière. Bonfigli the Italian national was under the civil authority of Italy. Bonfigli the priest, however, had served in Egypt as the primary representative of the Vatican, which was under the protection of France, although relations were somewhat strained.[97] Girard understood the delicate balance of his role as a French politician representing a civil state that claimed to be the religious protector of Catholics in a land in which France was not the preeminent colonial power. The relationship between Catholicism and the French Empire was both evident in the Ottoman Empire, as defined by the 1740 agreement, and complicated in that France had just acknowledged Egypt as British land.

The Italian consul approached Father Amato, insisting that the consulate had a right to be involved in Bonfigli's estate, as Bonfigli was an Italian national. Girard "knew" that the Italians would try to use this interaction between the Italian consul and the Vatican as a precedent to get involved with Catholic affairs in Alexandria. To maintain French control over Catholics in Alexandria, Girard offered the Italians "benevolent" assistance; he would be the one to interact with the Vatican on their behalf.[98] Girard noted a day later in a communication with La Boulinière, however, that such intervention might be problematic because of friction between the government of the French Republic and the Vatican.[99] La Boulinière was quick to respond, sending a reply just three hours later: the Italian minister would soon receive orders to desist from intervention in Bonfigli's estate, and Girard would thereafter be the estate's primary civil representative, able to represent not only the Vatican and Bonfigli but any claims to the estate as well.[100] Indeed, by April 11, Girard reported that the Italian consul of Alexandria had given up all claims on the estate of Bonfigli.[101]

The French government had worked behind the scenes in Europe to pressure the Italian government to accept the French local consulate in Alexandria as the primary political entity involved in the processing of the estate of the Italian archbishop. France's agreement with the Ottomans did not automatically give it control of the Catholic community, as politics did not necessarily translate into power within the mundane actions of governance. Rather, the French negotiated that authority in the specifics of this Alexandrian moment, turning Bonfigli into a French imperial body. "This sad event," Girard wrote, "gave us the chance to reconfirm that we are the protectors of Catholics in this city."[102] Claiming Bonfigli's body marked the French as important to Alexandria, despite British presence and power in Egypt. Indeed, the British are absent in discussions among French consular representatives about how to handle Bonfigli's death: the French cast as their competitors only Italian and papal diplomats. Perhaps the British loomed so large that Girard maneuvered to be their top competitor. Or perhaps the British simply were not and could not be protectors of Catholics, despite the numerous Maltese and other Catholics who were British subjects in Egypt. Regardless, the French continued to use religion to challenge British power, using their role as protector of Egypt's Catholics to indicate not only that Egypt was still a contested space but also that the British, by default, were not capable of protecting all the Europeans who lived there.

Finally, the day of the funeral arrived. *La Réforme* described the atmosphere of anticipation surrounding such a public spectacle: "From the early hours crowds of Europeans and natives gathered on the street. The crowds were there to see the important people in their uniforms. The poor police had to maintain order in this human swell that kept growing and growing to watch the funeral cortege."[103] Girard's insistence on uniforms had served him well. According to *La Réforme*, the many people in uniform caught the eyes of the crowd. The parading of uniforms was not about honoring Bonfigli but rather about the spectacle that uniformed officials would make on the streets of Alexandria. The uniforms attracted the crowds, and the crowds increased and elevated the stature of the mourning community. The funeral was more than an isolated procession; the city at large mourned.

Bonfigli's funeral procession took over city space. Businesses along the funeral route put their flags at half-mast and/or closed their doors in signs of respect.[104] The consulates also flew their flags at half-mast. Thus, the physical space of mourning was demarcated by people, the police, the halting of commercial transactions, and the spectators. The space of mourning was also demarcated aurally, as those who could hear the funeral marches or the funeral bells ringing from the church were included in the mourning community, however ephemerally.[105]

With the mounted police of the city at its head and foot, the solemn procession passed through several main streets and in front of the khedival bursary, a primary symbol of Egyptian governance.[106] Immediately following the police and leading the procession was the band of the Salesian Fathers, who filled the streets of Alexandria with the funeral march. Next came Catholic schoolchildren, both girls and boys, along with the sisters and orphans of the convent of Saint Vincent of Paul. Various representatives of the Christian communities of Alexandria followed the students. The Catholic clergy marched next, behind a cross; after them came the coffin, decorated in liturgical purple. In the position usually reserved for family, directly behind the coffin, stood La Boulinière with Girard by his side.[107] The consul of Italy, a representative of the khedive, and the governor of Alexandria joined them.[108] Behind the French and Italian consuls came the rest of the diplomatic and consular communities, followed by state administrators, city notables, and administrators of the municipality.[109]

Differences across accounts of the procession and its hierarchy point toward the underlying purpose of the public parade of mourning. The French Consulate archived three lists of the procession: the article in *La Réforme*, the consular report written by Girard, and the list provided by the apostolic delegation.[110] The newspaper article represents what was perhaps the most public account of the funeral procession. After celebrating the Catholic schools, sisters and brothers, and orphans, the article mentions the role of French officials as "chief mourners" alongside Egyptian and Alexandrian officials. The Italian consul and those walking behind the consular corps are not mentioned, nor is any other European nation. This omission by *La Réforme*'s editorial staff is indicative of the help the French Consulate received from the local French-language newspaper in positioning the funeral as a French event. The apostolic delegation list highlighted the children as part of the delegation, adding schoolchildren and orphans to a group that included governmental and business notables. This inclusion elevated the children to the level of the city's notables. Moreover, because the large procession of business elites from Alexandria was included in its list of representatives, the Catholic community, here represented by the apostolic list, heralded its importance to the city's religious life, financial well-being, charitable institutions, and educational infrastructure. The Catholic community thus grounded itself symbolically in Alexandrian soil, using death as a moment to celebrate its life.

In Girard's report, he noted the internal politics of planning the procession, such as the Mixed Courts' refusal to walk when it learned its judges would be behind the consular representatives. Girard mentioned neither the students nor the Catholic and Christian communal representatives marching ahead of Bonfigli's coffin. However, the apostolic list of the procession, which Girard claimed to be more hopeful than realistic, contained representatives from many more city groups and organizations and does not mention any European representatives by name.

Thus, *La Réforme* made Bonfigli's funeral procession through the streets of Egypt's main port city a story of French imperial political power, leaving out the city notables, as they were not necessary to the narrative. The apostolic delegation did not single out the specific political representatives but instead focused on how important the Catholic community was to Alexandria. Girard's report assesses what the French Consulate did and did not accomplish in arranging the procession. It, too, emphasizes French imperial power, although it is focused on civil power in the city, leaving the Catholic and Christian organizations out of the story and highlighting the role of other government officials and notables. In each account, the British are displaced as rulers of this particular Alexandrian moment.

Inside the church, the seating arrangement for the funeral replicated the hierarchy of the funeral cortege. The most prominent seats in the house, on the right of the chapel, opposite the representatives of the khedival government, who sat on the chapel's left side, were saved for the minister of France and the French consul in Alexandria.[111] The Italian consul sat immediately below the French. Across the church, next to the khedive's representatives, was the president of the Mixed Courts of Alexandria, who joined the funeral even though the members of the court refused to walk in the procession. The funeral clearly matched the representatives of France with those of the Egyptian government, while the British colonial and Italian governmental representatives were relegated to a position of lesser importance. Likewise, by elevating the Mixed Courts, the symbol of civil justice for foreign nationals in Alexandria, above the British colonial system, the French honored an institution that had equalized power between the various European states and that represented secular law, linking Egypt to the French Republic. The section of the church to the right of the Italian consul was filled by other members of the consular courts, followed by representatives of the British administration, army, and Anglican Church, as well as the chief rabbi of Alexandria. Behind them sat vice consuls, and behind the diplomats sat the city's notables. Members of the magistrate rounded out the first section, with rows of people from the municipality behind them and, in the final section of the left side, the religious clergy. The row of seats in front of the catafalque was saved for women. In this section, Mrs. Girard was given a position of honor.

The French priest of Alexandria, Reverend Father Paul d'Orléans, delivered the eulogy, which was later published in *La Réforme*. His presence was another coup for Girard in the planning of the funeral; the parish priest was an Italian national and thus, quite unusually, not invited to give the funeral oration.[112] Father d'Orléans gave a long and rousing eulogy, framing Bonfigli's life as a struggle for the love of Jesus against the temptations of flesh and material goods. Bonfigli, as the priest described him, was someone who earned his position of holiness through sheer force of will and who continually evolved into a person who could represent Catholicism to a broader world. In his service to Aleppo, Jerusalem, and Egypt, Bonfigli acted as Catholicism's messenger to the Arab Ottoman world. But Bonfigli's death, in this account, was more than a European and Ottoman loss; it was an Alexandrian one as well: "And now, farewell, sweet and Saint Pontiff, sleep your last sleep beside your children! Revered successor of Mark, the first bishop of this city, sleep at the feet of its altar, as a son close to his father. . . . We are proud to guard your mortal remains."[113] D'Orléans here references Mark the Evangelist, who founded the Church of Alexandria in 42 CE, thus marking Bonfigli as a part of a long succession of Christian leaders predating Muhammad as well as all modern nation-states. Alexandria, as the guardian of Bonfigli's "mortal remains," is his final home and thus the city to which he is connected. The French priest, speaking as both a Catholic representative and specifically because he holds French nationality, was thus able to speak for the communities that can claim Bonfigli, and, by extension, claim Alexandria from the days of Mark. The French were subtly positioned here as the real inheritors of the city, the consummate natives.

But d'Orléans did not linger in Alexandria's ancient past. The city was a Catholic city in his present as well. Alexandria at large, d'Orléans recounted, had celebrated Easter together, ringing happy church bells on April 3 of that year, three days before Bonfigli fell ill. The morning of the funeral, d'Orléans said, Alexandrians heard those bells once again, but in mourning. The city that just previously had celebrated as one was now mourning as one.

In Alexandria, funerals served to underscore the complexity of the population and the unique space within which they lived and died. Funerals were a celebration of cross-national and cross-religious interactions, in the form of mourners and those who provided funeral services. At the same time, funerals allowed consulates to claim the bodies of Alexandrians as their own—to turn dynamic, complicated once-living people into static, defined imperial bodies. The role of the individual consulates in giving those imperial bodies a decent death underscored the importance of consular activities to the city. The dead, both unknown and famous, allowed the British and the French to use the provision of needed, mundane services to assert their imperial power.

Thus, the funerals served a larger purpose. They were events through which European rivalries played out, where the French could challenge the British and their rule in Alexandria through a spectacle of France's making, despite whatever treaties had been signed by governments far removed from the everyday of empire. Funerals were also a ritual, the act that consecrated a body into the ground. Cemeteries, as the physical space in which the body was buried, were equally representative of belonging and identification in Egypt. We turn to them now.

3 A HOUSE FOR THE DEAD, A HOME FOR THE LIVING

AT FOUR IN THE MORNING on September 4, 1897, police in the small Nile Delta town of Kafr al-Dawar informed the Ramla police station in Alexandria that a double murder had been committed. Police officers were dispatched from the station, and at 8:30 that morning they found the bodies of Alexander Welch, a twenty-four-year-old British engineer, and his groom, Mohamed Ahmet, at their farm. The police immediately arranged for the bodies of Welch and Ahmet to be autopsied: Welch at the Deaconess Hospital, and Ahmet at the government hospital.[1]

When it arrived in Alexandria, Welch's body was made part of a British consular strategy for accounting for and protecting (legally, socially, and otherwise) its deceased expatriate subjects. Constable Whitfield went immediately to the farm to begin the inventory of Welch's belongings. Dr. Morrison, the consular doctor, performed a detailed autopsy. Consular employees engaged the SdPF and began to make funeral arrangements. The police worked with the consulate to arrest three Bedouins for the murders.

As the consulate staff organized Welch's possessions, they also organized the disposal of his body. Within the archives collected in the flurry of activity surrounding Welch's murder is a receipt for the British Protestant cemetery, where the consulate purchased a grave the day of Welch's death.[2] Placing Welch's body into a grave in the British Protestant cemetery was both an act of necessity—he had to be buried somewhere—and a statement about his belonging to the British community. Welch now took up permanent physical space in Alexandria and thus made the small piece of land in which he was buried hallowed British and Protestant ground.

Whereas Welch's death generated a variety of memoranda, Mohamed Ahmet's demise sparked nary a mention in the archival records once his native body was separated from Welch's imperial one. His death was not of concern to the British; his body could not be claimed as theirs. Likewise, it is the foreign-national and religious-minority cemeteries that concerned the British and French, not the Muslim ones. Their many Muslim subjects are lost to their consular cemetery records.

The primary foreign and non-Muslim cemeteries of Alexandria during the nineteenth and early twentieth centuries were located in the Shatbi neighborhood, by Bab Sharqi, the Gate of the Sun, also called the Rosetta Gate. Unlike foreign hospitals, which served the population of Alexandria as a whole, foreign cemeteries, built on parcels of land designated as sacred space and designed to outlast the living, specifically marked the city's population as divided by creed and nationality. The cemeteries marked those who were not Muslim as different from Muslim Alexandrians, creating physical borders between the communities. Yet while imperial bodies were interred in plots labeled "British" or "French," the soil that enveloped them was Alexandrian and Egyptian. Like sickness, death united foreign and local; death allowed the imperial to claim presence in Alexandria.

This chapter tells the story of how imperial cemeteries created permanent spaces of exclusion and empire in Egypt. Alexandrian cemeteries differed from the city's hospitals, imperial inquests and registries, and funerals in that they divided the population by religion first and thereby lumped Ottoman/Egyptian non-Muslims alongside foreign-national non-Muslim communities, in one large area of land set aside for non-Muslim cemeteries. These non-Muslim Ottoman/Egyptians, like the foreign-national communities, had to petition the Egyptian government for a piece of this private land in which to bury their dead. Non-Muslim cemeteries, in this sense, were aligned with empire in its many forms.

Cemeteries were not always located on private land. Although the Egyptian national government clearly saw utility in creating separate cemeteries, it also maintained perpetual ownership over the burial lands of foreign nationals and religious minorities, in a marked contrast to its approach to foreign hospitals, for which these same communities bought or received their land outright. The largest contiguous foreign cemetery block, at Shatbi, was located among military fortifications, and the Egyptian government would not relinquish its hold on the land. Perpetual governmental ownership of cemetery land points to the cemeteries' municipal role as both a site for burying the dead and protecting the living from the health hazards surrounding close contact with dead bodies. By securing its control of the cemetery land, the Egyptian government ensured that the needs of the living would always trump the needs of the dead. And by making burial of foreign dead its responsibility, the Egyptian government made the foreign living its responsibility as well.

The Egyptian state had a long history of utilizing others to take care of its own.[3] However, unlike a hospital, cemeteries carried with them the aura of perpetuity.[4] Thus, that the Egyptian state maintained control of land while creating permanent space for imperial bodies is of interest. This state was subordinated to both the British and Ottoman Empires. Yet within the limited scope of its authority, the politics of burial gave it life.

The same foreign communities that worked to make themselves vital to Alexandria through their hospitals also pushed the Egyptian national government to count them as Alexandrians through burial in private cemetery space. The same consulates that helped organize funerals of all religions and helped document and compress diverse, full lives into categories of nation and empire stood ready to push for exclusive cemeteries upon request from the religious and lay communal leadership. Cemetery space was a moment when inclusion, ironically, required exclusion. The Egyptian government, weak though it may have been, was the key actor in determining and granting cemetery space.

Cemeteries were the key physical site in the process that took Alexandria's imperial bodies and placed them, permanently, in set categories. Thus, the cemeteries were physical reminders that imperial involvement in Alexandria went beyond the activities of the British and Ottoman Empires. When Alexander Welch was buried in the British Protestant cemetery, his corpse became evidence of both a British, Protestant death and a British, Protestant life in Alexandria. Its presence proved the vitality of the many communities living there. The same could be said for the many French and other imperial subjects who lived and died in Alexandria. Foreigners could—and did—claim to be Alexandrians because their dead were buried there. The land in which corpses were interred allowed for a declaration of the presence of the French, British, Protestants, Catholics, and others on Egyptian, Ottoman, Muslim land.

The non-Muslim cemeteries illustrate what philosopher Henri Lefebvre called the "conceptual triad" of spatial practice, representations of space, and representational space.[5] Spatial practice, he contends, is, loosely, the actual use of space in an urban area; the representations of space are the ways in which space is conceived, how city planners and others determine the usage of space; and representational space is the approximation of what space means (and in this sense it is what happens when space becomes place, in geographer David Harvey's usage).[6] Any given urban space is a combination of all three. In Alexandria, the process of negotiations between the various Egyptian governmental agencies and the different foreign and non-Muslim communities determined the representations of cemetery space. But it is the final element of the triad, the representational space of cemeteries, that helps explain how foreign and non-Muslim communities used the cemeteries to make pointed arguments for the inclusion of their exclusive communities in the broader patchwork of Alexandria. The intricacies of working with the government bureaucracy for the acquisition of land and burial rights underlined the physical and intangible connections of the foreign communities with Alexandria. Cemetery space fulfilled a material obligation to the living population in the municipal planning and public health function: it served the representation of space for the dead. Cemetery space also created and sustained a link between the government of Alexandria, the city's living inhabitants, and the buried dead, becoming representational space. And it did so both before and after the British occupation in 1882, for Egyptian non-Muslim subjects and European communities alike.

NINETEENTH-CENTURY EGYPTIAN CEMETERIES IN LITERARY IMAGINATION

Cemeteries were everyday spaces for the living in Alexandria. In nineteenth-century Egypt, as recounted in famous works by contemporary authors such as the British Edward Lane or the Egyptian Muhammad al-Muwaylihi, residents regularly utilized cemetery space for social and religious occasions. Lane's *An Account of the Manners and Customs of the Modern Egyptians*, a book both celebrated as one of the most thorough accounts of life in nineteenth-century Egypt and disparaged as the quintessence of Orientalist writing, hints at the use of cemeteries by the living in early to mid-nineteenth-century Egypt.[7] Lane talks of the "poor at the tomb," waiting for bread and food from funerals.[8] He describes how "the Coptics, both men and women, pay regular visits to the tombs of their relations three times a year: ʾeed el-meelad, ʾeed al-gheetas, and ʾeed el-kiyameh. They go to the tombs on the eve of each of these ʾeeds and there pass the night."[9] The cemeteries served a social function as an open, public space, with visits to them consisting of all-day picnics and gatherings.[10]

The Coptic cemeteries, as well as the Muslim, also discussed by Lane, fall under the rubric of Ottoman/Egyptian; Lane does not mention foreign communal cemeteries and might very well have argued that they were not an "Egyptian" space. He was, after all, deeply embedded in the Orientalist tradition. Nonetheless, in his brief description, the relevance of the cemeteries to communal social life is evident. This relevance distinguishes the cemeteries from the hospitals, which served the sick but were not gathering sites for the healthy. The cemeteries, however, served both to house the dead and to home the living. That is, they held the corpses of the dead, but they also created space for the social connections of the living.[11] Using the cemeteries for burial or funerals or simply walking through them served to validate the communal presence of the living in Alexandria.

That the cemeteries were homes for the living is evident in Muhammad al-Muwaylihi's novel *Hadith ʾIsa ibn Hisham*, which was serialized in newspapers from 1898 to 1903 and which opens with a scene in a Cairo cemetery. ʾIsa ibn Hisham has come to the cemetery for solitude and reflection and instead encounters a pasha who, after rising from the grave, fumbles through a "modern" Egypt he does not understand. The cemetery is a peaceful space for the living, and Ibn Hisham uses it to escape from the chaos of the living world and commune with his thoughts. In this way, the cemetery is part of the built environment of the city while simultaneously providing a space that removes the visitor from the city. Ibn Hisham wanders the cemetery without purpose or a specific relative to visit, but the ease with which he wanders about suggests a kind of possessive feeling on his part. By virtue of his sharing an ethnic, religious, and national background with those buried, his world is integrated into their burial grounds. The cemetery is the site of Egyptian history and the marker of belonging for the dead: the pasha, having been buried in, and then emerging from, a grave on Egyptian soil, is immediately recognizable as a tangible part of Egypt's history. Thus, he plays the role of the credible commentator on the past. Egypt is his because his body is Egypt's.

While scholars have characterized al-Muwaylihi as working within a nationalist tradition, however vaguely defined that might have been at the time, his representation of the cemetery as a site of belonging seems applicable to the cemeteries of foreign-national and religious minorities, despite their connection to agents of imperialism.[12] That is, having a specific cemetery wherein members of a religious minority and a distinct nationality are buried would allow living people holding the same affiliations to use the cemetery as a claim of the same type of belonging in Egypt that the pasha and 'Isa ibn Hisham enjoyed.

We see from *Manners and Customs* and *Hadith 'Isa ibn Hisham* that the cemetery was integrated into Alexandria's public spaces. It was a "heterotopia," to borrow Michel Foucault's terminology, a space that was at once both real and unreal.[13] The cemetery was very much a part of everyday experience but concurrently removed its visitors from the quotidian world of whichever culture, society, or city they were part of. Alexandria's most famous poet, Constantine Cavafy, a Greek national who was born in Alexandria in the late nineteenth century, repeatedly referred to the city's cemeteries as sites that marked the Alexandrianness of those buried or places that connected the living to their history and their dead.[14] The cemetery was a special and emotional space, intricately connected, as this literature suggests, to the surrounding worlds of members of all the nationalities, religions, and ethnicities that found themselves in Alexandria.

CEMETERIES FOR WHOM? THE CREATION OF COMMUNAL CEMETERIES

It was not always the case that a religious community would have its own discrete cemetery. As cemeteries moved from churchyards and private land to public gardens in the nineteenth century, questions of how, and whether, to divide cemetery land along communal lines plagued governments in various regions of the world. As late as the 1880s in Cuba, for example, non-Catholics could not be ritually buried. Instead, their bodies were either lumped together in mass "potter's fields" or tossed out at sea.[15] In England, cemetery and church were divorced in the mid-nineteenth century when the mass accumulation of discarded bodies and unregulated burial grounds proved to be a health and sanitation hazard that resulted in the creation of new cemeteries not on church property. Religious communities would now contend with arranging for cemetery space within a large, public burial ground rather than on church property.[16] France struggled with the move between religious and secular cemeteries throughout the nineteenth century; the phenomenon of private burials in early nineteenth-century France was, at least in part, due to a desire by French Catholics and Protestants not to be buried next to each other.[17] By the end of the century, French cemeteries were legally a religiously neutral space.[18] Even in areas in which the ethnic, national, or religious-minority cemetery was the norm in the nineteenth century, such as Nebraska, where a number of Czech cemeteries were established,[19] cemeteries were often the result of that minority community having formed a majority in a geographically isolated territory. So these cemeteries were arguably a necessity rather than a choice by a government to promote, pay for, honor, or protect minority communities.

In Alexandria, before the completion of the foreign cemetery complex at Shatbi, foreign communities used private lands to bury their dead. The presumably first British cemetery in Alexandria was on 'Abd al-Mun'im Street, on the site of the garden of the British consul general Henry Salt. The consul general was buried there after his 1827 death, and the garden remained an active burial ground through the 1830s, when the British community opened a second cemetery in the Shatbi neighborhood near the Rosetta Gate, among the military fortifications known as Bab Sharqi, as part of the newly opened cemetery block regulated by the Egyptian government. The property on 'Abd al-Mun'im Street was soon thereafter considered British communal property and later converted back into a garden.[20]

In 1866, the Cemetery Committee of the joint Anglican and Scottish Churches requested and received permission for an expansion of their cemetery on land already owned by the British Consulate; although the exact site of the cemetery is not mentioned, it is presumably the Shatbi burial grounds.[21] The request was presented to the British residents of Alexandria at a general meeting. The minutes of the meeting record a resolution proposed by the treasurer:

> Seeing that the permission to enclose a further piece of land adjoining the burial ground has been in possession of the consulate for some time (as would appear by the [Alexandrian] governor's letter) and that Protestants have been buried outside the walls of the present burial grounds, HM's Consul is requested to take immediate steps to put the affair in order with the local authorities.[22]

This resolution is worth parsing in full. In the opening statement, we learn that there has been permission to expand the cemetery by the governor of Alexandria, an Egyptian governmental official. Moreover, we learn that this permission was granted to the British Consulate, not to the Cemetery Committee, and that the British Consulate may not have transmitted the information promptly. Next, it is noted that Protestants—not British, but Protestants—are already buried in the land that is now approved of for burial. Additionally, there is a call for the consul to remain the liaison between the British residents of Alexandria and the Egyptian government. Finally, we learn that the British Consulate owned the cemetery land (unlike in later years, when land in the area would be loaned to, rather than owned by, foreign communities). The Protestant Cemetery Committee thus both used the Egyptian government to legitimize their burials by placing themselves under the auspices of the municipal government, whom they want to "put the affair in order with," while also bypassing the government by using the land as they wished prior to getting approval. The Cemetery Committee simultaneously appealed to the Egyptian government as arbiter of what land can be used and disregarded its authority. The Protestants are both within and beyond the Egyptian government's reach. And the consulate stands as the conduit between the two, continuing its role of guaranteeing a good death by ensuring that its subjects would not only have the proper funeral but also a sacred, specifically Protestant, ground for interment.

The communication regarding this resolution, wherein the consulate allowed burials by the Cemetery Committee to continue before receiving formal permission from the Egyptian national government suggests both the weakness and strengths of the Egyptian state. That is, the Protestant community was comfortable enough with its own position in Egypt to bury bodies without permission from the governing authorities yet cautious enough to seek the protection of its dominant consulate nonetheless, a full fifteen years before the British occupation and ten years before France and England would take over the Egyptian economy. The Egyptian state was not to be feared, and European informal empire protected the foreign population; yet the state could not be completely discounted.

As noted, by the mid-nineteenth century non-Muslim cemeteries were grouped together in a block of land in the Shatbi neighborhood, chosen by the Egyptian government specifically to be used as burial grounds.[23] As were hospitals, these cemeteries were built with the help or oversight of the Egyptian government, and religious and national communities often overlapped. Individual communities maintained the foreign cemeteries, usually with the subvention and aid of the Egyptian national and Alexandrian municipal governments. Through World War I the creation and maintenance of foreign cemeteries involved an intricate bureaucratic process that required the participation of multiple departments of the Egyptian state, including the Interior Ministry, the Public Works Ministry, the Finance Ministry, the Health Ministry, the military, and the national Council of Ministers. The Alexandria municipal government was also involved in the process, often as a liaison between the national government and the city's foreign cemetery committees. The cemetery committees were made up entirely of members of the lay or religious communities, not members of the consulates.[24] Recall that a European consul always held the presidency of the European Hospital. These committees were the primary group responsible for communication with the Egyptian government. The consulates stepped in to help push the Egyptian government to move on cemetery decisions, but only after the lay committees communicated with the government on their own.

To build or expand a cemetery, representatives of a foreign community would typically lobby for a parcel of land that was part of a larger plot on the outskirts of the city that the Egyptian government had already designated for use by foreign communities to build cemeteries. The community would submit the request to the Interior Ministry, which would then involve the Public Works Ministry to determine if the land was appropriate for burials, and the Finance Ministry to calculate if the government could afford to give away the land. The Health Ministry would turn to subcommittees, such as the Sanitation Department or Commission,[25] to decide if the community's current cemetery was indeed overcrowded and therefore potentially posed a citywide health problem. The question of the land's suitability would be put to the Council of Ministers. Once the government approved of a foreign community's use of a parcel of land, the community usually received the rights to build on the land for free.[26] Questions of public health, city planning, bureaucracy, and belonging determined which communities were allowed to build cemeteries among the designated Shatbi lands.

As an early 1880s memo regarding the request for a Catholic cemetery expansion noted, the Egyptian government considered it the duty of the Council of Ministers to protect the land at Shatbi, which was adjacent to, and cordoned off from, the Bab Sharqi Fort and shooting range. Although some of the land, most likely including the land for the original British Protestant cemetery, had been sold before the Egyptian government had built the military fort, the remainder was protected military land that was to remain in government hands, specifically the Egyptian navy, regardless of its intended future purposes.[27] The Egyptian government would not only hold on to the land but would also control the expansion of the cemeteries.

Foreign communities, though minorities within the city population as a whole, were growing in the 1880s. As their populations grew, they became more and more invested in the idea that they were part of Alexandria and subject to Alexandrian laws. They understood, for example, that they could no longer simply will their garden to their greater community, as Henry Salt had done, and that they had to follow the same rules as others, including Egyptian subjects.[28] In 1876, the Egyptian government established regulations for the creation of cemeteries, after which point all Alexandrians would have to comply.[29] The new regulations designated control and maintenance of cemeteries to a designated sanitation commission. Burial grounds were to be kept as far as possible from any water source or supply. Likewise, the regulations delimited the depth of burial, and all burials outside prescribed cemeteries had to have the approval of the Sanitation Department.[30] For example, a cemetery had to be five hundred meters from the edge of the city and two hundred meters from other structures; in addition the cemetery had to be fenced in and contain three times the amount of space that was needed for the expected five-year decomposition time of corpses. Foreign burials and cemeteries were subject to the same regulations. Regardless of where one was buried in Alexandria, as of 1876, the technicalities of how one was buried were the same.

It is worth noting that the regulations requiring cemeteries to be moved to the city's outskirts also stipulated waiting periods before bodies could be shipped internationally for burial. Exhuming a corpse for such a purpose was strictly forbidden unless agreed to by the sanitation authorities.[31] While the very existence of the law suggests that the practice of shipping bodies was possible, I found no indication in archival research of foreigners who lived in Alexandria requesting burial anywhere other than Alexandria. Whether that absence reflects a preference or prohibitions due to cost, public health concerns, and/or bureaucratic complications, imperial corpses belonged to the city.

While foreign cemeteries were built on government-owned land, Muslim cemeteries were private enterprises, built on land donated by individuals or deeded in *waqfs*.[32] Muslim burial had long been a ritual that both symbolically and spatially distinguished the Muslim community.[33] Whereas an official community buried foreigners, an informal neighborhood and family net-work buried Muslims.[34] The government was available to help with burial of both Muslims and non-Muslims only as a last resort for all peoples and then only because dead bodies represented a public health issue.[35]

While funerals were primarily religious affairs, in the placement of Alex-andria's foreign cemeteries, religious concerns commingled with national af-filiation. There were not, however, any Muslim "foreign" communities listed within the foreign cemetery land, suggesting that all Muslims in Alexandria were buried together, regardless of origin.[36] Indeed, a 1911 map of the ceme-teries drawn up by the British Consulate of Alexandria shows an unspecified "Mohammedan" cemetery near the non-Muslim burial grounds, set off to the right beyond the foreign cemetery block.[37] Thus, the North African French subject would not be buried in a French-protected cemetery. Likewise, Said Basselm, the British Indian Muslim whose funeral the British Consulate ar-ranged, would not be buried in a British cemetery. Instead, his body, like other Muslim imperial bodies, faded from the consulates' view after he was buried; his cemetery was not protected imperial space and would not be advocated for or protected by the consulates. The British and French Consulates would claim Muslim subjects such as Basselm in inquests, registries, estates, and fu-nerals, but they would not bury them in their cemeteries; in burial, religion trumped nationality, and the status of being foreign, or imperial, was associ-ated exclusively with non-Muslims. At the same time, however, the alignment of foreign and non-Muslim in these cemeteries brought new groupings to the fore, as evidenced by burial of Ottoman/Egyptian Maronites, Coptic Chris-tians, Armenians, and Jews alongside the foreign-national communities.[38]

The difference between Muslim and foreign cemeteries suggests that the formal communal structure was more important to the foreign, non-Muslim communities than it was to local and foreign Muslims. Muslims, assumed to be native to the region, most likely did not rely as much on an identified of-ficial community to assert their belonging to Alexandria.[39] This is true even among the many North Africans in Egypt; their religion put them in the ma-jority in regard to their place of burial. In other words, a specific commu-nal cemetery was necessary only when the community was not the major-ity, and the assumption of belonging was not automatic. Consequently, the existence of the communal cemetery secured a place, a home for those as-sumed to be outside the population. The creation of a cemetery by a commu-nity, then, actually defined that community as belonging to the city and thus emphasized the insecurity of empire. That is, rather than an assumption of imperial strength or the presumption that being the European power would mean that one had control and access unavailable to the Egyptian Muslim— not only in a legal or political sense but also tangibly, in the ability to take land as desired—the need for cemetery space can be read as the need to prove that the community had the presence and importance necessary to be recognized as belonging to the jumble that made up Alexandria. Empire was not all-powerful but rather was constituted on the ground through day-to-day actions within the built environment of the city.

It is here, then, in the bureaucratic negotiations over where to inter the dead, that we see Lefebvre's representations of and representational space in action. The codification of a specific community through the process of requesting burial space actually facilitated inclusion within the broader population of Alexandria.

THE SHATBI CEMETERIES: IMPERIAL BODIES, EGYPTIAN GOVERNANCE

Over three decades, both before and after the British occupation, at least eight communities tried to build or expand cemeteries in the Shatbi area, involving at least twelve government agencies, the British and French Consulates, and numerous lay committees. The process was not an easy one; the cemetery lay committees and different government departments expressed constant confusion and frustration as they tried to work through land requests. The archives of the division of land are incomplete; we only know the end of the story because the cemeteries remain in Alexandria today.

An unknown department of the Egyptian government in 1878 sketched a blueprint of the cemetery lands in the Shatbi neighborhood; these are the non-Muslim cemeteries of Bab Sharqi.[40] The map shows a square (*midan*) to honor the military dead alongside a reserved section for soldiers, as well as designated land for Europeans (*afrangi*), European Catholics, Copts, British, Armenians, Syrian Catholics, Roman Orthodox, and Jews. The blueprint also includes sections for future growth as well as for burial of members of an unnamed benevolent association, space for fortifications and agriculture, and land privately owned by a foreign national.[41] A surviving 1911 map of the same foreign cemeteries from the British Consulate shows a different composition.[42] While the 1911 map marked Jewish, Coptic, Roman Orthodox, and Roman Catholic cemeteries, all other cemeteries are identified by nationality: two Greek cemeteries, two British civilian cemeteries, and one British military cemetery, two Armenian cemeteries, and a Free Masons cemetery rounded out the foreign cemetery section. A Muslim cemetery sat nearby.

Jewish, Coptic, Armenian (unspecified Catholic or Orthodox), and British cemeteries appear in both cemetery maps. The first three are Ottoman/Egyptian minorities; what is marked as British on each map is actually the Protestant cemetery and held people of various nationalities.[43] And while the Egyptian governmental map of 1878 speaks of European cemeteries, the British Consulate map of 1911 does not. As it does for the patient nationalities documented by the European and Deaconess Hospitals, terminology matters. While we do not know how or why the British consular employees labeled the cemeteries as they did, the result of these choices leaves a map that writes out competing European national cemetery space and, with it, claims of Alexandrian belonging for their living. Indeed, the only nationalities mentioned aside from the British are Greeks and Armenians, those associated with the Ottoman Empire. Britain stands alone as the sole European power with a permanent home in Alexandria's cemetery space.[44]

The cemetery blueprints diagram the intricacies of Alexandria's population. The allocation of land to the communities depended on the availability of land and was therefore somewhat random; the Greek cemeteries were split up, for example. The British Protestant cemetery traded lands with the Jewish cemetery to form one of its several cemetery sections.[45] Clearly, one community could not assume it would have contiguous lands in expansion. The name and definition of the community might have differed between the Egyptian and British blueprints, but the fact of the community did not. There was no open burial section, no potter's field. The government would involve itself with a burial only if the communities failed in their duty to bury their own and then only because dead bodies were a public health issue.[46]

In the inclusion of Ottoman *millets* next to foreign-national communities, these graves highlight the multivalence of the Ottoman Empire. In their division by nationality and religion, the cemeteries are a spatial manifestation of European empires' ability to establish communities in that multivalent Ottoman Empire and impact the physical layout of the cities in which they lived. As anthropologist Engseng Ho writes, "What is important is not where you were born, but where you die."[47] This statement was as true for recent migrants and settled families in Alexandria as it was for the diasporic communities of Hadrami Yemenis throughout the Indian Ocean that Ho describes.[48]

These cemeteries were imperial markers for imperial bodies, including those of the Ottoman Empire and the various European empires. These empires built and claimed imperial space not only through bureaucracy but body by body, corpse by corpse.

The maps demonstrate the results of land negotiations that began in the 1870s and lasted for decades. Who was buried where at Shatbi was the result of negotiations of power and claim making at work in the context of continued cemetery expansion.[49] By the late 1870s, numerous communities had either expanded beyond their assigned cemetery space or attempted to create new cemeteries within the allotted lands in Shatbi.[50] Those communities turned to the Egyptian government, just as they turned to that government for subventions with their hospitals. And like the back-and-forth correspondence around suspension of hospital subventions in the 1870s, so, too, did solutions to cemetery land requests drag on for years, thus spanning the period both before and after the British occupation. Throughout the decades, the Egyptian national government remained the final arbiter of who could bury where and of which communities could have land. And at a time when the government could have used the money earned by selling land (to offer help to the hospitals if for no other reason), it chose to maintain sovereignty over its land. The government stopped selling land at Shatbi by the 1870s and 1880s; all future cemetery land was to be leased instead.[51]

The creation of the cemeteries was not directly an act of empire. The European foreign communities wielded no special powers; they were given no special opportunities. At the same time, the cemeteries represented the spatial claims of empire, the marking of Alexandria, and by extension, Egypt, as a home to Europeans. British and French communities, through the Protestant and Catholic cemeteries, claimed both land and belonging. The various European communities competed with each other for recognition and cemetery space, yet at times they worked together in united blocs to present their needs to the Egyptian national government.[52] The cemeteries therefore indirectly served empire. They disrupted the Muslim majority with physical reminders of the many others who also made up Alexandria, of the many imperial bodies that needed to be buried.

EUROPEAN CATHOLICS, FREE THINKERS, AND THE EGYPTIAN GOVERNMENT

The Latin Catholic community established its cemetery at Shatbi on or before 1850, the first year for which there are statistics available.[53] The Franciscans took care of the Latin cemetery, which was alternately referred to as their cemetery, the Latin cemetery, and the European cemetery in correspondence between the Egyptian government ministers; this is the Roman Catholic cemetery on the 1911 British Consulate map.[54] Between 1864 and 1878 there was an average of 422 Catholic burials a year, and in 1865, a cholera year, 870 Catholics died.[55] By 1863, numerous families were reserving land together for family burial, and less room remained for individual burial. The space in the cemetery was quickly depleted.[56]

Whereas the early nineteenth-century Latin Catholic community was composed of single émigrés, by the 1860s it was constituted primarily of families, thus further rooting it in the city. Scholars have argued that the "cult of the dead," which included a family's burial together, was a route to stability and comfort during an era when the meaning of both families and work was in flux.[57] Planning for family burial can be read as the Catholic community's commitment to Alexandria and as the municipal government's commitment to the Catholic community. Even if these family plots were nothing more than prominent families attempting to assert themselves,[58] they are nonetheless evidence of a community attempting to establish itself and its history in Alexandria. The cemetery was integrated into the lives of the living in that blood relatives and in-laws, not just others of the same religion and nationality, were buried together in Alexandria.

By the early 1870s, the Latin Catholic community, represented by the Franciscan Brothers, had approached the Council of Ministers and asked for help expanding its cemetery.[59] The land was at the brink of being overcrowded, and the community faced a public health crisis if it could not find new burial grounds. Internal Egyptian governmental correspondence about the Catholic cemetery uses "Catholic" and "European" interchangeably and as two parts of the same community.[60] In other words, the problem of overcrowding was imagined by the Egyptian national government to be a problem of an imperial, foreign-national community as much as that of a religious community in Alexandria.

The conflation of European and Catholic within the cemeteries emphasizes their flattening effect on national and religious distinctions. Cemeteries were defined spaces, housing what were understood to be defined bodies; that those buried in the cemeteries might not match the definitions did not matter. The European Catholic community was understood by both its lay committee and the Egyptian government to be growing in part because of the crowding of its cemetery. Its living were defined by the bodies of its dead. The move from Catholic to all of Europe, which suggested that the European community at large would be understood in terms of the number of Catholic dead, was not surprising. As the case of Archbishop Bonfigli's funeral showed, the French had long asserted themselves as the protectors of the Catholics of the Orient and used that position to claim dominance over other European powers in Alexandria. The prevalence of Maltese in Alexandria furthered the connection between Catholics and Europeans; due to its numbers in Egypt, the British community was more Catholic than Protestant.[61] And the European Hospital was the Catholic hospital of Alexandria. That Catholicism, and therefore the Latin Catholic cemetery, represented all Europeans would have been obvious in late nineteenth-century Alexandria.

The primary problem concerning the European Catholic cemetery, noted a Ministry of Health report on the cemetery crisis, was the family plots; they required significantly more space in the cemetery than a single grave might.[62] It is telling, however, that the report did not suggest that the Catholic community cease selling family plots but rather that the Catholics integrate the family plots into a larger cemetery plan on a larger cemetery plot of land. That is, the Ministry of Health subcommittee (also known as the Health Commission) charged with determining who would get which cemetery space recognized the changing composition of the Catholic community in Alexandria. The Catholic cemetery had eight interlocking plots left by the 1870s, and rather than maximize who could be buried there by requiring individual burials, the Health Commission proposed that additional land be given, free of charge, to the community. Both the Sanitation Commission and the governor of Alexandria agreed. The Egyptian national government determined that whatever the final decision of land reviews by the Health, Finance, and Public Works Ministries, the land would be given to the community for free, as a new Catholic cemetery would be "for the public benefit and the public health."[63] Thus, from the start, questions of city planning, public health, and landownership overlapped. The Catholic community was offered a plot of land next to the existing Shatbi burial grounds.[64]

But that land was already claimed. In 1873, a group calling themselves the Free Thinkers—alternately called the Free Party in Arabic (Hizb al-Hurra), Free Thinkers (Libre Penseurs) in French, and variously Free Masons, Free Thinkers, and Civil International in English[65]—had asked for the same land to build a civil cemetery under local governance. The Free Thinkers had become established enough to want recognition as their own community in the

Shatbi cemeteries. They did not want to be affiliated with European powers but to be considered part of the Ottoman/Egyptian order. The Free Thinkers entered into negotiations with a family named Saba to use its private land next to the existing cemeteries.[66] However, this land was the same land that the government later offered to the Latin Catholic community. The Saba family land was contested: Although the Egyptian government insisted that it had settled all claims to the land by 1856 and was the rightful owner, the Saba family would nonetheless keep the government in court for decades.[67] Until the dispute between them could be settled, the Saba land was not available for cemetery usage.

In June 1876, the Egyptian government offered the Free Thinkers a different plot of land and asked the Saba family to turn over its deed to the land. Both parties refused. The Free Thinkers insisted on building a cemetery on that one piece of land, and the Saba family insisted that the land was its to do with as it pleased.[68] An August 1876 khedival order to the governor of Alexandria urged the municipal government to make finding land for the Free Thinkers its first priority in regard to the Shatbi cemetery grounds. All else was to wait. This meant, as government employees acknowledged, that the overcrowding of the Catholic cemetery was being neglected.[69]

The Latin Catholics were at a loss and turned to the French Consulate,[70] which lobbied the Egyptian government.[71] Here, once again, the consulate was the guarantee of a decent death or, in this case, a decent burial. The consulate intervened with the Ministry of Health, arguing first that the Catholics needed cemetery land as soon as possible and, when that proved fruitless, that the land promised to the Catholics was different from the Saba lands promised to the Free Thinkers. The Catholics, argued the consulate, should therefore be given access to that land immediately. Under pressure from the French Consulate, the governor of Alexandria pushed the minister of the interior to clarify the cemetery land distribution.[72]

At this point, the deputy director of the Bab Sharqi military fortifications that abutted the cemeteries intervened. The Catholic land, he said, was indeed different from the Saba land. But it was also needed for a military shooting range and therefore unavailable to both the Catholics and the Free Thinkers. Moreover, argued the deputy director, any available land for cemeteries in the future had to be leased rather than owned. The Egyptian government was to remain the legal owner and needed to inform the French Consulate that the land was not, and never would be, theirs.[73]

This change in ownership regulations reopened questions of landowner-ship and governmental responsibility. The government's public health and public works duties required it to provide appropriate burial grounds for its subjects, and it also oversaw the management of resources, including land, for the living population. The government had to ensure that the representa-tions of space, to borrow from Lefebvre once again, matched the representa-tional space in that the land served the needs of the living. The Egyptian gov-ernment worried about outside ownership in or near military fortifications. While the military might easily be able to relocate a church, it was signifi-cantly more difficult to gain public approval for the reinterment of dead bod-ies.[74] Maintaining that cemetery land was government land guaranteed the government the final word in questions of land use, allowing the Egyptian government to give priority to the needs of the military specifically and, more generally, to all of the living population within its territory.

But the Egyptian government of the 1870s was struggling and was unable to settle the cemetery crisis. The Catholics were not offered the Saba lands or other new land; several years passed without resolution for the public health crisis of the Catholic cemetery.[75] The president of the Committee to Expand Catholic Cemeteries wrote to Riyad Pasha, who was then minister of the inte-rior, in July 1881. He informed the minister that yet another Health Commis-sion had been established to study the need for an expansion of the Catholic cemetery. An increase in "Europeans," he said, made the enlargement neces-sary. He did not specify here that the Europeans were Catholics, and he did not need to do so. The link between the two was accepted.

As the Catholic community continued to struggle for new cemetery land, the Egyptian government remained focused on finding land for the Free Thinkers, who continued to press for the Saba land.[76] Again, there was no potter's field. Therefore, those who identified as Free Thinkers must have been buried in some other community cemetery; this was not a case of un-buried bodies piling up. The space crisis within the Catholic cemetery meant that the Catholic community was running a high risk of breaking the city's health regulations that required a certain amount of excess space to allow for "breathing room" in each cemetery,[77] but the Egyptian government pri-oritized communal recognition of the Free Thinkers over public health. The choice indicates that the question of recognition was primary to the relation-ship between the city and its diverse populations. The Catholic request could wait, in this instance, even at the risk of public health, as the Alexandrian municipal and Egyptian national governments already had a secure relationship with this established community. Requesting a cemetery for the first time, however, was not a question of public health but of belonging, of wanting recognition for one's religious, ethnic, or, in this case, civil beliefs as a part of the living, breathing city. So this process of negotiating for the land was a process of spatial inclusion into the social fabric of the city, and the Egyptian government deemed the Free Thinkers' request of primary importance.

The Free Thinkers began their quest for cemetery land as a community under local auspices, specifying that they wanted to be considered Ottoman/Egyptian. By 1883, however, ten years after their first request, they joined with the Greek Catholics and the Greek Orthodox in asking for a rectangular "European" block of land, to be divided into three parts: half for the Greek Orthodox and a quarter for the Free Thinkers and Greek Catholics each.[78] The Free Thinkers seemingly abandoned their commitment to being seen as an Ottoman/Egyptian community in their pursuit of cemetery land. Yet from their first request in 1873 through the 1880s, the Egyptian government had consistently sought to persuade them to assent to land other than the original Saba land.[79] The Free Thinkers clearly were not in a rush to accept whatever cemetery space was offered. Instead, they negotiated and demanded specific land, suggesting that they were secure enough in their position within the city to insist on what they wanted rather than simply what they could get. Burial lands, then, were part of a process of recognition rather than the starting point of it.

In their negotiations, the Free Thinkers played with the terminology of being both under local governance and joining forces with other European groups in their request. They did not accept distinct boundaries between belonging to Egypt and belonging to Europe and instead affiliated with multiple power structures.[80] The ease with which they presented themselves as part of both the local and foreign communities was a privilege of being primarily European imperial subjects. Indigenous Muslims and Copts would not have had license to call themselves Europeans when it benefited them. Nevertheless, even if this advantage was available only to European subjects, how the Free Thinkers navigated the play between local and European governance is revealing. The act of requesting a separate cemetery space in Alexandria was an act of belonging to both an exclusive community and the city. It was a sign that a community was recognized as populous enough to protect its dead, both in their burial and in the upkeep of this presumably permanent

hallowed ground. It was a sign of longevity, of a community's belief in its future in Alexandria. The Free Thinkers' request, as well as the protracted negotiations that ensued, is also a reminder that they imagined their future in Alexandria as being under both British and local rule.

In early 1884 the Egyptian government was still trying to figure out how
to satisfy the Free Thinkers. They had finally gotten the needed documents
from the Saba family enabling them to use the land for cemeteries, but now
the American Mission was asking for the Saba lands, and the minister of public works was inclined to give it to them.[81] The archival trail turns cold after a series of letters in mid-October 1884 in which the interior minister declared to the president of the Council of Ministers that the cemetery divisions
were a mess, that the government as a whole was confused, and that no one
knew which community had been promised which plots of land. Although we
know today that somehow the Free Thinkers got their cemetery, as you can
visit it in Alexandria's remaining Shatbi burial grounds, the issue remained
unsettled at the time. Despite more than a decade of working on questions of
cemetery land, everything, declared the interior minister, must begin anew.[82]

OTTOMAN CHRISTIAN CEMETERIES
AND THE EGYPTIAN GOVERNMENT

Although the Latin Catholic cemetery was synonymous with the European
community, Ottoman Catholics were also buried there, as were Maronites.[83]
The Maronite community was a sect of the Syrian Christian population that
first settled in Egypt in the seventeenth century and grew steadily in the late
nineteenth century.[84] In the early 1880s, at the same time that the Committee to Expand Catholic Cemetaries was arguing that the overcrowding of the
Latin Catholic cemetery was an Alexandrian crisis, the Maronite community
put in a request for a private cemetery. It was no longer acceptable to the Maronites to bury their dead among the graves of Latin Catholics.[85]

The Maronites requested ten thousand square meters of land abutting
the Jewish cemetery. It is possible that this request was simply the result of
the growth in the Maronite population and lack of space in the Latin Catholic cemetery. However, by asking for a separate burial space alongside other
recognized religious communities, the Maronites, like the Free Thinkers, attempted to secure communal recognition for their living population in Alexandria. In addition, the land the Maronites requested was significantly
larger than that of other communities: the plot the Greek Orthodox com-

munity sought as part of its collective request with the Greek Catholics and Free Thinkers, for example, was only forty-four hundred square meters.[86] The minister of public works declared the forty-four hundred square meters sufficient to hold off the need for expansion by the Greek community, Alexandria's largest foreign-national and religious-minority community, for the foreseeable future.[87] Thus, by asking for land more than twice the size of the Greek Orthodox's requested plot, the Maronite communal leadership was insinuating not only that it was a bona fide minority community but also that it was a significant, growing part of the Alexandrian population. The Maronites leveraged their dead as reason to believe in their future in the city.

The Egyptian government was not immediately sympathetic to the Maronites and insisted at first that the Latin community would have to decide for itself if it wanted to give land from within its cemetery allotment—that same cemetery deemed so crowded as to be an impending public health disaster— to the Maronites. That the Egyptian government insisted that the Maronites first speak with the Latin Catholics was most likely a result of broader diplomatic arrangements: the French were long connected to the Maronites of Syria, so it is not necessarily surprising that Maronites would be buried in Latin Catholic cemeteries.[88] Recall that the French Consulate negotiated for the Latin Catholics when the Egyptian government was not forthcoming in new land for the Latin Catholic cemetery. The Maronite communal request bumped up against questions of governance and imperial power.

If the Latin Catholics would not or could not find space for the Maronites, said the Sanitation Commission, then there might be some land available to the east of the Jewish cemetery.[89] That is, the government had land available and could give the Maronites a cemetery but would prefer to have the Catholic communities negotiate among themselves.[90] The archival trail peters out after this exchange, and we do not know how the Maronites finally managed to get their cemetery, but we do know that they did. On the 1911 map of the cemetery lands, a Maronite cemetery abuts that of the Greek Orthodox.[91] Far away from the Jewish cemeteries and across the street from the Latin Catholics, the community succeeded in finding its space.

We can parse out at least two different historical narratives at play in the story of the Maronites and the Latin Catholic cemetery beyond the story of recognition for the living community. First, as we have seen in the multiple cases this chapter examines, the Egyptian government maintained control of its land. It could choose to grant or reject cemetery requests, and it could choose to engage or disengage with questions of Catholic intracommunal issues. At a time when the British occupation limited the autonomy of the Egyptian government, the power to control these land resources and to arbitrate between and manage the populations, at least in the realm of burial, remained firmly in the hands of the Egyptian powers. Second, that the Maronites are buried in the Latin Catholic cemetery at the same time that the overcrowding of that cemetery is marked as a sign of European growth once again shows the importance of, yet lack of uniformity in, terminology. Like the amorphous "Arab" category of the European Hospital, the presence of the bodies of Ottoman Catholics in European Catholic burial grounds bolstered claims about the sheer number of Europeans in Alexandria and the importance of Catholic, French, and European presence in Alexandria. Death makes people more manageable and governable. Administering the dead in hospitals, in autopsies, in civil registries, in funerals, and in cemeteries produced flattened categories that purported to define an imperial population. Yet again and again, evidence demonstrates that imperial categories remained messy after death. Processing death is a tool of empire and a reminder of both the possibility and confusion created by the movement of peoples and governing bodies in this imperial age.

In *Alexandria: A History and a Guide*, E. M. Forster included the cemeteries at Shatbi as sites to see in a tour of the city.[92] They were an open public space that connected the living and the dead, the tourist and the resident, and all Alexandrians. André Aciman similarly experiences the cemetery as a site of connections when writing of his return to Alexandria. He describes his confusion and disappointment at the size of the city and his alienation from the land. It is only when he remembers the cemetery and returns to where his grandfather is buried that he again feels a part of the city, a citizen of Alexandria. The separate Jewish cemetery symbolized the simultaneous segregation and integration of the community into the broader city population. The cemetery reminds him that even as a foreigner, he can tangibly mark his connection with the city.[93] He, too, finds inclusion within the cemetery, but only within the exclusive cemetery of his ancestors. He belongs to Alexandria through his ancestors' Alexandrian deaths.

Cemeteries were the last stop in the processing of the imperial dead. Cemeteries are a basic social necessity yet symbolize much more as they are created and expanded. In nineteenth-century Alexandria, burial of the dead helped define which communities belonged to the city, to the empires, and to the Egyptian state. Communal cemeteries placed non-Muslim communities under the governance of the Egyptian state. The cemeteries that were exclusive spaces of empire also engendered inclusion in the state. That is, they constituted a space in which both the Egyptian and foreign governments had responsibilities to the dead imperial subjects. Moreover, those burial grounds, as land enshrined as sacred and reserved for those who could claim the port city as theirs, were physical sites of belonging for the living foreign communities. The negotiations between those communities and the Egyptian government over the handling of the dead led not only to new physical markers in the city but also to more clearly defined categories of belonging among the living. These categories were reflected in the documentation of the dead to which we now turn.

4 DYING TO BE FRENCH, DYING TO BE BRITISH

ON NOVEMBER 1, 1908, at approximately 9:00 a.m., Pauline Françoise Elisabeth Borivent was born in Alexandria to Pierre Borivent, a confectioner who had previously lived in Algeria, and his wife, Anna Catharine Becker. The next morning, Pierre went to the French Consulate with two other confectioners as witnesses and registered his daughter as a French subject.[1] The act of registration was a brief physical ritual: Pierre and his friends went to a specific locale and stood in front of the consul general, while a consular employee wrote down their words. All present then signed their names or made a mark in the register, thereby completing the ritual.

Pauline Borivent's registration was also a documentary act. Her name was entered into a civil-status register: entry number 118 for the year 1908, listed on page 302 of a registration book that spanned from 1907 through 1908. She was made official in the French records, with information gathered according to a proscribed bureaucratic formula and written down in words that mirrored those of all other entries in the registers. Upon her registration, Pauline Borivent became known to the French Consulate.

Over the next ninety-five years, Pauline Borivent remained the charge of the French Consulate. Notations made by consular officials in the margins of the register in which Pauline's existence was first recorded mark several of her life events. She was married in 1960 in Boulogne-Billancourt outside Paris and died in Magnanville, northwest of Paris, in 2003. The consul general of France in Alexandria signed each notation, making the tracking of Borivent and the certification of her death an official written act as well.

Pauline Françoise Elisabeth Borivent is but one example of the thousands of names that appear in the French civil-status registers documenting the births, deaths, and marriages of French subjects in Alexandria. Alongside each individual's name appear notations that detail profession, parental lineage, geographic origins, and, often, nationality (mostly notable if the individual is a citizen or subject or held protégé status) as well as that of the person's parents and those who served as witnesses. The information documented by consular officials is limited; rarely do we learn why someone died, or what led to a divorce, or if the person registered had siblings or children. Documenting strategies were meant to be universal, following rules and regulations passed by the French state that set out exactly what information needed to be collected and how the register entries had to be written. The French state thus decided which details were necessary for a subject to be properly registered as French, just as the French state delineated the scope of information gathering. The French state outlined the written markers of its imperial subjects. And by doing so, the consular employees became unwitting archivists not only for the French imperial project but also for the Egyptian state.

We have thus far followed imperial bodies through sickness, memorialization, and burial, learning that to know the dead is to know the living. The consular mechanisms to bury and process the dead reflect the makeup of Egypt under the multiple empires of the late nineteenth and early twentieth centuries. Foreign-national and religious institutions served the needs of empire and local populations simultaneously, providing fodder for imperial rivalries while attending to individual Alexandrians in need. Funeral services venerated the individual within the geographically bound space of Alexandria while turning consulates into power brokers through the celebration of the dead. The cemeteries made the relationship between corpses and Egypt permanent: markers placed in the built environment of the city made specific foreign and religious-minority communities part of the eternal fabric of Alexandria. As a corpse made its final journey to the grave, it would be protected by a singular consular jurisdiction and, therefore, be permanently tied not only to the port city but also to the country that claimed it. These steps marked the transformation of an imperial subject into an imperial body.

This final stop on our journey, and on the journey of the imperial body, is the written archive, wherein the dead were made permanent subjects of one or another nation. The implications of writing death, which I define as collecting information about the personal life of the dead, varied depending on the process of documentation.[2] In some cases subjects had to come forth and announce their dead. In others, the consulate chose whose death to investigate. In this chapter, the death registers of the French Consulate are juxtaposed with the inquest reports of the British. Whereas most research into personal status focuses on the legal aspects of protection, with the registries appearing inasmuch as they support broader arguments about what personal rituals such as marriage and divorce teach us,[3] this chapter takes the death registrations and the inquests as representative of the process of documenting death. Civil registers and inquests helped empires know their subjects, imperial bodies that could be divided into the categories that the empire might need.[4] There was always a desire to delineate in empire; the imperial state needed to know the difference between citizen, subject, and protégé in order to function properly. The institutions of such divisions created "liminal subject of empire," the person who crosses those legal lines.[5] In Alexandria, it was often the consulates that moved those lines in attempting to capture the body of that liminal subject. The French Consulate used registers to document, divide, and manage its dead. By doing so, it showed that the barriers between citizen, subject, and protégé were at times firm and at times supple. Nonterritorial empire moved and shifted as needed to fill the pages of its registers, to claim its subjects, including protégés, and citizens.[6] The inquests, in memorializing British subjects who lived far beyond the boundaries of British community, did much of the same work. Together the registers and inquests reveal that the process of investigating and recording death intertwined the consulates with local space and governance. Thus were consulate bureaucrats turned into archivists of Egypt even as they produced the building blocks— or, rather, the building bodies—of imperialism.

GOVERNANCE AND JURISDICTION IN DOCUMENTING THE DEAD

Through hospitals, public funerals, and negotiations over burial lands, British and French consular officials were intimately involved in monitoring the lives and deaths of their subjects. International treaties had guaranteed them jurisdiction over the bodies of foreign subjects in death as in life. The imperial consulates had a vested interest in claiming bodies in a show of the necessity of consular power. While they were alive, these subjects existed between, among, and around imperial categories but not definitively within them.[7]

Procedures for the tracking of the dead were an important part of the social and legal bureaucracies of death. Both civil-status registers and inquests were crucial state practices that allowed the government to know who had died and (sometimes) how. With such information, consular officials could surmise what impact these deaths might have on broader living populations. Consular officials sent their compiled statistics along to European home governments and to the Egyptian national government.[8] In the late nineteenth century, the Egyptian government had its own interest in the compilation of births and deaths and tried to require Europeans to register with them as well, but consular officials negotiated to continue to collect data themselves and, in turn, submit it to the Egyptian government.[9] In this way, writing about the dead had an immediate impact on imperial and Egyptian governance.

The French civil-status registers are individual books, with each citizen register consisting of one year's worth of reports about births, deaths, and marriages; registers for subjects, protégés, religious minorities, and deaths at sea, however, were filled with several years' worth of information.[10] The dates of the entries reflect when the ritual of registration took place, not necessarily the date of the act being registered. There is a register for citizens; another for Algerians (subjects) and protégés; and a third, somewhat repetitive set of registers for religious authorities, consular agencies, and ships, which is filled primarily with protégés and subjects and covers only the 1880s and 1890s.[11] Despite these divisions, each book often mixed within its pages information on citizens, religious minorities, subjects, protégés, and those who died on French ships. Prior to 1890, deaths outside Alexandria, primarily in the Nile Delta or on ships crossing the Mediterranean, pepper the registers of all collections.[12] The 1871 citizen register, for example, consists of 148 deaths, 84 of which occurred in the provinces of the Nile Delta area, outside Alexandria, and most of which took place long before 1871, as deaths and births from outside the city often took years to make it into the registry. Of the 143 live births, 79 were documented from places like the Suez Canal region, Port Said, Isma'iliyya, Mahalla al-Kubra, and Mansura. Even Khartoum found its way into the Alexandrian registers when, in 1871, Louis Édouard Lelubois's 1868 death by dysentery was recorded.[13]

Most often, the registration consisted of a straightforward paragraph or two, listing the birth, marriage, or death of someone with a French connection, including information about parents, professions, and geographic heritage. Some notations, most often marriage contracts, copied information provided by religious organizations. A birth, death, or marriage may have been written down in both a religious and civil register, but not within the registry of two religions or two national consulates. The exception that proves the rule was the death of Michael Erlanger in 1886. Marked in the registry for religious authorities and consular agencies, Erlanger was a four-year-old Jewish child whose death entry was half in French, half in Italian and was marked as coming from the Jewish community wherein the Austro-Hungarian consul general had signed on behalf of the legal protections of that community; this was the only case in which I saw that a second national consulate certified a death. Ironically, despite the Italian language in the entry, the Italian Consulate was not involved.[14] Original death certificates from religious organizations were periodically clipped into the registers, per consular regulations that detailed the handling of translated and transcribed documents from religious authorities.[15]

While the civil registers also covered birth and marriage and the related events of adoption, recognition of illegitimate children, and divorce, it is the death entries, in the form of death registrations and as marginal asides to birth announcements, that we focus on here. Birth announcements and marriage contracts could guarantee someone access to French imperial protection during his or her lifetime. They could mean that the legal benefits of French affiliation could become available, on some level, to those registered with the French Consulate, although that protection could change. There was no guarantee that one would have access to the consulate in life, just as there was no guarantee that one would stay within the same consular jurisdiction.[16] One might marry someone of a different nationality or move to a new country,[17] or perhaps one could be part of a broader political change such as decolonization. The legally protected status of someone born or married as a French subject, in other words, was not a lifetime guarantee. If one's death was registered as French, however, that was a final act, an unchangeable placement of the imperial dead under the auspices of French protection and governance in Alexandria.

Like the French, the British also compiled personal-status registers. But theirs did not find their way into the British National Archives and unfortunately are missing.[18] Nonetheless, we know they existed. The British government began collecting national registries of personal status after the 1836 Registration Act. As part of the act, all residents of Wales and England were required to register births within six weeks and deaths ideally within five days; marriages, too, would be recorded by the state.[19] With the civil register, the job of collecting data on the population shifted from the church to the state, a shift that allowed for nationality-based, rather than religion-based, personal status. Abroad, consulates were responsible for the personal-status data of their subjects. In Alexandria, data from the death certificates informed discussions of public safety and public health, helping document ways in which both the imperial and Egyptian governments could better protect the living. In this sense, the certificates served a similar purpose as the inquests, which were saved and archived by the British state yet are not found in the French archives.[20]

The British inquests were housed within individual consular court case files, adjudicated by the British consular courts. Any one case could include documents such as witness reports, receipts, or letters from parents and family in England, with some cases containing a few pages of documentation and others containing well over a hundred. By the 1890s, a universal inquest form summed up most cases. This typewritten blue form asked for the date and location of the inquisition and noted that the judge of the consular courts and the coroner for the British Consulate should both be present. Jurors selected from the eligible list of men within the Alexandrian British community would be listed as well, along with the name of the deceased and the cause of death. All of the jurors would sign the form at the conclusion of the investigation, much like the official signing of the death-register entries.

The inquest was thus a ritualistic and a documentary process, much like the registration of a death. The inquest reports, like the registry notations, were formulaic and limited in their information. The supporting witness reports and other evidence tell broader stories about Alexandria's people and the social and economic relations between them. The inquest forms may have missed the very intimate family relations captured by the death registers, which detailed parental lineage, but they provided a prose map of the Alexandria inhabited by the dead. Both the registers and the inquest cases serve, therefore, as the final reckoning of the imperial body, the permanent documentation of the consulate's protection of, and responsibility to, subjects in death.

The inquests and the civil-status registers predate the British occupation of Egypt, and their rituals and formulas remained the same after the occupation. In the case of the British, the consulate followed a detailed bureaucratic process that included conducting autopsies and holding inquests in cases of suicide, murder, or deaths that concern matters related to the public good, such as infectious disease and drowning. The French registers covered all deaths and often did not include a cause of death in their notations. The British operated through a relic of a series of Order in Council agreements between the British and the Ottoman government that delineated consular jurisdiction and extraterritorial sovereignty; the French operated through their own series of consular rules and regulations.[21]

Both in life and in death, British and European nationals were subject to a legal system separate from that of indigenous Egyptians. The Capitulations, the consular court system, and, after 1876, the Mixed Courts system fostered an environment in which foreign nationals were not necessarily subject to Egyptian law.[22] In regard to foreign nationals in post-1882 Ottoman British Alexandria, consular courts had jurisdiction over all civil and criminal cases in which parties were of the same foreign nationality and all criminal cases with a foreign defendant as well as cases of foreign civil status. The Egyptian government thus had no authority over autopsies and inquests of foreign residents, despite the importance of these tools of investigation for policing and public health.[23] Likewise, the rights of civil status remained firmly in the hands of the foreign consulates, despite attempts by the Egyptian government to collect the data themselves.[24]

The Order in Council of 1873 detailed how the British Consulate in Ottoman territories should process the deaths of British subjects. It described the procedures for probate, the administration of wills, and the property of those who died intestate.[25] A subsequent Order in Council mentions a 1910 agreement that sets out the detail of the limits of British jurisdiction within Ottoman territory and names inquests as a specific British consular duty, although British consular control of British inquests predates these orders by decades.[26] This particular Order in Council is based on an 1890 Foreign Jurisdiction Act, suggesting that the British understanding of their rights and responsibilities dates back at least to that time.[27] As there are inquests in the first consular court files dating back to 1880, we can mark consular control of inquests as beginning before the British occupation.[28]

In regard to inquests, the Order in Council states that the consular court "shall have and discharge . . . all the powers and duties appertaining in England to the office of the Coroner in relation to the deaths of British subjects."[29] It claims jurisdiction over any British subjects who died at sea en route to Alexandria, whether on British or other ships.[30] Inquests are requested for any suspicious deaths, but nowhere in the charge to act as coroner is there a determination to order an autopsy. It follows, however, that if coroners in England were in charge of determining the need for postmortems, then the British Consulate abroad would have that same right to perform autopsies on its subjects.[31] British consular jurisdiction does not appear to have changed much after the occupation, despite the extension of British authority.

The French registers were mandated through a variety of civil codes and circulars updated throughout the nineteenth century by departments of the French government.[32] At risk of unnamed penalties, the registers had to be a certain size, with a certain binding, opened on the first of January, and closed every thirty-first of December, and they were always duplicated in real time. There is no mention in the codes of citizens and noncitizens having separate registers. The writing was to be formulaic, no abbreviations were allowed, all numbers had to be written out in letters, and the age and residence of the witnesses were needed to make the certificates legitimate. The last step in the process was the reading aloud of the registry notation by consular employees, followed by the signing of the register by the witnesses and the consul general before it was finalized and became a legal reference.

At the end of each year, a copy of the registers was to be sent to the Foreign Ministry in Paris, and a copy was to be kept in the consulate. In addition to the two identical registers, beginning in the early nineteenth century the consular officials sent copies of individual birth, marriage, and death certificates to the Foreign Office to be sent to the birthplace or last residence of those being registered. How to document the information in the margins was also regulated, although no mention is made of documenting death. Instead, regulations focused on marriages, divorces, or illegitimate children. Yet the notation in the margin of Pauline Borivent's death, as well as that of so many others, tells us that citizens of France were followed by the consulate through their deaths, that the birth registration often began a chain of care and responsibility that lasted beyond the grave.

The death certificates themselves, then copied into registers, were regulated. A death certificate had to be "written by a civil officer, in the presence of two witnesses."[33] Witnesses were to be the two closest relations, neighbors, or the people who had been with the deceased at the time of death. Name, age, profession, residence, marital status, and birthplace for the deceased and their parents were to be included, as well as the name, residence, age, and profession of the witnesses. If the deceased was a current resident in France, this was to be noted as well. With this collection of information, the French Consulate could map the reach of its empire in Alexandria. Administrators could know where people came from and if they were first generation in Egypt. They could track the movement of French nationals in nonterritorial French space.

But this information mapped more than just French imperial space, and those interested were not only servants of the French Empire. The Egyptian government also had a clear and direct interest in the information the French Consulate gathered. In 1891, Khedive Tawfiq issued a decree mandating the registration of all births and deaths in Egypt. Many of the decreed regulations mirrored those guiding the French registers. For example, two male witnesses were required, registrations were to be signed and sealed at the time of reporting, and marginal notes were to be supplied for any mandated changes.[34] This decree was not only for Ottoman/Egyptians; people with foreign nationalities would also be responsible for reporting births and deaths to the Egyptian government.[35]

The French Consuls in Egypt were angry; they referred to the Egyptian government as living in a "fantasy" and "pretending" that the French Consulates would turn over the information requested.[36] Couched as a concern over taxes that could be levied on French subjects and citizens, the consuls were determined not to allow their subjects to be "real" Egyptian subjects (*véritables administrés égyptiens*).[37] It was imperative, argued the French chargé d'affaires in Egypt on behalf of the different consulates, that consulates maintain control over their subjects and citizens. That meant that the French needed to be the only governing powers requiring registration of births and deaths. The French desire to protect its hold over personal-status registration was in direct conflict with the Egyptian government's attempts to corral the information contained within the registers. How many babies were born in Egypt? Who was dying, and how?

The two governments had been in communication about the decree before its implementation; myriad exchanges between different ministers and consuls of France suggest that the French government tried to alter the decree before its announcement.[38] When the Egyptian government nonetheless insisted that foreign residents register, the negotiations continued, and a compromise was reached before the decree's implementation. The French Consulates throughout Egypt would maintain control over the registration of their citizens and subjects but would send a summary of births and deaths weekly to the Health Ministry or the sanitation bureaus of the provinces and cities in which the consulates served. The case of the Khedival Decree of June 1891 is telling: The French were involved in questions of Egyptian governance before the announcement of the decree. Indeed, the French were in negotiations with the Egyptian government for at least six years before the decree.[39] There is nary a British name or reference in the discussions, which are framed as issues of European and French sovereignty and questions between the Egyptian national government and the French imperial state directly.

French submission of weekly reports of births and deaths did not end the friction between the two powers. In 1897 the Egyptian government complained to the consul general of France in Egypt, who was stationed in Cairo, that the French Consulate of Alexandria was not sending it the proper materials. The consul general, Amaury Lacretelle, quickly replied: the consulate sent the materials faithfully, and the complaint was unwarranted.[40] The complaint was not the first one; in 1892, within a year of the implementation of the agreement, the Health Ministry was not collecting the materials from the French, thus proving to at least one French consular employee that the motivations for asking for the birth and death counts were questionable.[41] If this were truly a matter of public health, the consular employee implied, the Health Ministry would have been eager to see the French numbers.

The struggle for control over the birth and death registrations points to the importance of the data contained within them. They served the immediate needs of the Egyptian state and the local population. They told stories of who was there and of what diseases were threatening the population, so they served the immediate needs of empire as well.

ARCHIVING IMPERIAL BODIES

In the 1870s, the Egyptian government revamped health regulations regarding dead bodies.[42] Under the new regulations, a death certificate, signed by a doctor, was required before a corpse could be buried, and postmortems were required in cases where the death was suspected to be caused by an epidemic or crime. Autopsies were hardly new to Egypt; long before these regulations, they had been a key component of inquest cases both inside and outside Egypt.[43] Some scholars even say that the autopsy originated in pharaonic Egypt.[44] By the nineteenth century, autopsies were regularly undertaken in Europe, mainly to advance scientific and medical knowledge,[45] though by the 1830s, if not earlier, they were used to investigate possible criminal activity and to support the pursuit of justice in wrongful deaths.[46]

The autopsy as a modern practice in Egypt evolved from a way to teach medical knowledge in the 1820s to an investigative tool by the 1850s.[47] As a means of establishing an intimate relationship between the individual and the state, autopsies highlight the state's increasing involvement in individual lives and individual deaths. The management of death as a secular process rather than a religious ritual was directly linked to the rise of medicine and law in urban centers.[48] Autopsies formed part of the secular state process surrounding death in which the state claimed the right to demand and host an autopsy and an inquest. Burial thus was no longer simply the decision of relatives or religious clergy. The work of the state in processing the dead served both the legal and political needs of the governing institutions as well as the personal needs of relatives and friends of the deceased.

The move from religious registers to civil registers for the French and British populations of Egypt was a part of a larger trend internationally, a trend that links to the importance of symbolic power in the creation of the modern state.[49] The state could use these compilations to give or deny protection or to provide rights even as it consolidated control.[50] In the nineteenth century, the Middle East saw the growth of the census and other means of population management, and extraterritoriality allowed European states control of their own populations.[51] Prior to civil registers, churches and synagogues kept lists of births and deaths.[52] The imperial consulates relied on their relationships with individual religious organizations to track their populations and to know whom to protect. With universal civil registers, the French state claimed the power of determining protection for itself.

Historian Edhem Eldem uses parish records from the Church of Saints Peter and Paul to reconstruct the community of French subjects in eighteenth-century Istanbul. "The fact that the church functioned as a parish for the French *nation* should not be taken to mean that it serviced *only* the French," he writes, noting that there were relatively few French subjects among the names and lives collected by the parish.[53] Eldem breaks down the data further to show that the majority of people under parish protection were actually local Catholics, primarily of Greek origin, a relic, he argues, of the linkage of Catholic protectionism and French empire. In this case, the state offered religious protection; imperial power was reliant on the church.

The emergence of the secular state as its own record keeper heralded the weakening of the church, as the state could track its charges without relying on church records. Indeed, as Bonfigli's funeral highlighted, the French state's relationship to the Catholic Church was often contentious and not presumed. In Egypt, consulates kept their own records from the early nineteenth century, long before they were mandated to do so by the state. In this way, the consulates became archives of the Egyptian state, going beyond the church to capture the multinational, multireligious population living in Alexandria.

That agreements allowing European consulates legal governance of their subjects in Middle Eastern lands proved to be contentious to both empires and nascent national states is the subject of several academic studies.[54] Historian Mary Lewis likens the dual legal systems to a "divided rule"; in the case of Tunisia, the French colonial rulers were challenged for dominance not only by the growing national movement but also by British and Italian protection of their sizable populations in the land.[55] The civil registers proved time and again to be a place to exercise and protect those legal agreements that enabled consular governance; by documenting the population, the consulate could manage it. Civil registers guaranteed that one's nationality—meaning personal status—rather than geographic place would determine protection.

In the nineteenth century, however, *where* one died mattered. The place of one's death would determine where one was buried, and it would mark the end of the personal/geographic distinction created by dual or more legal systems. If the cemeteries represented the perpetuity of foreign communities' land claims in Alexandria, the death registers and the inquests symbolize the permanence of their place in the city's written archives.

WHO WERE THE IMPERIAL DEAD OF ALEXANDRIA?

In his two-volume tome *Modern Egypt*, Evelyn Baring, Earl of Cromer, the consul general of Egypt, purported to know the living of Egypt and thus the foreign nationals.[56] Europeans in Egypt, he argued, were more often than not unattached to the actual European state whose citizenship they carried. They were not truly European and did not fully possess what he called the national characteristics. Such "half" Europeans he dubbed "Levantine," a term intended to be an insult.[57] In other words, a French person in Egypt, who has been determined to be Levantine, is not truly French. "The particular consulate at which the Levantine is inscribed is a mere accident," Cromer writes, and thus diminishes the imperial workings of other European states.[58]

Cromer likewise discounts the Maltese and other British imperial subjects in Egypt: "The permanent British colony in Egypt is small. It consists mainly of a few merchants who reside at Alexandria. . . . The Alexandrian Englishman, like most of his countrymen, is somewhat exclusive. He mixes little in foreign society."[59] Using "British" and "English" seemingly interchangeably, Cromer not only wrote out subjects of the British Empire but also described a British population in Egypt as separate from native Egyptians, the European foreign nationals, and the other populations of Egypt.[60] The British, Cromer wrote, did not become "Levantine," or "semi-orientalised Europeans."[61] One wonders what Cromer would have thought had he stumbled on the funeral request of British Sara Roca, wherein she requested prayers from churches throughout the Middle East. The imperial dead of Alexandria found in the written registers and inquest reports, and those of the hospitals, funerals, and cemeteries, did not for the most part fit into Cromer's vision of Egypt.

British subjects dying of questionable natural causes, suicide, drowning, murder, and disease are all included within the case files. Cases included characters such as Luigi Mifsud, a mentally ill chemist who threw himself out of a third-floor window in August 1903 before "the Greeks" could get him; he worked at a Greek-owned shop and was apparently worried about its upcoming sale.[62] Antonio Felice, a Maltese subject, died of natural causes after collapsing on the street in 1880 while leaving a coffee shop run by one Mustafa Aga.[63] Juan Carlo Caruana was run over by a train in 1895, and Giuseppe Bellante died of cancer at the Greek Hospital in 1892.[64] Giuseppe Mamo died of natural causes in 1880, causing a "local subject," a female bread baker he had been living with, to petition the British Consulate for money he owed her in back rent.[65] Joseph Falconer died in 1894 of "visitation of God in a natural way and not otherwise"; only after interviewing several of his colleagues did the coroner realize that Falconer was drunk.[66] Serafino Buhagi, a house painter, shot himself in 1901 rather than be forced into marriage with a young Maltese woman.[67] Alessandro Ataliotti died of internal hemorrhaging in 1896 after a night of drinking, a possible blow to the back of his head, and being run over by a cab. The postmortem could not determine if his death was an accident or murder.[68] Lilian Irlam died in a riptide in San Stefano in 1903; her inquest led to a request for more lifeguards at the beach.[69] These dead, and hundreds of others like them, were the British bodies of Alexandria. Their names alone, ranging from the Anglo-Saxon to Maltese, suggest the heterogeneity of the British community. Overwhelmingly although not exclusively poor, they lived among others of the same class.

A broad world is equally represented in the French registers. Alongside the majority born in France, Tunisia, Algeria, Switzerland, and Egypt, people from elsewhere in the Ottoman Empire, Europe, the United States, and even some Caribbean Islands are represented in the files. Within Europe, people come from Ireland, Great Britain, Prussia, Italy, Romania, Poland, the Netherlands, Macedonia, Spain, Austria, Albania, Luxembourg, and Greece. Dozens of people died on French ships: a Martiniquais, an American, a Romanian, a Russian, an Algerian, and a Chinese man.[70] Many of these were born in Alexandria; others had been born elsewhere and moved at some point in their lives to the bustling port city. Some were just traveling through.

Death notices show that they were César Rizzoni, a Roman subject born in Istanbul who opted for French nationality before he died in Alexandria in May 1886; and Laurent Louis Autofage, born to French parents in Alexandria and dying in the city in August 1890.[71] They were Fernand Négrier, a butter manufacturer from France who lived in Damietta in the Nile Delta and died on November 7, 1893; and Louis Martin, a nine-month-old baby, born to French parents in the Nile Delta as well, who died in June 1884.[72] They were Alcibiade Prodanus, the Greek police chief of the Egyptian railway, who died in Alexandria in August 1877; and Eliaho Ghebali, a Jewish doctor born in Alexandria in 1842 to Algerian parents and who died in the city in 1890.[73] And they were Claudine and Maria Agier, twin girls born to French parents in Alexandria in November 1890. Maria died less than two months later, on January 1, 1891, and Claudine had passed away by February.[74]

EMPIRE AND NATION IN THE FRENCH DEATH REGISTERS

On November 15, 1890, just two days before the birth of the tragic Agier twins, Osman Wacil, a naturalized French medical doctor, and his wife, Layla Alfy, welcomed their son, Mohamed Aly Wacil, and promptly registered him as a citizen with the French Consulate, with witnesses including a French doctor who was also a knight of the Legion of Honor, a high French distinction held by the consul general as well.[75] As in the file of Pauline Borivent, a notation in the margins leads to the registration of Mohamed's death, only twelve years later, when he was still a minor. Unlike Borivent's, however, Mohamed's death is not documented in the citizen registers; his status is now that of a French Algerian, his death lumped together with other subjects and protégés.[76] The reclassification of Mohamed Aly Wacil, most likely due to the loss of his citizen status on the death of his father a few years earlier, reflects the way people moved between citizen and subject in the realm of personal status.[77]

Death registration is one of the key ways in which consulates protected their citizens and subjects abroad. The registration of death ensured that whatever protection one might have had would be extended to one's children, estate, and burial, although, as we see in the case of Mohamed Aly Wacil, this was not always permanent.[78] Three entries in a row in the 1875 citizen register demonstrate how the registry was used to safeguard protection.[79] On May 10, 1875, Alfred Paul Ibrahim Rocheman appeared before the French Consulate to enter his paternal recognition of his illegitimate child, Henri Paul Rocheman, born in 1869. Standing before the consul general with witnesses, he officially recognized his child. This recognition was immediately followed by the presentation of his marriage certificate, in Latin, from the Catholic church of St. Catherine's in Alexandria.[80] Rocheman, a French citizen born in Alexandria, married the mother of his child, Irmine Adam, born in France. The church served as witness to the marriage and to the legitimacy of the child. Just two days later, Irmine died. One of the men who had witnessed her marriage declared her dead, with Juba L'Hotelliere, a prolific death witness for the French, serving as the second witness. The compact time line suggests that the registration of their child with the French government became important to the couple only on the brink of Irmine Adam's death. They had been together for at least six years, but it is in death that they needed French recognition of paternity and marriage so that their son could and would be protected.

The variety of people in these ledgers suggests that the French, in regard to their dead, acted both as the protectors of the Catholics in the Orient and as the governing power of French citizens born in France, and these two roles at times overlapped and contradicted each other. Between 1865 and 1915, more than 260 women and nearly 600 men were registered as French dead in the subject/protégé files. Of these, approximately 25 percent were Algerian and another 25 percent Swiss. Tunisians accounted for just fewer than 20 percent, with their numbers picking up significantly after the French occupation of their land in 1881. More than 50 percent of the dead have clearly Muslim names; around 13 percent have clearly Jewish names. This means that nearly two-thirds of the French dead are not Christians, and among the Christians, the majority are Swiss, suggesting that they may have been Protestants. Protection for Catholics abroad, a key part of French imperial policy in Egypt and elsewhere, does not account for the people of the French protégé registers.

Within the Catholic Church, frequently nuns and priests born in France, such as Sister Marie Louise, who died in November 1899, were registered with the protégés.[81] They were marked as French by way of empire, despite their birthright as French by way of national origin. Catholicism became their tie to France, trumping their nationality. They chose to live within religious orders, and dying within them placed them under the orders' protection first, which was itself under French protection. Yet this was not a clear, firm distinction, and a French-born member of the Catholic religious clergy might just as easily appear in the citizen registers, such as the entry for Michelle Soulfour, known as Sister Joséphine, who died in Alexandria in January 1875, or Father Kista Barthez, a Lazarist missionary who died on September 16, 1895.[82] In these examples, those who interacted with empire in any sort of capacity outside the state could be classified as either citizen or subject/protégé, suggesting both that the categories of imperial rule were not always rigid and that distinctions between citizen and subject/protégé were not always necessary. The back and forth between empire and nation-state reinforces the overlap between the two; the French state might mark associations by nation or by empire, but nation and empire were inherently and necessarily intertwined.[83]

But while these boundaries were at times porous, the legal differences between citizens of France and subjects of empire held for the majority of those registered. This was not surprising, as delineating between subject and citizen was a necessity in the maintenance of French empire.[84] Despite the example of Mohamed Aly Wacil and a few other cases, Algerians were rarely found outside the protégé files, even when their legal standing should have put them firmly in the citizen column.[85] Additionally, the title of the registers suggest that Algerians were separated from other kinds of protégés: all registers before June 1912 were titled *Algériens et Protégés Français*; the register that began in that month is marked *Algériens, Tunisiens, et Protégés*. Usually called *indigènes* in Algeria, the Algerian Muslims in Egypt were marked first by the land they came from and second by their religion. Algeria gave them access to the French Consulate, even as their status as Muslim or Jewish subjects kept them out of the citizen files.

The 1865 *Code de l'Indigénat* ostensibly gave all Muslims and Jews in Algeria the right to French citizenship, though it denied their religious personal-status protections should they choose to embrace it. Algerian Muslims and Jews could apply for citizenship individually, although collectively as communities "they would remain as simple nationals, benefiting from French protection but apart from the citizen body."[86] Few Algerians chose to become French citizens.

The status of Algerians grew increasingly complex in 1870 when under the Crémieux Decree most Jews of northern Algeria (and not of the Sahara) automatically became citizens of France—they were made to be French citizens as a collective rather than by individual choice.[87] From 1870 onward, the Algerian Jews in Alexandria should have been legally marked as French citizens; instead, they are found in the files of the Algerians and protégés, alongside the occasional Algerian Muslim marked as a "French citizen."[88] Clearly, being Algerian (and Jewish) trumped citizenship; Catholics born in Algeria, however, were consistently found in the citizen files.[89]

The relationship between citizens and subjects in North Africa was further complicated when the French conquered Tunisia in 1881. French officials in Tunisia went to extreme efforts to track the differences between Tunisians and Algerians.[90] Indeed, calling oneself Algerian in Tunisia opened the door for rights not available to the indigenous population. Protection could travel across political borders, and the peculiarities of French empire in Algeria and Tunisia required French governing officials to vigilantly monitor the population.[91] Yet as people moved eastward and outside French territorial control, the French imperial government's need to monitor the border lessened, and the imperial categories became less refined.[92] Tunisians and Algerians could be, and were, lumped together in Egypt. When they did not have territorial authority, the French did not concern themselves with the nuances of imperial citizenship and subjecthood of North Africans. Arguably, the lack of territorial sovereignty allowed the state to be more lax in its techniques of population monitoring and data collection. At stake were not rights to the French state but access to French protection, which was shared across the citizen/subject/protégé divides.

Algerians and Tunisians, both Jews and Muslims, regularly reported on one another's deaths. Haim Chantob Habib, a French Algerian peddler born in Tzfat, died at twenty-seven years of age in the European Hospital of Alexandria on July 19, 1897. Haim's name, meaning "life" in Hebrew, as well as his birthplace in one of four primary locations for Jewish residency in pre-Zionist Palestine, marks him as most likely Jewish. A day later, Shaykh Hassan Abu Harum and 'Abd al-Hamid al-Djogroni, whose names indicate that they were Muslims, witnessed Haim's death for the French Consulate, ensuring that he would be entered in the register.[93] Just two months later, Aly Karkar, an Algerian sheikh, and Hassan Ahmed Karam, a Tunisian sheikh, together reported on the death of a Tunisian woman named Fatouma, the wife of Hamida ben

Khalifa.[94] Toward the end of that year, in December 1897, an Algerian Jewish man and an Algerian Muslim man reported on the death of a one-and-a-half-year-old Algerian Jewish baby.[95] In regard to working with the French Consulate, North Africans crossed religious and national borders with regularity; these collaborations appear to be more the rule than the exception.[96]

Aly Mahmoud Echarafy, a Tunisian broker, reported at least forty deaths to the French Consulate in the last ten years of his life, 1892–1902.[97] He reported almost exclusively on Algerians and Tunisians, pairing up with members of both communities, as well as French nationals, Muslims and Jews, to serve as witness for the French Consulate. Echarafy was often listed alongside a relative of the deceased, suggesting he would stand in as an extra witness when necessary. Before his 1902 death, which was witnessed for the French Consulate by his brother-in-law, a chickpea and vegetable seller, and a Tunisian tailor who was not related,[98] Echarafy reported on the deaths of his mother and mother-in-law, a Jewish trader born in Egypt to Tunisian parents, textile workers, tobacco merchants, landlords, day laborers, widows, infants, and children.[99] He stood with the Hamouda al-Haddad family to witness the death of Mohamed Rajab Hamouda Haddad in July 1901, linking him to a family of several brothers that had lost three generations of family over the course of a few years.[100]

Echarafy also reported on the death of three different members of the Ben Dahman family, including two children.[101] Tracing deaths within the Ben Dahman family's large extended clan based in Alexandria, which the registers alternately noted as Tunisian and Algerian, shows the relationship between the family and other Tunisians and Algerians in the city.[102] Chehaté Hassouna joined Ahmed Salah ben Dahman to report on the death of Ahmed's mother, Hamida, in 1903.[103] A year earlier, a relative of Ahmed's, Younès ben Dahman, had joined with Abdel Aziz Salah, both of whom were marked as Algerian, to register the deaths of two children, one of whom was Chehaté Hassouna's three-week-old daughter.[104] Abdel Aziz had stood as witness to the death of Ahmed ben Dahman two weeks earlier.[105] The connections spiral outward and inward: this listing of who is connected to whom, who reported on whom, who died and was represented by whom could continue for pages. The point here is that the death registers detail an intricate, interconnected, overlapping network of Tunisians and Algerians whose lives repeatedly collided in the management and recording of the dead. In Alexandria, all had access to the French Consulate, which served as the "principal mechanism of social insertion—or exclusion—and therefore created opportunities for, as well as limitations on, protégés or nationals," or, in our case, imperial subjects.[106]

A side-by-side comparison of the different registers reveals immediately that far more people are registered within the collection reserved for French citizens than for subjects and protégés. Additionally, it is equally evident that the registers are woefully incomplete sources, reflecting the threadbare fabric of empire.[107] In 1865, the first year under review in this study, 266 death entries fill the citizen register, despite this being the year that an outbreak of cholera saw more than 850 buried in the Latin Catholic cemetery in Alexandria, when we might reasonably expect many more French-affiliated dead.[108] The protégé register for the same year records only nine deaths.[109] The small number of protégé deaths might mean that there were simply a few protégé deaths, or it may reflect a broad avoidance of registering with the French state, or a choice by the French state not to actively pursue the registration of protégés. We do not and cannot know why the numbers are low. One of the reasons that the citizens' register was much larger was its scope. French officials had been collecting data about citizens' deaths across the Nile Delta over a period of several years; these deaths were recorded within in the 1865 register. The protégés, however, who were primarily Swiss, all died in Alexandria in 1865.[110]

In 1871, the most deadly year in the protégé records, fifty-four of a total sixty-one protégés registered died on November 22 in a terrible collision in the Alexandria harbor; they were all Algerian pilgrims. Newspaper accounts of that night, however, report the number of dead as at least sixty-three, or more than the total for the year.[111] Using this tragedy and the cholera epidemic of 1865 as our guide, we know that the numbers of those registered in the archives must be underreported. This point is driven home by my inability to find several people in the registers, despite having their estate cases or other means of tracking them. (For example, Lisette Bohren, whose 1908 death opened Chapter 2, is not in the French death registers.) In comparison to the protégé registers, the citizen registers for 1871 marked 148 deaths, of which over half (84) were from the Nile Delta provinces and stretched back into the latter half of the 1860s.[112] As occurred in the subject and protégé registers, not all deaths were captured, and those that were listed in a given year's registry may have been from several years earlier. Making it even more difficult to find the dead, although French citizens such as Pauline Borivent were often followed from birth to death with updates given in marginal notes, Algerians and Tunisians and other protégés, as well as those registered as religious figures or as ship deaths, were not accorded the same concern.[113] The registers are imperfect sources for the dead of Alexandria, replicating the uneven reach and incoherence of imperial rule, even in its attempts to capture in writing those under French governance.

The inclusion of so many dead from the Nile Delta area and elsewhere in Alexandrian registers ended by the mid-1870s, and by 1875 the numbers of recorded dead had decreased dramatically, from approximately 150 a year to around 60.[114] The registers for citizens and those for Algerians and protégés from that year clearly delineated their different charges: "Today, first January one thousand eight hundred and seventy-five. We, the Agent and Consul General of France in Egypt, have, in accordance with the Order of October 23rd, 1833, opened in duplicate this register consisting of one hundred and fifty sheets of paper, signed and initialed by us, civil status of the French *citizens*, resident in Alexandria or in the conscription of this Consulate General during the present year."[115] The register for noncitizens reads as follows: "Today first January one thousand eight hundred and seventy five. The Agent of the Consulate General of France in Egypt has opened this continuation of this Register for the purpose of recording the records of the civil status of *protégés* during the present year."[116] In the register for citizens, the French Consulate lists the regulations that it will follow, gives the size of the register it will use, and notes that it has properly documented compliance with French law. This register covers all citizens of France living within the area that fell under the consulate of Alexandria. Here the legal boundaries and the geographic boundaries are clear. The charge of the protégé register, however, is vague. The register is ostensibly to cover all of Egypt, although we know it does not, as all of the dead listed by 1875 died in Alexandria; there are no regulations mentioned; there is no individual stamp of approval in the form of affixing a name or initials; and there are not separate notebooks for each year. The protégé register reads as an afterthought in comparison to the detailed adherence to regulations one finds in the citizen register. One might assume that the difference between the eleven recorded dead of the protégé files and the sixty-one dead (including stillborn babies, sixty-three) of the citizen files should be easily recognizable as the difference between French by empire and French by nation.[117] Instead, a close reading of the dead of 1875 reiterates that "citizen" and "protégé" or "subject" were primarily geographic, not necessarily legal, terms. Terminology reflected a combination of place of birth, parental lineage, and place of death.

So who were the protégé dead of 1875? They were, as were their witnesses and parents, workers, lawyers, bakers, lace dealers, painters, doctors, shoemakers, and tailors. They included Louis Marins Cloux, a Swiss officer with the Egyptian police who died without papers, leading the consulate to rely on two witnesses to establish his identity;[118] and Alexander Sergierviez, a Polish baker who died in the European Hospital on May 14.[119] Several other Swiss citizens under French protection in Alexandria died, as did three children, all born in Alexandria to Algerian parents. Yet nestled in between these protégé death entries was a birth announcement for Azar Cohen, a Jewish child born on January 22 to two Jewish Algerian parents.[120]

When we turn to the citizenship files of 1875, whom do we find? Of the more than sixty deaths recorded in 1875, over half were women, and approximately a third were children. The dead were born in France or in Egypt to French parents, with only one born in Algeria. They were French by nation, whether because they were born in the European land of France or their parents had been born there. Like the protégés, they were variously employed; among them were lawyers, merchants, traders, engineers, pastry chefs, blacksmiths, cooks, cashiers, lemonade sellers, lyricists, shoemakers, newspaper sellers, Egyptian government employees, and even a bodybuilder.

Citizens and protégés/subjects alike reported deaths to the consulate. Several men show up repeatedly in the registers, reporting on deaths across communities. Juba L'Hotelliere, the French worker who witnessed the Rocheman death, reported more than a dozen French deaths, as well as two Swiss deaths, in 1875 alone; his name is repeatedly found throughout both sets of registers across the years as he reported on the deaths of Algerians, Swiss, and others.[121] Was L'Hotelliere simply a gregarious man who knew many people in Alexandria, or was he somehow compensated for his work for the French Consulate in reporting deaths?[122] In other years, over the course of several decades, various names, such as Henri Jean Baptiste Ollivier, a French weaver, and his brother (?) Antoine Ollivier, show up repeatedly as witnesses in both citizen and subject registers.[123] And throughout the 1870s and 1880s, Charles Siouffi, a marine broker, reported, often alongside Juba L'Hotelliere, dozens of citizen deaths, including the 1871 death of the pharmacist Jules François Petit at the European Hospital in Alexandria, as well as the deaths of protégés, including Greeks, Italians, Algerians, Macedonians, Swiss, Maltese, recent arrivals from Constantinople, and people born and raised in Alexandria.[124] He even reported the death of another Italian-national apostolic clergy in 1880, before Bonfigli's death in 1904 and the struggle over claiming him as French, as discussed in Chapter 2.[125] And he served as a witness to very personal deaths, such as that of his infant son on August 1, 1871.[126] Siouffi served as a witness not only across the national and religious spectrums but also across institutions, reporting on deaths at the Greek, Deaconess, and European Hospitals.[127] Like those institutions, Siouffi was open to all nationalities and religions in the name of empire.

How Siouffi, the Olliviers, L'Hotelliere, and others became death reporters extraordinaire might be unanswerable. It may have been a side business or a favor done by those who worked near the consulate. But their presence suggests that the legal regulations set out by the civil code did not hold; it was not always the closest relative or the nearest person to the dead who reported deaths.[128] Indeed, Siouffi was not a witness when it came time to register his own wife's demise. Instead, on April 27, 1885, Naphtalie Solomon, a merchant, and Paul Blanche, a hairdresser, stood before Consul Alfred Kleczkowski to document the death the previous day of Marie Anne Nordio, the wife of Charles Siouffi, at the age of forty-one.[129]

Interestingly, while Aly Mahmoud Echarafy reported on dozens of North African deaths, his name is not to be found in the citizen registers, nor did he report on the death of Swiss or other protégés in Alexandria. This may suggest that the French Consulate or families of the deceased did not consider Echarafy, a Muslim Tunisian, an appropriate witness for Catholics or Europeans. Perhaps, however, Echarafy himself chose to operate in particular networks only, or it may have simply been a coincidence. No matter the reason, the death registers weave a web of imperial Alexandrian connections spanning the myriad national communities and, in some cases, the religious communities, within the web of French empire.

Entries from 1875 and in many other years are peppered with translations from Arabic-language death registrations, such as the entry recording the death of Mr. Guérin, a French subject found in the citizen registers whose case, like that of Mohamed Aly Wacil, illustrates the movement between citizen and subject or protégé.[130] Guérin died of a combination of tuberculosis and dysentery. Registration of his death consisted of the translation of an Arabic document from the province of Qena. It lacked the basic information of the French entries and contained superfluous information on his medical condition and the reasons of death. But in its existence and those of other Arabic-language documents produced by the Egyptian government in French registers, the governance overlap between the imperial consulate and the Egyptian government is once again evident. Not only were the French sending their information to the Egyptian state, but they were also requesting and duplicating bureaucratic work of the national government in the documentation of people they counted as French.

Regulations required original death certificates from religious authorities if the death had been registered elsewhere; the originals were to be clipped to the registers, transcribed, and translated.[131] The records of 1875 reveal that regulations were only guidelines. When Marie Jean Marthou died on March 8 at the age of fifty-five, her death was registered with St. Catherine's Church. The registry notation about her death simply states that it is a translation from the Latin. The original is missing, and there is no transcription. Such examples, in which consular representatives did not have the time, resources, or perhaps the desire to follow the regulations exactly, abound in the archives. The consular representatives on the ground in Egypt had the flexibility to write their dead as they needed to; empire was not the regulations from above but the day-to-day, register after register, collection of data and performance of consular responsibilities. The official regulations suggested what the consular officials might do, but the consular officials did what they needed, wanted, or decided to do.

While I have used 1875 as a model year, the patterns revealed here hold for other years, especially for the decades following the British occupation. As the registers move through the end of the nineteenth century and into the twentieth, there were significantly more deaths registered in the archival set for citizens with civil status than in those for protégés. Deaths far outpaced births in the 1860s; by 1908, the last year for which citizen registers were available, there are significantly more births than deaths.[132] The French population was younger than it had been, with a broader array of jobs and connections to Alexandria. French citizens, protégés, and subjects came from all socioeconomic classes, all of which mixed within each of the nationalities represented in the French consular registers. What the family connections were, how jobs were passed down, where people came from, and where they moved to are all evident in a close reading of the registers.

But information in the registers is limited to what the French deemed necessary, and it is the people they were concerned with, the workings of imperial connections, not the geographically bounded space of Alexandria. It was that tangled, alternative imperial geography that the French collected. The

French Consulate did not need to know where the people of Alexandria lived, worked, and died, for it was not responsible for governance in the city. That job fell to the Egyptian government, which would use the statistics collected by the French for its own purposes in the Health Ministry.

Together the citizen registers and the subject and protégé registers show us the tentacles of empire and the dead of the Egyptian state. They reveal not only the people of France but also the bureaucratic logic that necessitated the collection of data that would divide its registers according to tiers of closeness to the state. Yet the details captured within these divisions demonstrate reliance on broad overlaps to build that imperial community. They show that the network of protection extended beyond the consulate, building French empire through the connection of various strands of French community, imperial and national, to one another and to the Egyptian state.

INVESTIGATING THE BRITISH DEAD

On Sunday evening, February 1, 1880, several of Paolo Callus's friends stopped by his little shop near Rue des Soeurs in Alexandria. One of them was chatting with Callus, a Maltese long settled in the city, as he weighed macaroons for a customer. Suddenly, Callus pitched forward, collapsing dead on the floor.[133]

Before the British consular court could demand a full autopsy, Chief Consular Surgeon Mackie went to Callus's home, where his body had been moved, and examined him. He took notes on the temperature and look of the corpse and interviewed friends of the dead. Callus had suffered from rheumatism, leaving him with a cough and periodic swollen legs, he learned. Although Callus was generally in good health, Dr. Mackie had no doubt that there was a "lesion in his circular system," causing instant death either by heart attack or aneurysm. A full postmortem, one that would cut into the body, was not necessary.[134] Mackie enclosed this report to Charles Cookson, judge of the consular courts and British consul in Alexandria, with a more casual cover letter attached. In it, Mackie said that he had chosen to look at the body without waiting for a court order, assuming this would be the desire of the British Consulate. But he did not stop there: "If the Maltese continue to go off as they have been doing lately, the population will be thinned—they [have] kept well in post mortems." He continued: "I don't think there is the least necessity for opening the body in this case, after the evidence I have got, but if the court thinks it necessary, I shall have great pleasure in the interest of science in doing it, but I think that I obtained all the evidence that is to be got."[135] The official report and the chatty note shed light on the inquest process as a ritual documentation of cause of death that preserves an individual's last moments and, with it, a glimpse into his or her Alexandrian life. At the same time, the inquest process was dehumanizing, turning characters like Callus into corpses and into problems to be dealt with. The British men in charge, familiar with one another as they worked within and around the court systems, used the bureaucratic process to turn Callus into an issue to be solved and a death to be written.

A quick perusal of the British archival index indicates that there are more than 150 court cases titled "inquest" or "death enquiry" between 1880 and 1915.[136] Most years saw fewer than 5 cases titled specifically as inquests; only toward World War I were there more, with 1915 alone witnessing at least 26 such cases. It is quickly evident that there were more inquests than the number of cases specifically marked as "inquest" suggests. Several dozen other cases mention only the name of the person as case title in the archives, yet many of these included inquests as well, as did murder cases or other investigations.[137] The British subjected more male than female corpses to inquests, which might reflect the kinds of deaths the consulate chose to investigate: deaths by drowning, suicide, ravaging diseases, or other forms of bodily violence. It may also simply reflect that the general British population, with its many soldiers and seamen, was disproportionately male.[138]

Inquest folders contain death investigations, usually with a summary of the proceedings in one blue pamphlet, with blanks to be filled in and questions with spaces where answers could be written. The name of the dead, the names of the three male jurors who served with the consul general, and the date and means of death are always listed. Files might have witness statements, doctors' autopsy reports, or other corroborating evidence such as receipts or notes from the Egyptian police. The inquest sometimes included a recommendation (e.g., more lifeguards are needed; language training is a necessity) aimed at protecting the living from the same type of tragic death. At least one included an elaborate sting operation, aimed at finding the responsible party for the accidental poisoning death of a British military man.[139] Thus, the inquests, like the death registers, served a role in alerting the Egyptian government to issues of public health and safety.[140] Drowning was of great concern.[141] Nowhere was this more evident, perhaps, than in the many inquests that reported on the drunken deaths of British soldiers and seamen.

"There can be no doubt that this accident would not have happened had he been sober," wrote Consul General Donald Cameron in 1915.[142] The need for the troops to sober up underlay many an inquest and was a broad anxiety in governing the city.

Like the registration of a death, the inquest was a formulaic, ritualistic collection of knowledge. It was a multistep process presided over by the consul general, who, along with three British men chosen from a list of possible jurors to represent the consular court, would view the body at a morgue. In the case of George Caruana, who died by drowning, Allen Borman, Thomas Ecclestone, and John K. Clarkson joined Consul General E. B. Gould at the Deaconess Hospital mortuary on Tuesday, May 4, 1909.[143] There they saw the body and took evidence from the consular surgeon, Arthur Morrison. Morrison described the decomposition of the body, which had been pulled from the water after three or four days. The head constable, an Italian subject, had searched the body upon its discovery, locating the certificate of registration that marked Caruana as the responsibility of the British. Other witnesses called to give evidence were diplomatic employees of the British Consulate, consisting of those people who had dealt with George Caruana as he tried to secure passage back to his home in Corfu. Caruana, it was revealed, was broke, unemployed, and had struck out with the woman he loved. There was nothing left for him in Alexandria, and he wanted to go home to his Greek island. His former employer, for whom he worked as a marble mason, spoke of his dismissal at work and, like the consular employees, described Caruana as "queer in the head" and "likely to become insane." Despite the many people suggesting that Caruana killed himself, the inquest was inconclusive, determining that Caruana "was found drowned off the Quay of the Eastern Harbour at Alexandria but that there is no evidence to show how he came to get into the water." The inquest completed, all three jurors and the consul general signed the report.

We do not learn from this report who Caruana's parents were or how he came to be in Alexandria. The information provided in the report is routine in that it contains how Caruana died and who saw him last, but the report is not fixed in what it reveals about Caruana. Indeed, testimonies in the inquest files preserve many more details of the living than the death registers do. The documented inquests provide access to emotions: Caruana was sad, desperate, in love, and feeling defeated. We know where he worked and where he came from. Consular employees tried to get Caruana back home. Perhaps they wanted him out of their jurisdiction, only to be stuck with him in death. The inquest report is more revealing of the physical world of Alexandria than the death registers are. Alexandria emerges from the pages of the written inquest reports through the mention of cafés, streets, quays, offices, neighborhoods, hangouts, and patterns of movement within the city and its streets.

The British Consulate chose which deaths to investigate, thus deeming the bodies chosen as British. The British Consulate noted which deaths harbored bad omens for its community and investigated those deaths with an eye to protecting the living. Within the pages of the inquests, there were military men, nannies, nurses, petit bourgeoisie, gardeners, the chief of the fish market, doctors, café owners and workers, ironworkers, port employees, railway employees, nuns, and a monk, spanning the social and economic spectrum of Alexandria.

Death practices were a way to systematize the British population in accordance with British decrees on governance within the Ottoman Empire. Death practices, like the death registers, were also a way to gather data, most often using British resources to gather information on British bodies. Periodically, a doctor other than the British consular surgeon performed, or participated in, a postmortem on a British corpse, usually in cases of violent crime that might be tried in another consulate's court.[144] Likewise, the British consular surgeon might assist in postmortems performed on non-British corpses should a British subject stand accused of murder.[145] Overwhelmingly, however, despite these exceptions, the inquest and postmortem represented a specifically British space and a specifically British ritual, a process that played out, again and again, according to a regimented, predictable pattern regulated by legal treatise and consular norms. In this respect, inquests embodied the fiction of an insular separation between the British community and the rest of Egypt.

Yet that separation was nearly impossible to uphold. Some inquests concerned exclusively British worlds in Egypt, like that of Bessie Pinn, a twenty-year-old nurse brought from England to work with a wealthy British family, who committed suicide in 1894. Her employer, Susan Mould, followed up with the British Consulate during the inquest to ask for repayment of Pinn's passage to Egypt; Bessie was relatively new to the city when she killed herself and, as far as the inquest captured her Alexandrian life, did not associate with people outside British, specifically English, nationals. Most inquests, however, captured worlds wherein people of all nationalities and religions intermixed, which would have been a surprise neither to those living in Alexandria at the time nor to the consular officials of Great Britain.

British soldiers and seamen were in direct contact with and enforcers of colonial power. Arguably, they were not in Alexandria to intermingle or to be anything other than a foreign ruling force. Yet they still walked the streets, drank at pubs, and interacted with the city.[146] For many, Alexandria was not only where they served and lived, but also where they died. Although there were standing orders that the British Consulate could not begin an inquest into a military death without the military's written permission, that permission was clearly granted regularly, as the archives are peppered with inquests into military deaths.[147] And in death, these soldiers and seamen necessarily became of Alexandria, processed and buried in the city, and written into its archives.

The Alexandria police found the body of Thomas Maher, fireman on the SS *Marathon*, floating in the Alexandria harbor in May 1894.[148] Several other firemen attested to Maher's proclivity for drinking and swimming, and Dr. Mackie concluded that Maher died an accidental death by drowning after an autopsy revealed that all his organs were healthy, but filled with water. Maurice Hammond met a similar fate in 1906, when a policeman saw him staggering across the railway footbridge heading back toward his boat. Hammond plunged over the bridge, hit his head on the way down, and drowned.[149] Michael Swiney left his ship for a night in town with two friends in 1883; he, too, ended up drowned in the sea.[150] Daniel Bell's body was not found right away after he toppled into the harbor in 1892. His friends were surprised that he fell over and insisted he was sober: they remarked that Bell had drunk only six or seven beers that evening. Not until a boat pulled away from the dock did his body float to the surface.[151]

The majority of these stories tend to follow this same pattern: a British fireman or sailor or soldier leaves his ship, cavorts in Alexandria, gets drunk, and drowns trying to make his way back on board.[152] But members of the military moved across the city of Alexandria, and they died in multiple ways. Some died when military equipment malfunctioned, such as Lance Corporal H. Phillips, who was killed in 1913 when a pulley he was fixing broke, sending him crashing to the ground only seconds before a crossbar and pulley block smashed his skull.[153] Or they died when they sought a moment of privacy in a strange land, like the 1906 case of Thomas Dixon, a sapper in the Royal Engineers who toppled to his death while leaning off a steep slope in the middle of the night with an upset stomach. He was found with his neck broken, his pants around his knees, covered in his own feces.[154] In Alexandria the British seamen and soldiers were tangible signs of brute colonial power, but they were also individuals who lived and died in the city and its waters. They remind us of the diversity of British subjects in Alexandria who ended their careers in the British colonial administration as corpses under the British consular knife and pen. They, too, are a part of the social history of Alexandria, even as the British authorities alone claimed them, processed them, informed their families of their demise, and buried them in Alexandrian soil.

Claiming a body as British was not only important for the government but for some families and friends as well. Jessie Brown was a British woman who was living with and either married to, or about to be married to, John (Yannis?) Mindler, a Greek national, which would mean that she had either given up or was about to give up her British nationality.[155] The pair lived in the home of Muhammad Hassan, working on the various ships that came through the Alexandria harbor. Brown spent her free time with Lea Cohen, a "local" subject who celebrated Easter, despite her clearly Jewish family heritage, and Lea's daughter, Fanny, who worked at a nearby shop. The daughter of a Scottish man and a woman who may have been Spanish, Greek, or Syrian, Brown spoke broken Arabic, French, Greek, and Italian; she may or may not have spoken English. Far disconnected from the idealized "British" person Lord Cromer wrote of, Brown came under British charge only after she committed suicide in April 1906. The British Consulate, called into duty by the Cohens after Brown's death, immediately set about to learn about her life, as they had not known of her previously.

In death the British, her birth community, processed her body. Fanny Cohen turned over Brown's belongings to the British Consulate, not to Jessie's Greek husband, suggesting that somehow Fanny, too, understood Jessie to be British or perhaps that Fanny or Jessie did not trust her husband. The British consular court performed and documented her inquest and recorded her suicide. Even her burial in the old Greek cemetery did not abrogate the British Consulate's responsibility; the British facilitated a multitude of religious funerals as needed for their imperial subjects.[156] Jessie Brown's life may not have caught the attention of the British Consulate, and she may have been able to claim only one British parent and may have married into a different nationality, but in death, the consulate attempted to render Jessie Brown's life legible within a rigid matrix of colonial governance and communal boundaries that mandated categorizations. The friends who turned news of Jessie Brown's death over to the British Consulate for inquest and processing may or may not have shared the consulate's understanding of the category "British." Nevertheless, Jessie Brown's death turned her into an imperial body.

The inquest as documentary guide to life in Alexandria, to British Empire, and to the geographic space of the city comes together in the sad case of the death of Pietro Montano.[157] Montano had been in Alexandria for at least thirty years. Prior to his death, he lived his brother, Andrew Montano; they had two more siblings in Malta. One day in March 1909, Pietro Montano took a seat at Café du Quai, rigged up his shotgun with strings and pulleys, and shot himself through the neck. Furious with his brother, he had meticulously planned his death, dividing up prized possessions among his friends and nephew. He even left bonds to pay for his funeral in a bank box, giving the key to a friend. The worker who opened the café in the morning discovered his body.

Montano's inquest began at the Deaconess Hospital and ended a few days later at the British Consulate. The contours of the city are mapped onto the story of his last days. He worked and lived with his brother in the district of Ramla; their fights and Pietro's subsequent disappearances were a pattern. He may have stayed in Ramla when he left his brother; Andrew neither knew nor cared. Pietro was spotted at various cafés, playing trictrac and spouting off against his brother. The British Consulate, in documenting the geographic space of Pietro Montano's life, documented as well the patterns of the city it engaged with both as colonial ruler and as a local governing force.

While this public suicide may have been undertaken purposefully to humiliate his brother, as suggested by some of his suicide notes, it also had the effect of engaging the consulate, thereby making Montano a part of the Alexandrian archives. The investigation included the two Maltese brothers and the British consular employees, as well as the Greek café waiter, an Italian lifelong friend, and the police captain who identified the body as simply a "European."[158] Pietro Montano used the city of Alexandria to write his own story. Instead of being erased by death, Montano became inscribed in the consular records and thereby in the preserved history of the city.

British inquest reports reveal the desire of an imperial consulate to shoehorn complex peoples into narrow national categories at death, while the substance of the reports themselves reveals, ironically, the very complicated,

multifaceted, ambiguous lives of Alexandrians that the postmortem categories otherwise erased. These reports show that British subjects integrated into
the larger city, marrying Greeks, working for indigenous bosses, swimming
with other Europeans, buying and selling and loving and eating and dancing
and drinking and living with others. The categories used by official governing procedures to classify the dead were not necessarily accurate—and defi-
nitely not limiting—in life. It was death that reified categories of nationality
in a way that created, built, and reified empire.

Writing the dead of the British community in Alexandria conferred the
meaning of "British" as an imperial category. It created a means to monitor the population in a geographically bounded city and an unbounded empire, archiving an alternative geography with both. In harnessing that map,
in gathering the myriad peoples of Alexandria as its own, the British used the
inquests to bolster its city presence, using the imperial bodies to mark imperial presence.

French is as French dies, and British is as British dies. At the end of this journey through dying and death, our subjects have been cared for in hospitals, feted at funerals, and buried in cemeteries. And, finally, they have been
written.

The act of writing the dead predated the British occupation and continued, much the same, beyond it. The death registers and inquests illuminate
the stories of "foreign" British and French residents, whose lives often did not
conform to the narrative of imperial privilege, though they died within an
imperial framework. The French continued to collect their own civil-status
registers; the British continued to document their dead in inquests filled with
witnesses and peoples from all over Alexandria. These are stories of movement and migration, a privilege that often excluded the indigenous "Egyptian." However, it was a movement that was circumscribed. Algerians could
come to Egypt and claim French protection, yet they were marked as protégés
and could not be counted as citizen except in rare exceptions. Maltese might
have peppered the inquests, disproportionately "going off," as Dr. Mackie
noted, but they were not listed among the British in Lord Cromer's imagination of Egypt.

Death forced the consulates to contend with their charges. The writing of
death was both a ritualistic manner of keeping track of charges and, at the
same time, an archiving of stories. In the death registers and the inquests, we

can trace networks of imperial peoples and their spatial and human networks in Alexandria. We can make maps of empire and the city from the writing of death. Death was the building block, then, of empire.

It may very well be that the French Consulate opened its doors so widely in regard to registering the dead because a high number of dead allowed the French to stake their claim to Egypt, to be needed in a very tangible fashion. Processing the dead allowed the French to turn the local need of dealing with the dead into a challenge to British rule. And it may very well be that the British grudgingly subjected the bodies of Maltese and other imperial subjects to inquests as a part of a broader public health initiative in Egypt; they were likely not thinking about the effect of including these different subjects in the archives of the British and the Egyptian state.

Yet while the French and British Consulates may have acted on behalf of imperial subjects and as representatives of empire, those who died in Alexandria, ironically, could often most explicitly claim their imperial connections only in death. In documenting inquests and death registers, the imperial consulates memorialized their subjects and citizens as the dead of Britain and France. By tracking the bodies in the place of Alexandria, they memorialized them in the space of empire. And in doing so, they archived both the imperial peoples and the state of Egypt. Death in colonial Egypt was vital to the creation of the categories of the living and the definition—and confinement—of belonging.

CONCLUSION

The Death of Empire

GREAT BRITAIN DECLARED Egypt a protectorate in 1914, after the Ottoman Empire entered the First World War. In the years following the war, Egyptians waged a nationalist revolution, culminating in the declaration of Egyptian independence in 1922 and the subsequent "liberal experiment" of a constitutional monarchy.[1] The parliament solidified laws determining who was and who was not an Egyptian, and foreign nationals were identified as definitively outside the boundaries of the national community.[2] The British shared a condominium of rule until 1952 when the Revolutionary Command Council deposed the king, kicked out the British, and ushered in an era of nationalization that saw the exile or departure of most of Egypt's foreign-national and Jewish populations.

This book argues that 1882 was not a watershed year concerning the bureaucracy and maintenance of the dead; the foreign-national communities of Alexandria continued to care for their dead through the same institutions and means both before and after the British occupation of Egypt. The general structure of governance at the time, which included multiple imperial powers and a limited, nascent national government, remained the same. There were myriad actors vying for political and social strength in Egypt; imperial bodies were a tool of belonging and relevancy. In contrast, 1952 marked a sea change in the political power structure in Egypt, when the Egyptian national government became the sole power in charge.

With the changing political fortunes of Egypt came a marked reevaluation in the connection of the imperial living to their Egyptian-buried dead.

The British Protestant cemeteries serve as one example of this evolving relationship. As British rule in Egypt ended, the consulates had to determine how they would bury imperial subjects and citizens who died in Alexandria. Increasingly, upkeep of the many cemeteries became a financial drain on the former imperial powers. By 1930, eleven years after the Egyptian revolution and eight years after the declaration of independence, the British Protestant Cemetery Committee disinterred bodies in preparation for the sale of the land of the 'Abd al-Mun'im cemetery, the first British cemetery in Egypt.[3] Remains were moved to the British Protestant cemetery in Shatbi. The sub-Committee of the British Protestant Cemetery Committee released a report documenting the disinterment and laying out a path for future cemetery protection:

> The sub-Committee [of the British Protestant Cemetery Committee] desire to call attention to the special responsibility of the British community in this foreign land for the care of the last resting places of their dead. . . .
>
> The British Community in Egypt is ever-changing, and soon no representative of the families of a past generation is left to tend with affection to the graves of their dead. . . .
>
> They [the sub-Committee] venture to hope that with sustained effort and interest on the part of the British Community, present and future, the resting places of those who have passed away will bear witness to what should be a patriotic duty.[4]

The Cemetery Committee painstakingly saved the tombstones, moving them to Shatbi as well. These included the memorials of Henry Salt, the British consul general who originally willed the land to be used as a British cemetery; several soldiers; the two-year-old child of the Danish consul; and an American man. Those buried in this British cemetery were not all of British nationality; they were a Protestant mélange. The protection of their stones was nonetheless termed a British "patriotic" duty, and the British claimed the buried as theirs. These were imperial bodies.

Throughout the decades following Egyptian independence in 1922 and the subsequent coup of 1952, the Egyptian government repeatedly suggested moving foreign-national and religious-minority cemeteries out of Alexandria.[5] Arguments over the meaning of perpetuity broke out between the Egyptian government and the communities with foreign-national and religious-minority cemeteries: Could the nationalist Egyptian government appropriate foreign communal cemetery lands, once thought to be permanent, sacred sites in the city, for new public projects? Did the foreign consulates need to upkeep cemeteries of communities no longer living in Egypt? Who was in charge of the maintenance of the imperial dead when the age of imperialism had passed? All sorts of compromises had to be negotiated: Should civilian bodies be moved into military graves? Was the long-term upkeep of a military cemetery more sustainable than a civilian one? How could the imperial powers consolidate their dead into manageable cemetery spaces without enraging their domestic publics and descendants of the buried?[6] The British and other communities repeatedly struggled to preserve these cemeteries that had once symbolized the strength of inclusion and empire in Alexandria.

The negotiations between imperial powers and the Egyptian government went back and forth; protection of the military dead was a major concern for the Imperial War Graves Commission of Great Britain and the Commonwealth. Paying for war graves was more palatable to the domestic publics, as the protection of the body of soldiers, buried where they fell in battle, was considered a sacred duty. Plans to reinter civilian bodies within military cemeteries solved some questions of maintenance and space, but the cemeteries, once symbols of the ostensible permanence of imperial claims to Egypt and the belonging of people of all nationalities in Alexandria, were now a political aberration. A walk through Alexandria today shows that some of these civilian cemeteries still exist, serving as reminders of this power struggle, and ultimately of the compromises necessary, between empires and nation.[7]

As the framework of empire dwindled to its ignominious end, the imperial bodies of Alexandria may not have been important as claims of belonging, but they remained politically significant because they were a problem to be solved.[8] They were residues of empire, no longer needed to make claims of power and presence in Alexandria, turned from an asset into a burden. Likewise, the Egyptian government no longer included the foreign communities within the boundaries of the Alexandrian population; they held no political benefit. Instead, the Egyptian government saw their remnants, the colonial dead, as obstacles to the city's growing municipal needs.[9] The remaining burial grounds may have served to emphasize the definitive exclusion of the British and other imperial powers from newly independent, Egyptian Alexandria, but nonetheless they endured, a diminished, increasingly decrepit reminder.[10] Egypt was no longer theirs, and, more important, they were no longer of Egypt.

In this book I argue that death was a key factor in imperial politics. Death served to link the imperial bodies to Alexandria and beyond, in both tangible and intangible terms. It claimed land and money from the Egyptian government, just as it demanded money and time from the consulate. Death is ubiquitous, always present, yet it has rarely been the central focus of academic work on the Middle East.[11]

Death illuminates the obvious: people were buried, and management of the remains of citizens and subjects who died abroad was, and remains, a key consular function. Still, within the obvious, a study of late nineteenth- and early twentieth-century Alexandria through the lens of death parses out the local, immediate needs for government resources and land. This study shows that the necessity of hospitals and morgues; of public space and commercial resources for coffins, hearses, funeral programs, and funeral ceremonies; of land for burial; and of counting the dead and knowing what caused their demise demanded cooperation and negotiations between local and imperial authorities. The functioning of these institutions and rituals of death depended on collaboration among the Egyptian, French, and British national governments and between and among the individuals of Alexandria. Yet the final decisions on available land and resources often rested firmly within the hands of the Egyptian national government, both before and after the British occupation.

Death forces us to ask who has a claim to land. The public health and public utility implications of the dead and dying force a reconsideration of what it means to be local, of who holds what power in what space. The Shatbi cemeteries today are relics of an imperial past, when the British and French used death to create imperial bodies, putting them into the service of expanding empire's material and performative power. The British and the French did not as much claim Egypt as theirs as maneuver, manipulate, and cajole their empires into a part of Egypt.

Using death to understand the reach and limits of different forms of governance underscores the utility of religion to political entities. Death practices were intertwined with questions of the sacred, as someone who died in Alexandria had to be buried there, and one needed a religion for burial. Protecting religion, practicing religion, and representing religion all provided empire with reasons for ensconcing themselves in overseas lands. As the French government in particular enshrined secularism at home, it used religion abroad to justify its presence. In nineteenth-century Egyptian life, one might change religions or live without practicing religion in daily life. But there was no escaping religion in death.

And just as imperial subjects of late nineteenth-century Alexandria could not escape religion in death, they also could not escape their consulates. While the living had the ability to tap into consulates as necessary and by choice, these transimperial people needed a community for burial. While this population of late nineteenth- and early twentieth-century Alexandria did not live in national categories, they died in them. Imperial bodies existed as subjects after their deaths; in graves that needed to be maintained and protected; as statistics in death registries, court cases, and public health reports; and as concerns of their communities and of their consulates.

In that process of dying—in the morgues, the funerals, the cemeteries, and death documentation—this book reveals that European consulates and communities were in constant negotiation with the Egyptian government, just as they were with each other and with their own capitals across the sea. The Egyptian national government maintained control of land and institutions, even as it ceded them to foreign consulates and communities to build cemeteries or care for the sick and dying. That is, even in the acts of burying imperial bodies, acts I describe as building empire, the foreign consulates and communities were beholden to the decisions of the Egyptian administration. And after 1882, the British colonial state was almost nowhere to be found in these negotiations; the dead were the purview of the local, Alexandrian British and French Consulates and the Egyptian government alone. The imperial bodies were thus both bodies of empires and bodies of Egypt.

But 1952 marked the dawning of a new political framework, one in which the national state emerged as the dominant—and arguably the only—governing entity. Today the British and the French are guests in Egypt; the scramble for colonial control has ended. A list of doctors found on the website of the French consulate in Alexandria today includes only Arabic names.[12] The Deaconess, the Greek, and the European Hospitals have been nationalized and turned into military, university, or otherwise public Egyptian governmental hospitals. It is no longer possible to imagine a funeral such as that of Archbishop Bonfigli in 1904; even forming a core group of mourners is a challenge.[13] British citizens abroad are instructed to report deaths to the Egyptian authorities before turning to the British embassy.[14] Details on how to cremate or repatriate a body reiterate that burial in Egypt is no longer the only option for the dead, as it was at the turn of the twentieth century. And if foreign-national dead no longer have to be buried in Egypt, the foreign-national living, no matter the size of their numbers, no longer require that private, exclusive cemetery space.

Alan Banks, the British consul general of Alexandria in the late 1960s, was tasked with the maintenance of British-affiliated cemeteries in the face of declining resources. With a diminishing population to tap for donations, the British Protestant Cemetery Committee applied to the consulate once again for financial help. Consul General Banks forwarded the request to British officials in Cairo and London. E. K. Green of the Consular Department, Foreign Office, London, was quick to reply, noting that this was not simply a request for funding. It was, instead, a broader question of empire, challenging the British government to answer "whether the disappearance of the British community from Alexandria will involve Her Majesty's government in an open ended commitment to support the cemetery indefinitely."[15] The immediate response was no, and the request for money was denied.

NOTES

INTRODUCTION

1. Copy of memo from British Consul Edward Gould to Lord Cromer, 10 June 1899, estate of Miss Gertrude Beasley Woodward deceased, 1899, FO 857/29/28, TNA.

2. Estate of Miss Gertrude Beasley Woodward deceased, 1899, FO 857/29/28, TNA.

3. The consulate even engaged itself with her family's concerns. When her family in England accused Engell of stealing from her, it was employees of the British Consulate who tracked him down, "in true Sherlock Holmes fashion," interrogated him, located the pawn shops he used, and bought back her jewelry for her father. Equally noteworthy is that the consulate chose not to pursue actions against Engell. The doctor and others noted that while Engell had trouble paying his bills (and was therefore untrustworthy), he had cared for her diligently and lovingly through her sickness and death. Quote from Letter from Cameron, Consul of Port Said, to Gould, Consul of Alexandria, 25 June 1899, estate of Miss Gertrude Beasley Woodward deceased, 1899, FO 857/29/28, TNA.

4. This is a guiding principle in the field of death studies, where scholars from a wide variety of disciplines use death to study broad overviews of societal and political change and values. These are a few books of death studies that have influenced my thinking: V. Brown, *Reaper's Garden*; Faust, *Republic of Suffering*; Ho, *Graves of Tarim*; Kellehear, *A Social History of Dying*; Kselman, *Death and the Afterlife*; Laqueur, *Work of the Dead*; and Verdery, *Political Lives*. Two recent works offer overviews of the changing field of death studies: Malone, "New Life"; and Minkin, "History from Six-Feet Below."

5. See, e.g., the 1847 Orders of the Ottoman Porte about the protection of Protestants. L. Hertslet, *A Complete Collection of Treaties*, 11:551. The Hertslet volumes, published regularly by the British Foreign Office, were compiled by Lewis Hertslet through 1864 and thereafter by Sir Edward Hertslet for the remainder of the nineteenth century.

6. By Egyptian or Egyptian national government, I am referring to the khedive, the Council of Ministers and the included ministries, and the various commissions and departments that, while in flux, made up the national Egyptian government both before and after the British occupation. For more, see Goldschmidt and Johnston, *Historical Dictionary of Egypt*.

Although Egypt was nominally still a part of the Ottoman Empire at this time, I do not use the term "Ottoman Egyptian" in regard to the government because the Ottoman government in Istanbul was irrelevant to the realms in which the Egyptian national government exercised power discussed in this book. I do at times refer to the indigenous local population as "Ottoman/Egyptian" to signify that "Egyptian" was not yet a legal category of national classification.

7. Jennifer Derr writes that the revamped irrigation systems altered the agricultural capabilities of the state, precipitating the explosion of the cotton market that led to so much economic growth. Derr, "Labor-Time." For more on the military and the rise of the individual, see K. Fahmy, *All the Pasha's Men.*

8. Michael Reimer writes that "the efflorescence of Alexandria in the latter half of the nineteenth century is inconceivable apart from the water supply and improved communication made available by the Mahmudiyya canal." Reimer, *Colonial Bridgehead,* 59 (for quote), 90 (for population numbers).

9. Ibid., 93.

10. The original agreement negotiated between Sa'id Pasha and Count De Lesseps was a terrible agreement for Egypt from the beginning; Khedive Isma'il came to power stuck with the ramifications. Owen, *World Economy,* 123–127.

11. Roger Owen argues that this work shaped Cromer's engagement with Egypt and his thinking about Egyptian sovereignty. Owen, *Lord Cromer,* esp. chaps. 7, 8, 10, 11.

12. Owen, *World Economy,* esp. chap. 5.

13. Reimer, *Colonial Bridgehead,* 110, 160.

14. Cole, *Colonialism and Revolution.* Juan Cole is responding to Robinson and Gallagher, *Africa and the Victorians.* See also Mitchell, *Colonising Egypt*; and Todd, "Beneath Sovereignty."

15. That 1882 revolved around "foreign" and "local" clashes is generally accepted, although historians debate what "foreign" and "local" meant at the time. For one of the most intriguing discussions of foreign and local in late nineteenth-century Alexandria, see Khuri-Makdisi, *Global Radicalism.*

16. Nineteenth-century French politician François Deloncle harshly critiqued the British bombardment at the time of the invasion. Deloncle, "France and Egypt." Martin Thomas and Richard Toye argue that the French invasion of Tunisia stymied the ability of the French to respond to the British invasion. Thomas and Toye, *Arguing about Empire.*

17. See, e.g., FO 78/3733, TNA.

18. David Nirenberg argues that outbursts of violence allow for the diverse society to coexist rather than represent a rupture within it. Nirenberg, *Communities of Violence.*

19. Tignor, *Modernization. Modernization* was the standard political history of this time period until the recent work of Aaron Jakes: "State of the Field" and *Colonial Economism.*

20. Genell, "Empire by Law."

21. Owen, *Lord Cromer.*

22. Exceptions include times when the family writes to Lord Cromer, who then passes the letters on, such as the family of Gertrude Beasley Woodward did. Estate of Miss Gertrude Beasley Woodward deceased, 1899, FO 857/29/28, TNA.

23. Valeska Huber calls the canal both a "hub and a chokepoint" where those in charge could encourage and stop mobility to, within, and from Egypt. Huber, *Channelling Mobilities*.

24. Nicholas Roberts, in *Islam under the Palestine Mandate*, makes a similar argument regarding Palestine.

25. Jakes, "The Scales of Public Utility."

26. Ellis, "Anomalous Egypt?" and *Desert Borderland*.

27. The following books highlight some of the key texts of Egyptian nationalism in this time period, loosely divided for pedagogical purposes. For social and political organization, see Barak, *On Time*; Gasper, *The Power of Representation*; Hanley, *Identifying with Nationality*; Ibrahim, "Legitimising Lay and State Authority"; and Omar, "Tensions of Nationalist Modernity." For gender implications, see Baron, *Women's Awakening*; Pollard, *Nurturing the Nation*; and Russell, *New Egyptian Woman*. For culture and emerging ideas of Egyptianness, see Bashkin, "My Sister Esther"; Z. Fahmy, *Ordinary Egyptians*; and Gitre, *Acting Egyptian*. For education, see Kalmbach, "Training Teachers." For public health, see Abugideiri, *Gender and the Making of Modern Medicine*; and Hammad, "Regulating Sexuality."

28. See, e.g., Beinin and Lockman, *Workers on the Nile*; Chalcraft, *Striking Cabbies*; and Abul-Magd, *Imagined Empires*.

29. The cooperation was not solely diplomatic but also a matter of personalities. Owen, *Lord Cromer*.

30. Concerning the Suez Canal, see Huber, *Channelling Mobilities*. British occupation did not end French involvement but instead provided a more stable governing ground from which to increase French economic investment in Egypt; the French had more economic interests in Egypt than the British. Saul, *La France et L'Egypte*. Likewise, the legal reform that led to the international courts system in the mid-1870s "transformed rather than curtailed French influence" in Egypt. Todd, "Beneath Sovereignty," 109.

31. See, e.g., Clancy-Smith, *Mediterraneans*; and Mazower, *Salonica*.

32. The Ornato Commission, created in 1834, held many of the same responsibilities of the municipality; in 1879 a preliminary committee for the municipality took over for Ornato, which was concretized around 1890. The new municipality had twenty-nine members, of whom the Egyptian government appointed fourteen. The remaining fifteen consisted of nine men from export houses, three from import houses, and three general business owners. These fifteen were elected through their business "colleges." Ilbert, *Alexandrie*, vol. 1, chap. 5; and Reimer, *Colonial Bridgehead*.

33. Ilbert, *Alexandrie*, vol. 1.

34. Ilham Khuri-Makdisi asks, "What was the significance of *foreignness*, when many of Alexandria's foreign Greek, Italians, and other workers had known nothing but Egypt?" Khuri-Makdisi, *Global Radicalism*, 161, emphasis in original.

35. Zubaida, "Cosmopolitanism," 26.

36. See, e.g., Aciman, *Out of Egypt*; Durrell, *The Alexandria Quartet*; Forster, *Alexandria*; Haag, *Alexandria*; Ilbert and Yannakakis, *Alexandria*; and Mansel, *Levant*. Even books that touch on Alexandria tangentially rely on this stereotype of cosmopolitan Alexandria to describe the city. See Freundschuh, *Courtesan and the Gigolo*.

37. Jasanoff, "Cosmopolitan."

38. Ilbert, *Alexandrie*, vols. 1 and 2.

39. Hanley, "Grieving Cosmopolitanism," "Cosmopolitan Cursing," and *Identifying with Nationality*.

40. Hanley, *Identifying with Nationality*. See also Driessen, "Mediterranean Port Cities"; K. Fahmy, "For Cavafy," "Towards a Social History," "Essence of Alexandria Part I," and "Essence of Alexandria Part II"; Fuhrmann, "Cosmopolitan Imperialists"; and Mabro, "Alexandria." For literary criticism of cosmopolitanism, see Halim, *Alexandrian Cosmopolitanism*; and Starr, *Remembering Cosmopolitan Egypt*.

41. I borrow the phrasing from Ziad Fahmy in "Jurisdictional Borderlands." See also Carmanati, "Alexandria 1898." For the situation outside Alexandria, see Lessersohn, "Provincial Cosmopolitanism"; and Shields, *Fezzes in the River*.

42. Clancy-Smith, *Mediterraneans*.

43. Robert Ilbert writes that people used nationality like "credit cards," pulling out the one that would most benefit them in any given situation. Ilbert, "Citizenship"; and Ilbert and Yannakakis, *Alexandria*, 25. See also Z. Fahmy, "Jurisdictional Borderlands." For the situation outside Egypt, see Can, "The Protection Question."

44. I am inspired by Robert Vitalis's argument that capital originating in Egypt and concerned with Egypt, regardless of passport, should be considered local capital. Vitalis, *When Capitalists Collide*, 13.

45. This is prevalent in many Arabic-language histories of foreigners, such as Shalabi, *Al-'aqaliyat al-'irqiyyah*. Even Arabic-language work that attempts to argue that all nationalities were integrated into Egypt often insists on inherent, permanent foreignness. See, e.g., Sulayman, *Al-ajanib fi Misr*; or Rifa'at al-Imam's several books on the Armenians in Egypt: *Al-Arman fi Misr: Al-qarn at-tasi' 'ashar, Tarikh al-Jalia al-' Armaniyya*, and *Al-Arman fi Misr: 1896–1961*. For an argument about teleology and the history of Alexandria, see Hawas, "How Not to Write."

46. I am borrowing from E. Nathalie Rothman, who writes about early-modern Venetians that "the concept of trans-imperial subjects thus underscores the need to understand the perspective of those who were caught in the web of complex imperial mechanisms but who at the same time were essential to producing the means to calibrate, classify, and demarcate imperial alterities." Rothman, *Brokering Empire*, 13.

47. David Lambert and Alan Lester argue that viewing empire through the lens of a network connects metropole to colonies and decentralizes any specific place as the origin of empire. They employ the metaphor of a kaleidoscope to demonstrate that the networks themselves may have been constantly changing and temporary, but the interconnectivity they demonstrated was a constant of empire. Lambert and Lester, *Colonial Lives*; and Lester, "Imperial Circuits."

48. Cooper, *Colonialism in Question*, 11.

49. Cooper and Stoler, *Tensions of Empire*; and Burbank and Cooper, *Empires in World History*.

50. Thomas, *Colonialism's Culture*. Within Egypt, Eve Troutt Powell beautifully demonstrates the specificities of a place that was both colonized and colonizer. Troutt Powell, *A Different Shade of Colonialism*.

51. The organized Jewish community in Alexandria split into two factions in early 1871. One faction aligned with the Austrian Consulate; and the other, with the local—or Egyptian—government. The Austrian-affiliated Jewish community refused burial of those allied with the local government, leading to two communal cemeteries. The two factions reunited in 1878 under the protection of the Austrian Consulate. Krämer, *Jews in Modern Egypt*, 75–77; Haag, *Alexandria*, 139–140; and Hassoun, "The Jews," 44.

52. Ilbert, *Alexandrie*, 2:760–761.

53. Ibid.

54. Hanley, *Identifying with Nationality*, chap. 4. See also Cuno and Reimer, "Census Registers."

55. Reimer, *Colonial Bridgehead*, 160. See also ʿAshmawi, *Al-Yunaniyyun fi Misr* and "Perceptions of the Greek Money-Lender"; Glavanis, "Aspects of the Economic and Social History"; Kazamias, "Cromer's Assault"; and Kitroeff, *The Greeks in Egypt*.

56. Lazarev, "Italians, Italianity, and Fascism." Anthony Gorman argues that the Italian community should be understood as diasporic and not as a political colony. Gorman, "The Italians of Egypt."

57. Lanver Mak writes that the British population of Alexandria had nearly five thousand Catholics and fewer than three thousand Protestants in 1897; this discrepancy was due to the Maltese population. Mak, *The British in Egypt*, 39.

58. Ilbert, *Alexandrie*, 1:414. For the millet system, see Hourani, *Minorities*.

59. Ilbert notes that many communities were themselves divided between the "local" and the "European"; e.g., the Latin and Jewish communities both have "indigenous" and "European" branches in 1907. Ilbert, *Alexandrie*, 414–415.

60. Ibid., 417. See also the letter from the Greek Orthodox patriarch of Alexandria asking for help building a hospital for the "Greek Colony." Letter to Nubar Pasha from the Patriarch of Alexandria, 15 February 1884, 12/alif baaʾ, box 2, Al-tawaʾif wa-l-jaliat al-ajnabiyya, Majilis al-Wuzaraʾ, DWQ.

61. Can, "The Protection Question," esp. 689–691.

62. See the 1897 petition from the patriarch of the Armenian Catholic community in Alexandria to the Egyptian Ministry of the Interior for cemetery land. Finance Minister to the Council of Ministers, 8 February 1898, documents 125–128, box 4, Al-tawaʾif wa-l-jaliat al-ajnabiyya, Majilis al-Wuzaraʾ, DWQ. See also the books of death certificates of the French Consulate of Alexandria, 20 PO/2009041 7–9, Alexandrie, Consulat Supplement, CADN. CADN also houses boxes of wills and estates, e.g., 20PO/1 290 or 291, Alexandrie, Consulat.

63. There are multiple examples in both TNA and DWQ. See 1924 Report of

the Committee Appointed to Consider and to Make Recommendations concerning the Provision, Maintenance, and Disaffection of Cemeteries throughout Egypt, FO 141/454, TNA; testimony given to the Health Ministry, 21 July 1891, document 15, box 4, Al-tawaʾif wa-l-jaliat al-ajnabiyya, Majilis al-Wuzaraʾ, DWQ; Minister of Public Works to the President of the Council of Ministers, 26 Rabiʿ ʾAwal 1301/24 January 1884, documents 60 and 64, box 4, Al-tawaʾif wa-l-jaliat al-ajnabiyya, Majilis al-Wuzaraʾ, DWQ.

64. See 1924 Report of the Committee Appointed to Consider and to Make Recommendations concerning the Provision, Maintenance, and Disaffection of Cemeteries throughout Egypt, FO 141/454, TNA.

65. Pollard, "Egyptian by Association," 239–257.

CHAPTER 1

1. Estate of Lisette Bohren, 20 PO/1_290, Alexandrie, Consulat, CADN.

2. See, e.g., Re: the death of Julia Edwardes, 1880, case 26, FO 847/1, TNA; or Estate of Sarah Colwyn, 1892, case 28, FO 847/21, TNA.

3. Colonial institutions often became the foundations of local infrastructure. For examples outside Egypt, see Chopra, *A Joint Enterprise*; and Mazza, *Jerusalem*. In regard to colonial medicine, see Amster, *Medicine and the Saints*; and Arnold, *Colonizing the Body*.

4. Letter from French Consul of Alexandria Amaury Lacretelle to the Minister Plenipotentiary of France in Cairo, 23 March 1897, 353 PO/2_438, Le Caire, Ambassade, CADN.

5. Abugideiri, *Gender and the Making of Modern Medicine*; K. Fahmy, "Women, Medicine and Power," "The Anatomy of Justice," and "Medicine and Power"; Kuhnke, *Lives at Risk*; and Sonbol, *Creation of a Medical Profession*.

6. Ilbert, *Alexandrie*, vols. 1 and 2; and Reimer, *Colonial Bridgehead*.

7. This was also the case elsewhere. See Chopra, *A Joint Enterprise*, chap. 4.

8. K. Fahmy, *All the Pasha's Men*. See also Jagailloux, *La Medecine Moderne en Egypte*. For the medical system outside the Egyptian army, see Cooter et al., *Medicine and Modern Warfare*; Harrison et al., *From Western Medicine*; and Kelly, *British Army Medicine*, esp. chap. 3.

9. "Fundamental Statutes of the Hospital Modified in General Assemblies 22 November 1861 and Again 3 March 1875," published by Francis A. Moures Printer in Alexandria, 1876, 20 PO/1_28, Alexandrie, Consulat, CADN. Article 12 notes that there have been records of proceedings from the European Hospital for every year since 1816. Michael Reimer notes that both the Greek Hospital and the European Hospital were built before 1830. Reimer, *Colonial Bridgehead*, 88.

10. Inquest of Jacob Gherson, 8 July 1895, case 19, FO 847/25, TNA. Gherson was run over by a train at Ramleh Station, and his unidentified body was transported to the Egyptian Government Hospital. His case is discussed further in Chapter 2.

11. This is a repeated theme in the literature. See M. Brown, "Medicine, Reform, and the 'End' of Charity"; Cherry, "Hospitals and Population Growth," Parts I and II;

Imhof, "Hospital in the 18th Century"; Jones, *The Charitable Imperative*; and Rosenberg, "And Heal the Sick" and *The Care of Strangers*. For colonial hospitals specifically, see Harrison et al., *From Western Medicine*, 14.

12. Cherry, "Hospitals and Population Growth," Parts I and II; and Rosenberg, "Heal the Sick."

13. Gorsky and Sheard, *Financing Medicine*.

14. Cherry, "Hospitals and Population Growth," Parts I and II; and Rosenberg, "Heal the Sick."

15. Imhof, "Hospital in the 18th Century," 451.

16. Derr, "Labor-Time," 200–201; and K. Fahmy, "Medicine and Power," 39–46. Jennifer Derr notes that the number of patients in the government hospitals increased dramatically by the early twentieth century. She writes that this was not an improvement in the hospital conditions but was attributable to the rise of perennial irrigation and the changing agricultural landscape, which in turn gave rise to increased diseases: "Hospitals were crowded, in part, because Egyptians engaged in agriculture were notably sicker than they had been in the past." Derr, "Labor-Time," 201.

17. Ener, *Managing Egypt's Poor*, 92. See also Sonbol, *Creation of the Medical Profession*.

18. K. Fahmy, "Medicine and Power," 42–46.

19. See undated letter from the members of the Commission of the Hellenic-Egyptian community to Khedive Isma'il, document 56/2, box 2, Al-tawa'if wa-l-jaliat al-ajnabiyya, Majilis al-Wuzara', DWQ. Trouble with upkeep long haunted Egypt's foreign hospitals. Curtis, "Charity Begins Abroad," 93.

20. Dr. Arthur Morrison described the Deaconess Hospital as "a splendid building, fully equipped with all the modern appliances in surgery and in medicine. . . . I have seen no hospital to equal it in spaciousness and completeness." Report by Dr. Morrison, British Consular Surgeon, 18 April 1911, FO 891/1, TNA.

21. Reimer, *Colonial Bridgehead*, 110, 160.

22. Ilbert, *Alexandrie*, 1:146; and Reimer, *Colonial Bridgehead*, 88, 138.

23. Mubarak, *al-Khitat*, 7:197–198. The government hospital was by far the largest, serving thirty-three hundred of the fifty-eight hundred patients in 1870.

24. Mubarak, *al-Khitat*, 7:197–198.

25. In 1911, the Deaconess, Greek, and European Hospitals, as well as the Jewish Hospital, served a total of 7,999 inpatients. See Nizarat al-maliyya, *Ihsa' al-jam'iyat al-khairiyyin*, 22. It is worth noting that Nizarat al-maliyya claims 791 patients for the European Hospital, whereas the hospital claimed close to 1,800 in its 1911 annual report. See 20 PO/1_28, Alexandrie, Consulat, CADN.

26. Sonbol, *Creation of a Medical Profession*, 48.

27. This first hospital in Alexandria was attached to the naval yards and contained three hundred beds specifically for naval personnel and their families; it was not built for the urban poor.

28. Undated letter from 1880 to Riyad Pasha, President of the Council of Ministers, from the Administration Council of the European Hospital, document 7/2,

box 2, Al-tawa'if wa-l-jaliat al-ajnabiyya, Majilis al-Wuzara', DWQ. See also "Fundamental Statutes of the Hospital Modified," By-Laws, Article 12. Will Hanley maps the hospitals in "Foreignness," 111. The Daughters of Charity, who built the European Hospital, replicated the medical institutional setup of rural France in the Ottoman Empire. Curtis, "Charity Begins Abroad." This linkage of medicine and religion was not limited to Europe and the Middle East. See Nelson, *Say Little, Do Much.*

29. Hospital leadership and sponsor lists can be found at the end of every annual report.

30. The Daughters of Charity were invited to Alexandria by European consuls and merchants specifically to work in the European Hospital. Curtis, "Charity Begins Abroad," 93. The contract for the nurses as well as the "Rules of Procedure" for the hospital can be found in 20 PO/1_28, Alexandrie, Consulat, CADN.

31. The Deaconess movement was a product of German missions. Kaminsky, "German 'Home Mission' Abroad."

32. For the year, see Nizarat al-maliyya, *Ihsa' al-jam'iyat al-khairiyyin*, 22–23. For the location, see Mubarak, *al-Khitat*, 7:197; and Milne Cheetham to Earl Curzon, 6 February 1919, FO 608/214, TNA. For the structure, see report by Dr. Morrison, British Consular Surgeon, 18 April 1911, FO 891/1, TNA.

33. Report by Dr. Morrison, British Consular Surgeon, 18 April 1911, FO 891/1, TNA.

34. Milne Cheetham to Earl Curzon, 6 February 1919, FO 608/214, TNA.

35. For before 1830, see Reimer, *Colonial Bridgehead*, 88. For 1843, see Nizarat al-maliyya, *Ihsa' al-jam'iyat al-khairiyyin*, 22–23. For location, see Hanley, "Foreignness," 111.

36. Robert Ilbert writes, "Between the hospitals and benevolent societies, they [the elite] assured a permanent control on the whole of each colony." Ilbert, *Alexandrie*, 1:146.

37. Michael Reimer argues that the foreign hospital system was a separate, exclusive system and that the government hospitals were "the *only* medical facility frequented by the urban poor." Reimer, *Colonial Bridgehead*, 88, 138, emphasis added.

38. For example, in 1911, the European Hospital provided 454 free days of service to Italian patients while collecting money from the Italian Benevolent Aid Society for three hundred patients' care. See 1911 Annual Report of the European Hospital, 20 PO/1_28, Alexandrie, Consulat, CADN. That same year, the Jewish Hospital collected hospital fees from just 44 of 757 patients, or fewer than 6 percent. Nizarat al-maliyya, *Ihsa' al-jam'iyat al-khairiyyin*, 22. Archives do not explain how the breakdown of free days versus money collected from consulates and other societies worked.

39. Mubarak, *al-Khitat*, 7:197.

40. Ibid., 198.

41. For the Greek and Deaconess Hospitals, see Nizarat al-maliyya, *Ihsa' al-jam'iyat al-khairiyyin*, 22. Nizarat al-maliyya has 891 patients noted for the European Hospital, while the European Hospital annual report notes a total of 1,791 patients for 1911. See 20 PO/1_28, Alexandrie, Consulat, CADN. Nizarat al-maliyya consistently

put the number of patients at the European Hospital far lower than the tallies in the hospital annual reports. While it may have benefited the European Hospital to inflate its patient numbers, its account of patients and services is relatively consistent through the years of annual reports.

42. Abugideiri, *Gender and the Making of Modern Medicine*; and Kozma, *Policing Egyptian Women*.

43. Report to the Committee of the Deaconess Hospital of Alexandria, 1890, 20 PO/1_28, Alexandrie, Consulat, CADN. According to the report, men account for more than 76 percent of the hospital patients. Of the 1,112 patients, 848 were men, 195 were women, and 69 were children.

44. See 1909 Annual Report of the European Hospital, 20 PO/1_28, Alexandrie, Consulat, CADN.

45. Hanley, *Identifying with Nationality*.

46. The use of "Egyptian" is in direct contradiction to Philip Mansel's claim that Europeans in Alexandria did not think of Egyptians as "Egyptians" well into the mid-twentieth century. Mansel, *Levant*, 247.

47. Ellis, *Desert Borderland*.

48. Report to the Committee of the Deaconess Hospital of Alexandria, 1890, 20 PO/1_28, Alexandrie, Consulat, CADN.

49. See 1909 Annual Report of the European Hospital, 20 PO/1_28, Alexandrie, Consulat, CADN.

50. The French invaded Algeria in 1830 and Tunisia in 1881. The Italians entered Libya in 1911.

51. Regina v. Giuseppe Rosa, 1886, case 17, FO 847/11, TNA; and Juan Carlo Caruana, Coroner's Inquest, 1895, case 23, FO 847/25, TNA. This held true for other European Hospitals in Egypt; see Death of Judge Fagan in Suez, 1875, FO 78-2406, TNA.

52. Milne Cheetham to Earl Curzon, 6 February 1919, FO 608/214, TNA.

53. The British turned their affiliation from the European Hospital to the Deaconess at its founding in 1857. Reimer, *Colonial Bridgehead*, 219n89. Public health as a site for imperial competition predated the British occupation. See Boyle, "Cholera, Colonialism, and Pilgrimage."

54. Clancy-Smith, *Mediterraneans*; Khuri-Makdisi, *Global Radicalism*; Lorcin and Shepard, *French Mediterraneans*; and Makdisi, *Culture of Sectarianism*.

55. See, e.g., Schlöch, *Egypt for the Egyptians!*; Tignor, *Modernization*; and Vatikiotis, *Modern History of Egypt*.

56. Inquest on the Body of Capt. Samuel Fawcett, case 45, FO 847/52, TNA.

57. Report by Dr. Morrison, British Consular Surgeon, 18 April 1911, FO 891/1, TNA.

58. See 1909 Annual Report of the European Hospital, 20 PO/1_28, Alexandrie, Consulat, CADN.

59. Ibid. Italians and Arabs were consistently the largest categories of patients.

60. "The Fundamental Statues of the Hospital Modified," Article 1. The European Hospital in Suez required notification of the French Consulate or head doctor when

a British patient arrived. I found nothing similar concerning Alexandria's European Hospital. Death of Judge Fagan in Suez, 1875, FO 78/2406, TNA.

61. The 1894 subscribers included France, Italy, Austria, Belgium, Portugal, and Sweden. See 20 PO/1_28, Alexandrie, Consulat, CADN.

62. See 1909 European Hospital Annual Report and other annual reports, 20 PO/1_28, Alexandrie, Consulat, CADN.

63. See 1909 Annual Report of the European Hospital; "Fundamental Statutes of the Hospital Modified."

64. Undated letter from 1880 to Riyad Pasha, President of the Council of Ministers, from the Administrative Council of the European Hospital, document 7/2, box 2, Al-tawa'if wa-l-jaliat al-ajnabiyya, Majilis al-Wuzara', DWQ. Diversity of funders can be found in the many annual reports of the European Hospital in 20 PO/1_28, Alexandrie, Consulat, CADN.

65. See 1911 Annual Report of the European Hospital, 20 PO/1_28, Alexandrie, Consulat, CADN.

66. The Germans demanded "control" of the Deaconess in the negotiations for the Mixed Courts in 1876. Milne Cheetham to Earl Curzon, 6 February 1919, FO 608/214, TNA.

67. Mak, *The British in Egypt*, 39, 255.

68. Report to the Committee of the Deaconess Hospital of Alexandria, 1890, 20 PO/1_28, Alexandrie, Consulat, CADN.

69. The Greek Consulate and the Greek Orthodox patriarch were in a "bitter struggle" over who would control (and therefore define) Greek "community" in Alexandria during the second half of the nineteenth century. The consulate, with its ability to offer legal protections, won. Kitroeff, *The Greeks in Egypt*, 14–17.

70. Some 759 of the 910 patients identified as Greek in 1879 and 498 of 866 in 1882. Letter from the Secretary of the Hellenic-Egyptian community, 20 December 1883, document 11/alif baa', box alif baa', Al-tawa'if wa-l-jaliat al-ajnabiyya, Majilis al-Wuzara', DWQ. In 1882, the total Greek population in Alexandria was 18,688, suggesting that approximately 2.7 percent were inpatients at the Greek Hospital. Hanley, "Foreignness," 282.

71. The use of the term "Hellenic" was a victory for the Greek Consulate over the Greek Orthodox patriarch, made official in 1887. Kitroeff, *The Greeks in Egypt*, 17.

72. Letter to Nubar Pasha from the Patriarch of Alexandria, 15 February 1884, document 12/alif baa', box 2 alif baa', Al-tawa'if wa-l-jaliat al-ajnabiyya, Majilis al-Wuzara', DWQ.

73. Ibid., emphasis added.

74. "Statutes of the European Hospital of Alexandria: Financial Regulations, Internal Rules," published in Alexandria in 1894, 20 PO/1_28, Alexandrie, Consulat, CADN.

75. Nursing Contract for the European Hospital, between the Administrative Council of the Hospital and the Daughters of Charity, Article 4, 1844, 20 PO/1_28, Alexandrie, Consulat, CADN.

76. The single largest regular expenditure was for meat. Other expenditures included bread, vegetables, gas appliances, wine, utensils, fire insurance, beard and haircut instruments, linen, doctor and nurse fees, laundry soap, and printing paper. "Statutes of the European Hospital of Alexandria: Financial Regulations, Internal Rules," published in Alexandria in 1894; "Financial Regulations," Article 2, 20 PO/1_28, Alexandrie, Consulat, CADN.

A council member chosen from those who could vote in the hospital general assemblies held the hospital and the treasurer accountable; any check written by the treasurer from the hospital account had to have the signature of at least one other member whose specific charge was to oversee the public good of the hospital. "Fundamental Statutes of the Hospital Modified," Articles 4 and 7.

Extraordinary expenses included unexpected charges such as fixing a steam-pipe valve in the European Hospital in 1908. See 1909 Annual Report of the European Hospital, 20 PO/1_28, Alexandrie, Consulat, CADN.

77. See, e.g., Stanley to the Earl of Clarendon, 12 July 1866, FO 78/1941, TNA.

78. The British stopped donating to the European Hospital in 1844, when it was officially affiliated with the French Soeurs de la Charité, despite the many Maltese who used the hospital. Reimer, *Bridgehead*, 219n89. Although the British Consulate did not subscribe to the hospital, it did regularly contribute to hospital funds. See, e.g., the 1915 Annual Report of the European Hospital, 353PO/2_464, Le Caire Ambassade, CADN.

79. Stanley to the Earl of Clarendon, 12 July 1866, FO 78/1941, TNA. It is unclear if Stanley was referring specifically to the Deaconess Hospital or to whichever hospital a distressed British subject might use.

80. For example, the Italian Benevolent Aid Society paid for 300 of the 502 Italian patients in the European Hospital in 1911. Yet the hospital still gave away 454 free days of care to Italian patients. See 1911 Annual Report of the European Hospital, 20 PO/1_28, Alexandrie, Consulat, CADN.

81. Henry Calvert to the Earl of Granville, 15 June 1871; Dr. Mackie to James Sam, Judge of H. M. Consular Court, 9 December 1871; Henry Calvert to the Earl of Granville, 11 April 1872; and Henry Calvert to the Earl of Granville; all in 26 July 1872, FO 78/2232, TNA.

82. Margaret Hughes had a small savings in control of another British subject in Alexandria. The consulate unsuccessfully tried to recover its costs in sending her back to England. See 26 July 1872, FO 78/2232, TNA.

83. See 1911 Annual Report of the European Hospital, 20 PO/1_28, Alexandrie, Consulat, CADN.

84. Meeting of the Federation Royale des Associations Internationales d'Assistance Publique et de Secours d'Urgence en Egypte, 4–11 September 1926, in Amsterdam, box 204, Abdeen, DWQ. The British Consulate organized considerable charitable aid around the cholera donations, as did the French and Italian Consulates and a Maltese beneficent society. Help included paying for the destitute to return to their native countries and arranging for foreign doctors to work through the nights. See,

e.g., Stanley's letters to Foreign Secretary Earl Russell, 7 July 1865 and 27 July 1865, FO 78/1886, TNA.

85. "Terrible Explosion at Alexandria."

86. Unnumbered pamphlet, "Rapport concernant les Bonnes Œuvres Faites par l'Association des Dames de la Charité, d'Alexandrie depuis le 1er Mars 1880 jusqu'au 1er Mars 1881," 15 March 1881, box 2, Al-tawa'if wa-l-jaliat al-ajnabiyya, Majilis al-Wuzara', DWQ.

87. Undated letter from German Consul General Hartmann to the Prosecutor General of the Mixed Courts, approximately 1900, document 44/alif baa', box alif baa', Al-tawa'if wa-l-jaliat al-ajnabiyya, Majilis al-Wuzara', DWQ.

88. Nizarat al-maliyya, *Ihsa' al-jam'iyat al-khairiyyin*.

89. Currency table found in Hanley, *Identifying with Nationality*, 126.

90. "Fundamental Statutes of the Hospital Modified," Article 3.

91. The five subscribers were R. J. Moss & Co., Ludwig Muller, Barker & Co., Carver & Co., and G. Franger & Co. Report to Committee for the Deaconess Hospital, 1890; list of subscribers to the European Hospital, 1894, 20 PO/1_28, Alexandrie, Consulat, CADN.

92. Mansel, *Levant*; and Whidden, *Egypt*.

93. The family petitioned the British Consulate in Egypt to be considered natural-born British subjects, despite residing in Smyrna since 1760 and Alexandria since the early nineteenth century. Mansel, *Levant*, 254–255. Barker & Co. was a regular donor to the European Hospital. Annual Reports of the European Hospital, 20 PO/1_28, Alexandrie, Consulat, CADN.

94. The Austro-Hungarian, French, and Italian consuls served as presidents of the European Hospital. At least one German consul general served as president of the Deaconess. Undated letter from German Consul General Hartmann to the Prosecutor General of the Mixed Courts, approximately 1900, document 44/alif baa', box alif baa', Al-tawa'if wa-l-jaliat al-ajnabiyya, Majilis al-Wuzara', DWQ.

95. "Financial Regulations of the European Hospital," 1894, Article 3, 20 PO/1_28, Alexandrie, Consulat, CADN. Also found in the "Fundamental Statutes of the Hospital Modified."

96. List of subscriptions for the European Hospital, 1894, 20 PO/1_28, Alexandrie, Consulat, CADN.

97. "Fundamental Statutes of the Hospital Modified," Article 3.

98. See 1911 Annual Report of the European Hospital, 20 PO/1_28, Alexandrie, Consulat, CADN.

99. "Fundamental Statutes of the Hospital Modified," Articles 1 and 3. See also 14 June 1911 letter from Acting Consul of France to Vice President of European Hospital, 20 PO/1_441, Alexandrie, Consulat, CADN.

100. Report of the Committee of the Deaconess Hospital, 1890, 20 PO/1_28, Alexandrie, Consulat, CADN.

101. See, e.g., letter to Nubar Pasha, President of the Council of Ministers, from the Patriarch of Alexandria, 15 February 1884, document 12/alif baa', box alif baa';

and letter to Mahmoud Pasha Samy, President of the Council of Ministers, from Suz-zara, Consul General of Austria-Hungary and President of the European Hospital, 6 April 1882, document 24/2, box 2, both in Al-tawa'if wa-l-jaliat al-ajnabiyya, Maji-lis al-Wuzara', DWQ.

102. See, e.g., letter from Consul General of France to Riyad Pasha, Minister of Finance, 8 January 1880, document 5/2, box 2, Al-tawa'if wa-l-jaliat al-ajnabiyya, Ma-jilis al-Wuzara', DWQ. The literature on government medicine in Egypt (e.g., Abugi-deiri, *Gender and the Making of Modern Medicine*; or Sonbol, *Creation of a Medical Profession*) does not explore the impact of the financial crisis on the medical system.

103. Letter to Nubar Pasha, President of the Council of Ministers, from the Pa-triarch of Alexandria, 15 February 1884, document 12/alif baa', box alif baa', Al-tawa'if wa-l-jaliat al-ajnabiyya, Majilis al-Wuzara', DWQ. Mansel argues that 1882 brought with it an economic boom for the Greek community, which he says had two hospitals at the time. This is in direct contradiction to the words of the patriarch. Mansel, *Le-vant*, 137.

104. Ilbert repeatedly invokes foreign-national involvement in the building of city infrastructure as evidence of their belonging. Ilbert, *Alexandrie*, vols. 1 and 2.

105. Letter from Consul General of France to Riyad Pasha, Minister of Finance, 8 January 1880, document 5/2, box 2, Al-tawa'if wa-l-jaliat al-ajnabiyya, Majilis al-Wuzara', DWQ.

106. Undated letter from the European Hospital Committee to Riyad Pasha, Minister of Finance, approximately 1880, document 7/2, box 2, Al-tawa'if wa-l-jaliat al-ajnabiyya, Majilis al-Wuzara', DWQ.

107. Draft letter from President of the Council of Ministers to Minister of Fi-nance, responding to correspondence from 27 April 1880, document 31/alif baa', box alif baa', Al-tawa'if wa-l-jaliat al-ajnabiyya, Majilis al-Wuzara', DWQ. *Al-da'ira al-khassa* consisted of monies received from a loan guaranteed by khedival lands. The fi-nancial crisis of the 1870s was caused in part by defaulting on these loans. McCoan, *Egypt*; and Owen, *Cotton*.

108. Letter from the Governor of Alexandria to the President of the Council of Ministers, 20 June 1880, document 3/2, box 2, Al-tawa'if wa-l-jaliat al-ajnabiyya, Ma-jilis al-Wuzara', DWQ.

109. Letter from the Governor of Alexandria to the Council of Ministers, for-warded to the Finance Minister on 5 July 1880, document 8/2, box 2, Al-tawa'if wa-l-jaliat al-ajnabiyya, Majilis al-Wuzara', DWQ.

110. See 1911 Annual Report of the European Hospital, 20 PO/1_28, Alexandrie, Consulat, CADN.

111. Draft letters from the Council of Ministers to Mr. Baron, 7 July 1880, docu-ments 12/2–13/2, box 2, Al-tawa'if wa-l-jaliat al-ajnabiyya, Majilis al-Wuzara', DWQ.

112. Undated correspondence, linked to a letter from 6 April 1882, to Riyad Pa-sha, Minister of Finance, from the administration of the European Hospital, doc-uments 14/2 and 20/2, box 2, Al-tawa'if wa-l-jaliat al-ajnabiyya, Majilis al-Wuzara', DWQ.

113. Undated letter from Consul Suzzara to Riyad Pasha, attached to a letter from 1882, document 20/2, box 2, Al-tawa'if wa-l-jaliat al-ajnabiyya, Majilis al-Wuzara', DWQ.

114. See, e.g., draft letters from the Council of Ministers to Mr. Baron, 7 July 1880, documents 12/2–13/2, box 2, Al-tawa'if wa-l-jaliat al-ajnabiyya, Majilis al-Wuzara', DWQ.

115. Letter from the Secretary of State to the Minister of Finance, 24 October 1886, document 93/2, box 2, Al-tawa'if wa-l-jaliat al-ajnabiyya, Majilis al-Wuzara', DWQ.

116. Letter from the Minister of Finance to the Council of Ministers, 4 August 1880, document 33/alif baa', box alif baa', Al-tawa'if wa-l-jaliat al-ajnabiyya, Majilis al-Wuzara', DWQ.

117. Ibid.

118. This is a main point made by Ilbert, *Alexandrie*, esp. vol. 1, chap. 6.

119. In addition to the main hospitals, "François Joseph" asked for and received tax breaks on land purchased in 1900 to build a new hospital. Letter from the Finance Minister to the Council of Ministers, 18 December 1900, document 180/2; and government note, 29 August 1886, document 146/2, both in box 2, Al-tawa'if wa-l-jaliat al-ajnabiyya, Majilis al-Wuzara', DWQ. I have no evidence to suggest that this was a request from the French community as a whole, and I am inclined to believe it is the request of a specific religious organization for the building of a clinic. No hospital called "François Joseph" is found in the Nizarat al-maliyya statistics (see *Ihsa' al-jam'iyat al-khairiyyin*), but there is evidence of a "François Joseph" asylum built in 1906. Notes to the Council of Ministers, February 1906, documents 295-297/2, box 2, Al-tawa'if wa-l-jaliat al-ajnabiyya, Majilis al-Wuzara', DWQ.

120. While Ilbert and Reimer note the key role of the Ornato and municipality in building Alexandria, the municipality does not play a central role in my archives. Ilbert, *Alexandrie*, vol. 1, esp. chap. 6; and Reimer, *Colonial Bridgehead*.

121. Scholarship on landownership in Egypt has focused primarily on questions of peasants and agricultural land projects and are documented through the era of Mehmed 'Ali and post-British occupation. The years of the khedives are a topic yet to be explored in full. For Mehmed 'Ali, see Cuno, *The Pasha's Peasants*; for British Egypt, see Jakes, *Colonial Economism*.

122. Undated letter from European Hospital Committee to Riyad Pasha, Minister of Finance, approximately 1882, document 14/2; undated letter from Suzzara, Consul General of Austria-Hungary and President of the European Hospital, to Riyad Pasha, Minister of Finance, approximately 1882, document 20/2; letter from Suzzara, Consul General of Austria-Hungary and President of the European Hospital, to Sharif Pasha, President of the Council of Ministers, 27 April 1883, document 17/2; letter from the Secretary of State to the President of the Council of Ministers, 10 May 1883, document 18/2; and letter from the administration of the European Hospital, 1883, document 19/2; all in box 2, Al-tawa'if wa-l-jaliat al-ajnabiyya, Majilis al-Wuzara', DWQ. The hospital's beneficial role to the city at large was repeated regularly in the annual

reports. See Annual Reports of the European Hospital, 20 PO/1_28, Alexandrie, Consulat, CADN.

123. See, e.g., undated letter from European Hospital Committee to Riyad Pasha, Minister of Finance, approximately 1880, document 7/2; undated letter from European Hospital Committee to Riyad Pasha, Minister of Finance, approximately 1882, document 14/2; letters from Suzzara, Consul General of Austria-Hungary and President of the European Hospital, to Mahmoud Pasha Samy, President of the Council of Ministers, 6 April 1882, documents 15/2, letter from Suzzara, Consul General of Austria-Hungary and President of the European Hospital, to Mahmoud Pasha Samy, President of the Council of Ministers, 6 April 1882, document 16/2, 22/2, 24/2, 25/2; letter from Suzzara to the President of the Council of Ministers, 27 April 1883, document 17/2; letter from Secretary of State to the President of the Council of Ministers, 10 May 1883, document 18/2; letter from the European Hospital administration, 1883, document 19/2; undated letter from Suzzara to Riyad Pasha, approximately 1883, document 20/2; and note from the Governor of Alexandria, 6 May 1882, document 27/2; all in box 2, Al-tawa'if wa-l-jaliat al-ajnabiyya, Majilis al-Wuzara', DWQ.

124. See, e.g., letter from Suzzara, Consul General of Austria-Hungary and President of the European Hospital, to Mahmoud Pasha Samy, President of the Council of Ministers, 6 April 1882, document 22/2, box 2, Al-tawa'if wa-l-jaliat al-ajnabiyya, Majilis al-Wuzara', DWQ.

125. This point is reiterated in a letter from Acting Consul of France Finn Witnay to Monsieur Stagni, 14 June 1911, 20 PO/1_441, Alexandrie, Consulat, CADN. Stagni demanded the presidency of the European Hospital when the French consul took leave; Witnay countered that the position was not about the person but the relationship between the consulate and the hospital.

126. Report by Dr. Morrison, British Consular Surgeon, 18 April 1911, FO 891/1, TNA.

127. Letter from the Deaconess Hospital Committee to unspecified members of the Egyptian government, 14 May 1899, document 56/alif baa', box alif baa', Al-tawa'if wa-l-jaliat al-ajnabiyya, Majilis al-Wuzara', DWQ.

128. Ibid.

129. There is broad literature on public health and the logic of empire. A few texts that have been particularly central to my thinking, aside from Amster, *Medicine and the Saints*, and Arnold, *Colonizing the Body*, include Johnson and Khalid, *Public Health in the British Empire*; Keller, *Colonial Madness*; Mitchell, *Colonising Egypt*; and Peckham and Pomfret, *Imperial Contagions*.

130. The military cemeteries were due to be transferred to al-Maks; the Muslim cemeteries, to be moved elsewhere. Letter from Finance Minister to the President of the Council of Ministers, 27 June 1899, document 55/alif baa', box alif baa', Al-tawa'if wa-l-jaliat al-ajnabiyya, Majilis al-Wuzara', DWQ.

131. Letter from Deaconess Hospital Committee to Council of Ministers, 14 May 1899, document 56/alif baa', box alif baa', Al-tawa'if wa-l-jaliat al-ajnabiyya, Majilis al-Wuzara', DWQ.

132. Letter from Finance Minister to the President of the Council of Ministers, 27 June 1899, document 55/alif baa', box alif baa', Al-tawa'if wa-l-jaliat al-ajnabiyya, Majilis al-Wuzara', DWQ.

133. Report from Dr. Morrison, British Consular Surgeon, 18 April 1911, FO 891/1, TNA.

134. Ibid.

135. Letter from the Governor to the President of the Council of Ministers, 26 February 1878/23 Safar 1295, document 53/2; letter to Zaki Pasha, Governor of Alexandria, from C. M. Salvagos, Vice President of the Committee to Build a New Greek Hospital, 17 and 29 October 1878, documents 55/2 and 56/2; and undated letter from the members of the Commission of the Hellenic-Egyptian community to the Khedive Isma'il, document 56/2; all in box 2, Al-tawa'if wa-l-jaliat al-ajnabiyya, Majilis al-Wuzara', DWQ. See also report from Mohammed Marachli Pasha, Engineer of the Egyptian Fortifications, 7 February 1879, document 7/alif baa'; copy of Marachli report with attached note to the Minister of Public Works from the Minister of War 19 February 1879, document 8/alif baa'; letter to Sharif Pasha, President of the Council of Ministers from C. M. Salvagos, Vice President of the Committee to Build a New Greek Hospital, 15 April 1879, document 9/alif baa'; unsigned memo about the Greek Hospital in Alexandria, 31 May 1879, document 10/alif baa'; letter to Nubar Pasha, President of the Council of Ministers from the Greek Patriarch of Alexandria, 15 February 1884, document 12/alif baa'; letter from (signature unreadable) to Minister of Public Works, 23 January 1879, document 13/alif baa'; and letter to the Minister of Justice, European Department, from the Minister of Finance, 19 April 1905, documents 18–19/alif baa'; all in box alif baa', Al-tawa'if wa-l-jaliat al-ajnabiyya, Majilis al-Wuzara', DWQ.

136. Undated letter from members of the Hellenic-Egyptian community to Khedive Isma'il, approximately 1878, document 56/2, box 2, Al-tawa'if wa-l-jaliat al-ajnabiyya, Majilis al-Wuzara', DWQ.

137. Letter to Zaki Pasha, governor of Alexandria, from C. M. Salvagos, Vice President of the Committee to Build a New Greek Hospital, 17 and 29 October 1878, document 55/2, box 2, Al-tawa'if wa-l-jaliat al-ajnabiyya, Majilis al-Wuzara', DWQ.

138. Ibid. In addition to serving in a number of positions within the Greek community, Salvagos was the US consular agent in Alexandria. Z. Fahmy, "Jurisdictional Borderland."

139. Letter written to the Minister of Public Works, 23 January 1879, document 13/alif baa', box alif baa', Al-tawa'if wa-l-jaliat al-ajnabiyya, Majilis al-Wuzara', DWQ.

140. Letter to the President of the Council of Ministers, 17 November 1878, document 52/2, box 2, Al-tawa'if wa-l-jaliat al-ajnabiyya, Majilis al-Wuzara', DWQ.

141. Letter to the Minister of Public Works, 23 January 1879, document 13/alif baa', box alif baa', Al-tawa'if wa-l-jaliat al-ajnabiyya, Majilis al-Wuzara', DWQ.

142. Note from Minister of Public Works, February 1879, document 4/alif baa', box alif baa', Al-tawa'if wa-l-jaliat al-ajnabiyya, Majilis al-Wuzara', DWQ. It is not

clear that this was still an active cemetery, although the fort was part of the larger Bab Sharqi military lands that housed the foreign-national and religious minority cemeteries.

143. Note from Minister of Public Works, February 1879, document 4/alif baa', box alif baa', Al-tawa'if wa-l-jaliat al-ajnabiyya, Majilis al-Wuzara', DWQ.

144. Letter to Minister of Public Works, May 1879, document 2/alif baa'; note from Minister of Public Works, February 1879, document 4/alif baa'; and report from Chief Engineer to Minister of War, February 1879, document 7/alif baa'; all in box alif baa', Al-tawa'if wa-l-jaliat al-ajnabiyya, Majilis al-Wuzara', DWQ.

145. C. M. Salvagos, Vice President of the Committee to Build a New Greek Hospital, to Sharif Pasha, President of the Council of Ministers, 15 April 1879, document 9/alif baa', box alif baa', Al-tawa'if wa-l-jaliat al-ajnabiyya, Majilis al-Wuzara', DWQ.

146. Note about Greek Hospital land requests, 31 May 1879, document 10/alif baa', box alif baa', Al-tawa'if wa-l-jaliat al-ajnabiyya, Majilis al-Wuzara', DWQ.

147. Note from Ibrahim Fouad, Minister of Justice, to Council of Ministers, 19 April 1905, documents 18–19/alif baa', box alif baa'; note from Minister of Justice to Council of Ministers, 10 April 1905, unnumbered document, box 3 dell; both in Al-tawa'if wa-l-jaliat al-ajnabiyya, Majilis al-Wuzara', DWQ.

CHAPTER 2

1. Letter from Sister Dora Brooks to Edward Gould, H. B. Consul General, 9 May 1904, estate of Rose Northcote, case 1, PRO 847/34, TNA.

2. Olwig, "A Proper Funeral."

3. I am borrowing the terminology of the imperial nation-state from Wilder, *French Imperial Nation-State*.

4. Letter from Sister Dora Brooks to Edward Gould, H. B. Consul General, 9 May 1904, estate of Rose Northcote.

5. Notes from Constable Whitfield in file, 10 May 1904, estate of Rose Northcote.

6. SdPF receipt, estate of Rose Northcote. SdPF was an umbrella organization representing funeral parlors with at least three branches in Alexandria: in front of the Greek Church, by St. Catherine's, and on Rue Abou Darder.

7. Receipt from British Protestant Cemetery, Rosetta Gate, 10 May 1904, estate of Rose Northcote. The consulate reserved a grave without long-term property rights.

8. Receipt of stay in Deaconess Hospital for Miss Rose Northcote, 11 May 1904, estate of Rose Northcote. Port, cherry wine, and champagne would be included in the daily costs of first-class rooms. That a half bottle of champagne is a separate charge is a sign that Rose Northcote was in a second-class room. Conditions for Admission to the Deaconess Hospital, included in the Report to Committee, 1891, 20 PO/1_28, Alexandrie, Consulat, CADN.

9. Estate of Rose Northcote.

10. In the nineteenth century, various Christian sects laid out the specific understandings of death and burial needed for a good death; funerals were an important part of the process. What it meant to have a good death is amply covered in several

broad works on death, including Jalland, *Death in the Victorian Family*; Kellehear, *A Social History of Dying*, esp. chap. 8; Kselman, *Death and the Afterlife*; and La-queur, *Work of the Dead*. This was not limited to Christians; see Omar, "Snatched by Destiny's Hand," for how obituaries were used to mark good Muslim deaths in late nineteenth- and early twentieth-century Egypt. The quest for a good death was used to challenge religious rituals as well. See DiGirolama, "Newsboy Funerals"; Gewald, "Flags, Funerals and Fanfares"; Ranger, "A Decent Death"; and Rosenow, *Death and Dying*.

11. Report from Constable Whitfield to Consul General Charles Cookson, 2 March 1893, estate of Said Basselm, case 9, FO 847/23, TNA.

12. Ibid.

13. "Règlement sur les Cimetières, Inhumations, Exhumations et Transport de Cadavres." Not all bodies were buried. Bodies in England could be marked as do-nated to science immediately upon death, per the Anatomy Act of 1832. Laqueur, *Work of the Dead*, 353–361. Amira Sonbol writes that unclaimed bodies from hospi-tals in Egypt were donated for dissection in the early nineteenth century; this is still the norm at the time of the printing of her book in 1991. Sonbol, *Creation of a Medi-cal Profession*. Because foreign consulates were vigilant in protecting their dead sub-jects, it is unlikely that bodies of foreigners would have been donated for dissection.

14. Puente, "Consular Establishment."

15. Henry White notes that consuls in the Levant had to study language and pass an exam before appointment, thus marking them as professionals. White, "Consular Reforms," 716. D. C. M. Platt writes that plans to professionalize the consulate were largely ignored. Platt, *The Cinderella Service*, 164. Gordon Iseminger argues that Brit-ish consuls of this time often became "pro-Turkish" and thus no longer reliable for the British. Iseminger, "The Old Turkish Hands."

16. Keating, "Empire of the Dead," esp. chap. 2.

17. "The Consular Service," 561.

18. Orders in Council were unilateral statements by the British government de-tailing how to govern abroad; they were not negotiations between two or more coun-tries. Oakes and Maycock, *British and Foreign State Papers*, 1045–1105.

19. Ibid., 1079.

20. "'The Court,' except when the reference is to a particular Court, means any Court established under the Order, subject, however, to the provisions of this Order with respect to powers and local jurisdictions." British Order in Council of 1899, Ar-ticle 3, ibid., 1046.

21. British Order in Council of 1899, Articles 113–121, ibid., 1104.

22. See, e.g., estate of Moise Abeasis, 1910, case 6, FO 847/44, TNA.

23. The chief constable, a rank in the British police force, was also a consular po-sition in charge of many basic social services for British subjects living in Alexandria. Platt, *The Cinderella Service*.

24. Letter from Sister Dora Brooks to H. B. M. Consul General of Alexandria,

28 January 1910, Late Miss Aurelia Gardner Estate and Administration Thereof under Art. 121 of O. in C. 1899, case 15, FO 847/44, TNA.

25. Probate Jurisdiction, H. B. M. Consular Court at Alexandria, 14 April 1904, estate of Massaoud Daoud Hayou, 1903, case 26, FO 847/33, TNA.

26. Account of execution of will (*Dossier de la Succession*) of Massaoud Daoud Hayou by the Grand Rabbinate of Alexandria, 23 March 1904, estate of Massaoud Daoud Hayou, 1903, case 26, FO 847/33, TNA.

27. Late Miss Aurelia Gardner Estate and Administration Thereof under Art. 121 of O. in C. 1899, case 15, FO 847/44, TNA.

28. See, e.g., letter from Consul Stanley to the Earl of Clarendon, 29 January 1869, FO 78/2095, TNA. See also estate of Marshall Williams, July 1880, case 20, FO 847/1, TNA.

29. Letter from G. U. Diaper to the British Consul, 29 January 1890; response from Cookson to Diaper, 10 February 1890, estate of William Beach, 1890, case 12, FO 847/18, TNA.

30. Not counting Beach as a British employee may also have been a move to assuage the fears of the nascent Egyptian nationalist movement. Thank you to Aaron Jakes for pointing this out, as well as for talking through the Beach case with me.

31. Inquest of Jacob Gherson, 1895, case 19, FO 847/25, TNA.

32. In chapter 7 of *Identifying with Nationality*, Will Hanley argues that exhumations represent a preoccupation with individual status.

33. Eventually the consulate found his relative, who identified Gherson and, interestingly, spoke only Italian.

34. Questions of death and perpetuity pepper research on the dying and the dead. See, e.g., Dubisch, "Death and Social Change."

35. See, e.g., Hodes, *Mourning Lincoln*; and Jindra and Noret, *Funerals in Africa*.

36. Thomas Laqueur writes that "the pauper funeral became the final stamp of failure" in nineteenth-century England. The movement from churchyard to park cemetery correlated with the growth of class-based funerals and the removal of a safety net that provided funerals for all. Laqueur, *Work of the Dead*, 323–325.

37. Brophy, "On Church Grounds"; Kedourie, "Death of Adib Ishaq"; Minkin, "Simone's Funeral"; Trice, "Rites of Protest"; and Verdery, *Political Lives*.

38. See, e.g., de Chaparro and Achim, *Death and Dying*, esp. chap. 7; and Warren, "Medicine and the Dead."

39. See, e.g., Fox, *Lincoln's Body*; and Hodes, *Mourning Lincoln*.

40. Letter from Mr. Buch, Treasurer of the British Burial Ground in Suez, to Consul General Gould, 5 June 1903. Additional notes in the estate case show that the Egyptian government sought repayment. Estate of Thomas J. Baldrock, case 8, FO 847/33, TNA.

41. Jean Antoine Marius Autran, 15 June 1909, 20 PO/1_291, Alexandrie, Consulat, CADN. Failure to provide a decent funeral was a serious offense in the eyes of the consulate. In 1875, the British consul in Suez neglected his "duty" to bury Judge

Fagan, a British judge in India, who died shortly after arriving in the port city. Subsequent correspondence within the Alexandria consulate determined his behavior to have been "scandalous" and "offensive," as burial was both a consular and a "moral" duty. Death of Judge Fagan in Suez, 1875, FO 78/2406, TNA.

42. Jean Antoine Marius Autran, 15 June 1909, 20PO/1_291, Alexandrie, Consulat, CADN. Within this estate case, bills collected include those relating to sickness, pharmacy, and doctor's fees alongside the funeral charges. His extensive medical costs suggest he was ill for a long time.

43. Printing funeral invitations to mark a middle-class or wealthy funeral was neither unique to Egypt nor an invention of the nineteenth century. Kreiger, "Dutch Cemeteries," 85; and Kselman, *Death and the Afterlife*, 224, 228.

44. Meredith Chesson writes that "mortuary rituals provide a sensuous arena in which the dead are mourned, social memories are created and (re)asserted, social bonds are renewed, forged, or broken, and an individuals make claims for individual identities and group memberships." Chesson, "Social Memory," 1.

45. Laqueur, *Work of the Dead*, chap. 5; Bullock and McIntyre, "The Handsome Tokens"; and Gott, "'Onetouch' Quality."

46. Laqueur, *Work of the Dead*; and Curl, *Victorian Celebration*.

47. There was widespread concern over changing funeral costs, especially the new trend of clergy charging for their role in funerals, in nineteenth-century France. Kselman, *Death and the Afterlife*, chaps. 6, 7.

48. Probate Jurisdiction, H. B. M. Consular Court at Alexandria, 4 June 1909, estate of Helen Pauline Demench, died 26 April 1909, case 19, FO 847/42, TNA.

49. Probate Jurisdiction, H. B. M. Consular Court at Alexandria, 12 April 1910, estate of Moise Abeasis, 1910, case 6, FO 847/44, TNA.

50. Probate Jurisdiction, H. B. M. Provincial Court at Alexandria, Schedule 2, 29 August 1911, estate of the Late Eugenia Phillips, 25 July 1911, case 35, FO 847/46, TNA.

51. SdPF receipt, Rue Abou Darder, 22 April 1909, succession Yehuda Nahom 1909, 20PO/1_291, Alexandrie, Consulat, CADN. Khaled Fahmy notes that following ritual Islamic burial in mid-nineteenth-century Egypt would mean that a body was "washed, shrouded, and buried." Coffins were not used. Fahmy, "The Anatomy of Justice," 242. See also Halevi, *Muhammad's Grave*, esp. 165–168. In twenty-first-century Egypt, Jewish bodies, too, are buried in shrouds without coffins. Minkin, "Simone's Funeral."

52. One exception is Aurelia Gardner, whose funeral included a hearse but no horses. SdPF receipt, Rue Abou Darder, 28 January 1910, Late Miss Aurelia Gardner Estate and Administration Thereof under Art. 121 of O. in C. 1899, case 15, FO 847/44, TNA.

53. Separate charges for moving the body to and from the morgue (usually in a hearse) are noted in several funeral cases.

54. Letter from Sister Dora Brooks to the Consul General of France, 9 November 1908, Marguerite Lancon, 9 November 1908, 20 PO/1_290, Alexandrie, Consulat, CADN.

55. Probate Jurisdiction, H. B. M Provincial Court at Alexandria, 29 August 1911, estate of the Late Eugenia Phillips, 25 July 1911, case 35, FO 847/46, TNA. Having several members of the clergy participate in one's funeral was a mark of "moderate wealth" in late eighteenth-century France. Kselman, *Death and the Afterlife*, 224. Only two cases in the archives showed evidence of multiple clergy involved in an Alexandrian funeral: Eugenia Phillips and estate of Sara Roca 1885, case 36, FO 847/10, TNA.

56. Will of Sara Roca, certified at the British Consulate, translated from the Arabic, on 27 May 1885, estate of Sara Roca 1885, case 36, FO 847/10, TNA.

57. One of the relatives who received a bequest from Sara Roca was accused of stealing belongings slowly out of her home while she lay dying. The British assumed him to be a local subject, like most of Sara's other relatives, and only later realized he was the dragoman for the Terre Sainte and had French protection. Estate of Sara Roca 1885, case 36, FO 847/10, TNA.

58. The British Order in Council of 1899, which details the testamentary process of British subjects in the Ottoman Empire, does not address what might happen if the consulate is named executor. Oakes and Maycock, *British and Foreign State Papers*, 1045–1105.

59. Estate of Moise Abeasis, 1910, case 6, FO 847/44, TNA.

60. Hanley, *Identifying with Nationality*. A large percentage of the Jewish community was under Austro-Hungarian protection from 1881 until World War I. It is therefore not surprising that the sister who remained in Alexandria had Austrian protection; it is more unusual that Moise held British protection. Krämer, *Jews in Modern Egypt*, 75.

61. Benedict Anderson demonstrates the political and economic benefits of birth certificates and passports. Anderson, *Spectre of Comparisons*, esp. 69–70. The same benefit would pass to the family in possession of the death certificate from desirable consulates.

62. Report from Constable Whitfield to Acting Consul General Alban, 18 July 1892, estate of Maria Mondello alias Maria Camilleri, Italian Subject, case 51, FO 847/22, TNA.

63. Baldwin, "Subject to Empire," 525.

64. "The Murder of Captain Fawcett," *Egyptian Gazette*, 28 April 1914. Found in Inquest on the Body of Capt. Samuel Fawcett, case 45, FO 847/52, TNA.

65. Laqueur writes: "The funerals of the great were essential rituals of inclusion for a small band of men and a show of status that expressed the deceased's place in a well-defined, if sometimes contested, community of superiors, equals, and dependents." Laqueur, *Work of the Dead*, 320. See also Flaks, "Death of the Monarch"; and Necipoglu, "Dynastic Imprints."

66. Noorani, "A Nation Born in Mourning"; and Wilson, "Representing National Identity."

67. Fenton, "The Day They Buried"; and Wein, "The Long and Intricate Funeral."

68. Tombs and Tombs, *That Sweet Enemy*, 442–443.

69. "La Maladie de Mgr. Bonfigli," *La Réforme*, 30 March 1904; and "La Maladie de Mgr. Bonfigli," *La Réforme*, 31 March 1904; both in 20 PO/1 449, Alexandrie, Consulat, Solemnities, CADN. *La Réforme* had a daily circulation of approximately fifteen hundred. *Newspaper Press Directory*, 473.

70. "La Maladie de Mgr. Bonfigli," *La Réforme*, 31 March 1904, 20 PO/1 449, Solemnities, Alexandrie, Consulat, CADN.

71. "La Maladie de Mgr. Bonfigli," *La Réforme*, 30 March 1904; and "La Maladie de Mgr. Bonfigli," *La Réforme*, 31 March 1904; both in 20 PO/1 449, Solemnities, Alexandrie, Consulat, CADN.

72. A 1740 agreement between the Sublime Porte and the French stated that "France could invoke a French Catholic Protectorate over all Latin rite Catholics, thus becoming the official representative of the pope in a predominately Muslim empire." De Dreuzy, *The Holy See*, 45, 48.

73. This debate culminated in the 1905 law enshrining a separation of church and state. Elizabeth Foster writes: "The issue of whether republican *laïcité* should apply in the empire played a key role in the definition and elaboration of the relationship between the metropolitan republic and its colonies just after the turn of the century." The question of application of *laïcité* laws enacted between 1901 and 1905 would demonstrate "the degree to which theoretically immutable republican principles such as *laïcité* were objects of negotiation and compromise across the frontiers of metropole and colony." Foster, *Faith in Empire*, 72, 73.

74. Daughton, *An Empire Divided*, 221–223. The pushback against the *laïcité* laws by British Protestants in Madagascar "saved" the French Catholic missions from the wrath of the French state.

75. The expansion of French missions in Egypt was designed to challenge the British. Ibid., 14.

76. "Oraison Funèbre," *La Réforme*, saved without date (presumably 10 April 1904) by the French Consulate; and Bonfigli funeral program; both in 20 PO/1 449, Solemnities, Alexandrie, Consulat, CADN.

77. See an engaging example of the Ottoman ideal in Palestine in Campos, *Ottoman Brothers*.

78. "Oraison Funèbre," *La Réforme*, saved without date (presumably 10 April 1904) by the French Consulate; and Bonfigli funeral program; both in 20 PO/1 449, Solemnities, Alexandrie, Consulat, CADN.

79. Obituary of Mgr. Gaudenzio Bonfigli, *La Réforme*, 6 April 1904, 20 PO/1 449, Solemnities, Alexandrie, Consulat, CADN.

80. Mak, *The British in Egypt*, 39.

81. Tombs and Tombs, *That Sweet Enemy*, 442–443.

82. Telegrams between Girard and La Boulinière, 6–7 April 1904, 20 PO/1 449, Solemnities, Alexandrie, Consulat, CADN.

83. "Father Ammadio Amato, the Provicar of the Franciscans, has not always been so good about the French consular authorities, but he had me intimately involved in the organization of the funeral," wrote Girard to his home office in Paris

following the event. Copy of letter to L. E. M. Déclassé from Girard, 16 April 1904, 20 PO/1 449, Solemnities, Alexandrie, Consulat, CADN.

84. Copy of letter to Graham Bey, Administrator of the Municipality, from Girard, 6 April 1904, 20 PO/1 449, Solemnities, Alexandrie, Consulat, CADN.

85. Ilbert, *Alexandrie*, vols. 1 and 2.

86. "La Mort de Mgr. Bonfigli," *La Réforme*, 7 April 1904, 20 PO/1 449, Solemnities, Alexandrie, Consulat, CADN.

87. Letter to Girard from Atelier de Photographie Artistique, 8 April 1904, 20 PO/1 449, Solemnities, Alexandrie, Consulat, CADN.

88. See 20 PO/1 449, Solemnities, Alexandrie, Consulat, CADN.

89. Girard's notes to file, 11 April 1904, 20 PO/1 449, Solemnities, Alexandrie, Consulat, CADN.

90. Letter from British Consul General Gould to French Consul General Girard, 8 April 1904, 20 PO/1 449, Solemnities, Alexandrie, Consulat, CADN.

91. Ibid.

92. Letter from Girard to Graham Bey, 8 April 1904; letter from Vice President of the Municipality to Girard, 8 April 1904; and additional notes in file, regarding the gas company, 8 April 1904; all in 20 PO/1 449, Solemnities, Alexandrie, Consulat, CADN.

93. Telegrams between La Boulinière and Consul Girard, 6–7 April 1904, 20 PO/1 449, Solemnities, Alexandrie, Consulat, CADN.

94. Consul Girard's Report of the Bonfigli Funeral transmitted to La Boulinière in Cairo and from Cairo to Paris, 16 April 1904, 20 PO/1 449, Solemnities, Alexandrie, Consulat, CADN.

95. Letter from Girard to La Boulinière, 6 April 1904, 20 PO/1 449, Solemnities, Alexandrie, Consulat, CADN.

96. Ibid.

97. A few months after the Bonfigli funeral, the French state would break off diplomatic relations with the Vatican over the republican sympathies of two French priests. This would alter the relationship between the French and the Vatican in Alexandria, and future public memorials at St. Catherine's would be more contentious. The French Consulate was hypervigilant about disrespect from the apostolic delegation and involved various Catholic European countries in its struggle. See for example the documents covering the 1909 death of King Leopold of Belgium, 20 PO/1 449, Solemnities, Alexandrie, Consulat, CADN.

98. Letter from Girard to La Boulinière, 6 April 1904, 20 PO/1 449, Solemnities, Alexandrie, Consulat, CADN.

99. Letter from Girard to La Boulinière, 7 April 1904, 20 PO/1 449, Solemnities, Alexandrie, Consulat, CADN.

100. Telegram from La Boulinière to Girard, 7 April 1904, 20 PO/1 449, Solemnities, Alexandrie, Consulat, CADN.

101. Note from Girard to file, 11 April 1904, 20 PO/1 449, Solemnities, Alexandrie, Consulat, CADN.

102. Report by Girard submitted to La Boulinière, 16 April 1904, 20 PO/1 449, Solemnities, Alexandrie, Consulat, CADN.

103. "La Mort de Mgr. Bonfigli," *La Réforme*, 9 April 1904, 20 PO/1 449, Solemnities, Alexandrie, Consulat, CADN.

104. Ibid.

105. "Oraison Funèbre," *La Réforme*, saved without date (presumably 10 April 1904) by the French Consulate; and Bonfigli funeral program, 20 PO/1 449, Solemnities, Alexandrie, Consulat, CADN.

106. Program of Funeral Procession of Archbishop Bonfigli, 20 PO/1 449, Solemnities, Alexandrie, Consulat, CADN.

107. Ben-Amos, *Funerals, Politics and Memory*, esp. chap. 11.

108. Note from Girard, 11 April 1904, 20 PO/1 449, Solemnities, Alexandrie, Consulat, CADN.

109. Program of Funeral Procession of Archbishop Bonfigli, 20 PO/1 449, Solemnities, Alexandrie, Consulat, CADN.

110. Ibid. Note from Girard, 11 April 1904; "La Mort de Mgr. Bonfigli," *La Réforme*, 9 April 1904; both in 20 PO/1 449, Solemnities, Alexandrie, Consulat, CADN.

111. Seating chart for Archbishop Bonfigli funeral, 20 PO/1 449, Solemnities, Alexandrie, Consulat, CADN.

112. Report by Girard to La Boulinière, 16 April 1904, 20 PO/1 449, Solemnities, Alexandrie, Consulat, CADN.

113. "Oraison Funèbre," *La Réforme*, saved without date (presumably 10 April 1904) by the French Consulate; and Bonfigli funeral program, 20 PO/1 449, Solemnities, Alexandrie, Consulat, CADN.

CHAPTER 3

1. Murder of Alexander Welch, 1897, case 1, FO 847/27, TNA.

2. Welch's grave came with "right of property," a right linked to the length of time the body could stay in the grave; the vast majority of grave purchases were without right of property, so graves could be exhumed or moved, within limits. A 1911 letter from representatives of the Greek community in Cairo to the president of the Council of Ministers asked for government intervention against the Greek Orthodox patriarch because of his removal of bones from graves if the family did not pay him extra monies. Letter from representatives of the Greek Orthodox community to Mohamed Pasha Said, President of the Council of Ministers, 10 August 1911, documents 65–66/4, box 4, Al-tawa'if wa-l-jaliat al-ajnabiyya, Majilis al-Wuzara', DWQ.

3. Ener, *Managing Egypt's Poor*; and Pollard, "Egyptian by Association."

4. Although bones were dug up and graves were reused, the cemetery itself was considered permanent. For the situation outside Egypt, see Dubisch, "Death and Social Change." For a look at how states use the destruction of cemeteries to assert state control, see Willis, "Governing the Living and the Dead."

5. Lefebvre, *The Production of Space*, 38–39.

6. Harvey, *Justice*, chap. 11; and Lefebvre, *The Production of Space*, 38–39.

7. Edward Lane is a repeated example for Edward Said in *Orientalism*; see also J. Thompson, "Edward Lane in Egypt."

8. Lane, *Manners and Customs*, 522.

9. Ibid., 553.

10. This was not unique to Alexandria in this time period. See, e.g., Marcus, *Middle East*, chap. 7.

11. This was not only in Egypt. Orhan Pamuk writes: "Of all the losses [from the nineteenth century], I think the hardest for Istanbullus has been the removal of graves and cemeteries from the gardens and squares of our everyday lives to terrifying high-walled lots, bereft of cypresses or views." Pamuk, *Istanbul*, 240.

12. See, e.g., Rastegar, *Literary Modernity*, 93–100.

13. Foucault, "Of Other Spaces."

14. See, e.g., "Tomb of Lanis," where Markos spends "lingering hours on end" looking for his friend, "an Alexandrian." The Cavafy Archive, accessed 23 November 2018, http://www.cavafy.com/poems/content.asp?id=82&cat=1.

15. Martinez-Fernandez, "Don't Die Here."

16. The movement from private churchyard to public, often nonreligious, "modern" cemeteries is amply covered in writings about the cemetery in England. See Laqueur, *Work of the Dead*, esp. chap. 4; and Rugg, *Churchyard and Cemetery*.

17. Ariès, *Hour of Our Death*, 520–524.

18. Kselman, *Death and the Afterlife*, 9.

19. Kiest, "Czech Cemeteries." Even within the confines of the Czech cemeteries, the community was subdivided into Catholics and Free Thinkers.

20. Outline of history of Abd el Moneim Cemetery by C. E. Heathcote-Smith, Consul General of Great Britain and Chairman of British Protestant Cemetery Committee, 19 December 1935, FO 891/60, TNA. Andrew Keating writes that the first British cemetery in Alexandria opened in 1839; 'Abd al-Mun'im predates this. Keating, "Empire of the Dead," 44.

21. Minutes of the meeting of the Cemetery Committee of the Joint Anglican and Scottish Churches of Alexandria, 1 February 1866, FO 78/1941, TNA.

22. Ibid.

23. The British consul general writes that the Shatbi cemeteries opened in 1835. British Consul General of Alexandria to Her Majesty's Principal Secretary of State for Foreign Affairs, 17 April 1950, FO 369/4478, TNA.

24. An 1885 letter from a chaplain affiliated with the British Consulate appealed for help in securing land for the Protestant community. The chaplain noted that the trustees of the cemetery have been trying without success. One of the two trustees was affiliated with the British Consulate; notably missing were the consul general or other top officials. Even the chaplain was only standing in for a lay leader who was traveling in England at the time. Letter to Director General du Cadastre from E. G. Davis, Chaplain of St. Mark 6th Co. and HM Consulate, 18 August 1885, document 1/3, box 3, Al-tawa'if wa-l-jaliat al-ajnabiyya, Majilis al-Wuzara', DWQ.

25. Sanitation Commission and Sanitation Department are used interchangeably in government correspondence.

26. The process is documented throughout the correspondence saved in box 4, Al-tawa'if wa-l-jaliat al-ajnabiyya, Majilis al-Wuzara', DWQ.

27. Memo from Minister of Interior to Council of Ministers, no date, connected to 1881 report, documents 13/4, 14/4, and 17/4, box 4, Al-tawa'if wa-l-jaliat al-ajnabiyya, Majilis al-Wuzara', DWQ.

28. Only after World War I did the Egyptian government end the practice of offering free use of land, tax breaks, and/or significantly reduced prices to foreign communities in establishing their cemeteries. While foreign communities were not required to pay for land already in use, any expansion of the old or creation of new cemeteries would now require buying land, and all cemetery lands under public domain were to remain under public domain. In other words, the land deeded to the cemeteries would always stay open to the public as a park or a garden. Private cemeteries would revert back to the person or community involved. There was some confusion (and worry!) within the British Consulate about which category a foreign cemetery, built on land donated by the Egyptian government, would belong. See 1924 Report of the Committee Appointed to Consider and to Make Recommendations concerning the Provision, Maintenance, and Disaffection of Cemeteries throughout Egypt, FO 141/454, TNA.

29. "Règlement sur les Cimetières, Inhumations, Exhumations et Transport de Cadavres."

30. Much of this mirrors the French Decree of 23 Prairial, Year XII (12 June 1804). Ariès, *Hour of Our Death*, 516–520; and Kselman, *Death and the Afterlife*, esp. chap. 5.

31. "Règlement sur les Cimetières, Inhumations, Exhumations et Transport de Cadavres."

32. See 1924 Report of the Committee Appointed to Consider and to Make Recommendations concerning the Provision, Maintenance, and Disaffection of Cemeteries throughout Egypt, FO 141/454, TNA.

33. Halevi, *Muhammad's Grave.*

34. Official communities buried the foreign dead, even when the cemetery space was not yet sanctioned. Minutes of the meeting of the Cemetery Committee of the Joint Anglican and Scottish Churches of Alexandria, 1 February 1866, FO 78/1941, TNA.

35. See, e.g., Re: Alfred Baldacchino, 1880–1881, case 17, FO 847/2, TNA.

36. Similarly, there are no Muslim "foreign" charities or hospitals listed in Nizarat al-maliyya, *Ihsa' al-jam'iyat al-khairiyyin.*

37. See 1911 map, FO 925/41172, TNA.

38. See also the "Egyptian Protestants," whose cemetery was maintained by the American Mission, 1928 map of Alexandria's foreign cemeteries, FO 141/454, TNA.

39. Muslims who took French nationality were ostracized from Tunisian Muslim cemeteries as part of the struggle for national independence in the early twentieth century; the cemeteries were eventually divided by both religion and nationality for

the Muslim population. In this example, Muslim burial reflected the political implications of power and control of land. Lewis, *Divided Rule*, chap. 5.

40. See 1878 map, unnumbered document, box 4, Al-tawa'if wa-l-jaliat al-
ajnabiyya, Majilis al-Wuzara', DWQ.

41. The land is owned by a man named "Bolanki." I was unable to find any other
details of his existence.

42. See 1911 map, FO 925/41172, TNA.

43. This was the norm beyond Alexandria. "It goes without saying that Protes-
tants of all nationalities may be buried in this cemetery [in Port Said]." H. B. M. Sd.
Chas. McDonald, one of the Trustees of the British Protestant Cemetery, to H. B. M.
Vice Consul, Port Tewfik, 30 March 1924, FO 454/6, TNA.

44. A 1928 map shows that cemeteries affiliated with Latin and Greek Catholics,
Syrian and Coptic Orthodox, and Egyptian Protestants (affiliated with the American mission) were all created after 1911. Interestingly, this map also suggests that the
Greek Orthodox and Syrian Orthodox (Maronite) cemeteries swapped locations
shown on the 1911 map and that the Free Thinkers were linked to the British cemetery rather than the Coptic one. See 1928 map of Alexandria's foreign cemeteries, FO
141/454, TNA.

45. Letter from the British Consul General of Alexandria to Her Majesty's Principal Secretary of State for Foreign Affairs, 17 April 1950, FO 369/4478, TNA.

46. See 1924 Report of the Committee Appointed to Consider and to Make Recommendations concerning the Provision, Maintenance, and Disaffection of Cemeteries throughout Egypt, FO 141/454, TNA; and testimony given to the Health Ministry,
21 July 1891, document 15/4; testimony given to Health Ministry, 23 June 1881, document 16/4; copies of a letter to the President of the Council of Ministers from the Minister of Public Works, 26 Rabi' 'Awal 1301/24 January 1884, documents 60/4 and 64/4;
all in box 4, Al-tawa'if wa-l-jaliat al-ajnabiyya, Majilis al-Wuzara', DWQ.

47. Ho, *Graves of Tarim*, 3.

48. In distinction from imperial Alexandria and its rooted foreign populations,
Engseng Ho writes that diasporas form "the society of the absent" and focuses on the
role of absence in defining the diasporic experience, in terms of both emotional and
financial situations. Ibid., 19.

49. Letter from the British Consul General of Alexandria to Her Majesty's Principal Secretary of State for Foreign Affairs, 17 April 1950, FO 369/4478, TNA.

50. Ibid.

51. This was related to the need to preserve nearby military land. Copies of undated report from the Minister of the Interior to the Council of Ministers, documents
13/4–14/4, 17/4, box 4, Al-tawa'if wa-l-jaliat al-ajnabiyya, Majilis al-Wuzara', DWQ.

52. In addition to the Greek Orthodox, Greek Catholic, and Free Thinkers' joint
request for a "rectangle" of land discussed here, a General Earl represented both Protestant and Catholic communities in a quest for new cemetery land in 1884. This request for Catholic cemetery land was different from that of the Franciscans discussed
here. Correspondence from Minister of Interior to the President of the Council of

Ministers, 21 Safar 1301/21 December 1883, document 78/4, box 4, Al-tawa'if wa-l-jaliat al-ajnabiyya, Majilis al-Wuzara', DWQ.

53. The report of the commission to study the enlargement of the Catholic cemetery of Alexandria, 23 May 1881, documents 7/4–8/4, box 4, Al-tawa'if wa-l-jaliat al-ajnabiyya, Majilis al-Wuzara', DWQ.

54. See 1911 map, FO 925/41172, TNA; correspondence from the Health Ministry to the Interior Ministry, 12 July 1881, documents 15/4–16/4, box 4, Al-tawa'if wa-l-jaliat al-ajnabiyya, Majilis al-Wuzara', DWQ. The Franciscans were the original Catholic missionaries to the Middle East, arriving in Alexandria by the late seventeenth century. Meinardus, *Christians in Egypt*, 72–73, 80.

55. Correspondence from the Health Ministry to the Interior Ministry, 12 July 1881, documents 15/4–16/4, box 4, Al-tawa'if wa-l-jaliat al-ajnabiyya, Majilis al-Wuzara', DWQ.

56. Ibid.

57. Kselman, *Death and the Afterlife*, paraphrasing Ariès, *Hour of Our Death*, 205.

58. There is lively academic discussion of graves as markers of separation (especially in regard to family, class, and religion) within the cemetery. Some of the abundant literature that has particularly resonated with me includes Carpenter and Murphy, "Churchyard and Cemetery Sculpture"; Karus-Friedberg, "Across the Pacific"; Kselman, *Death and the Afterlife*; Laqueur, *Work of the Dead*; Lim, *Forgotten Souls*; Meyer, *Ethnicity and the American Cemetery*; Podoler, "Death as a Nationalist Text"; and Tzortzopoulou-Gregory, "Remembering and Forgetting."

59. Copies of undated report from the Minister of the Interior to the Council of Ministers, documents 13/4–14/4, 17/4, box 4, Al-tawa'if wa-l-jaliat al-ajnabiyya, Majilis al-Wuzara', DWQ.

60. Letter from D. Salem, President of the Committee to Expand Catholic Cemeteries to Riyad Pasha, Minister of the Interior, 12 July 1881, documents 5/4–6/4; report of the commission to study the enlargement of the Catholic cemetery of Alexandria, 23 May 1881, documents 7/4–8/4; correspondence from the Health Ministry to the Interior Ministry, 12 July 1881, documents 15/4–16/4; all in box 4, Al-tawa'if wa-l-jaliat al-ajnabiyya, Majilis al-Wuzara', DWQ.

61. There were 4,923 Catholics and 2,718 Protestant British subjects in Alexandria in 1897. Mak, *The British in Egypt*, 39.

62. Correspondence from the Health Ministry to the Interior Ministry, 12 July 1881, documents 15/4–16/4, box 4, Al-tawa'if wa-l-jaliat al-ajnabiyya, Majilis al-Wuzara', DWQ.

63. Ibid.

64. Copies of undated report from the Minister of the Interior to the Council of Ministers, documents 13/4–14/4, 17/4, box 4, Al-tawa'if wa-l-jaliat al-ajnabiyya, Majilis al-Wuzara', DWQ.

65. See 1928 map of Alexandria's foreign cemeteries, FO 141/454, TNA. The Free Thinkers' origins in Egypt may be linked to Italian anarchists who arrived in Egypt

by the 1860s. It is highly unlikely that these Free Thinkers were, in actuality, linked to the Free Masons of Alexandria. The masonic secret societies contained members of the royal family and other upper-class Muslim Egyptians. While these Free Masons were not necessarily separate from religion, Free Thinkers worked for civil society. "At the end of the last [nineteenth] century, between French and English culture, the literate Egyptian youth and the professional classes were much stirred by rationalism, and much in need of a reasoned ethical culture." Robertson, *History of Free Thought*, 601–602. For discussion of Free Thinkers, see Gorman, "Internationalist Thought," 243–245. For discussion of Free Masons, see Landau, "Prolegomena"; and Wissa, "Freemasonry in Egypt."

66. Samir Raafat writes of a Syrian native of Alexandria named Joseph Saba who was postmaster general of Egypt 1887–1907 and later promoted to Minister of Finance in 1910. The Saba family who owned these lands may have been related to this branch of the family; that would help explain why they were able to confound the government time and again. Raafat, "A Snapshot of Egypt's Postal History."

67. The archives do not specify which courts dealt with the Saba family and the government's competing land claims. Correspondence from the Minister of Public Works to the President of the Council of Ministers, 26 September 1884, documents 52/4, 55/4–56/4, box 4, Al-tawa'if wa-l-jaliat al-ajnabiyya, Majlis al-Wuzara', DWQ.

68. Booklet by the Ministry of Finance, 28 August 1883, documents 38/4–44/4 and 45/4–51/4, box 4, Al-tawa'if wa-l-jaliat al-ajnabiyya, Majlis al-Wuzara', DWQ.

69. Undated letter from the Minister of Interior to the Council of Ministers, documents 9/4–12/4, box 4, Al-tawa'if wa-l-jaliat al-ajnabiyya, Majlis al-Wuzara', DWQ.

70. The Franciscans took care of the Latin Catholic cemetery in Alexandria. They had long turned to the French for help in the Middle East and Ottoman Empire. See, e.g., Mazza, *Jerusalem*, esp. chap. 2. There were exceptions: the Franciscans of Port Said were under Austrian protection. Carmanati, "Bur Sa'id/Port Said."

71. Copies of undated report from the Minister of the Interior to the Council of Ministers, documents 13/4–14/4, 17/4, box 4, Al-tawa'if wa-l-jaliat al-ajnabiyya, Majlis al-Wuzara', DWQ.

72. Booklet by the Ministry of Finance, 28 August 1883, documents 38/4–44/4, 45/4–51/4, box 4, Al-tawa'if wa-l-jaliat al-ajnabiyya, Majlis al-Wuzara', DWQ.

73. Copies of undated report from the Minister of the Interior to the Council of Ministers, documents 13/4–14/4, 17/4, box 4, Al-tawa'if wa-l-jaliat al-ajnabiyya, Majlis al-Wuzara', DWQ.

74. The movement of graves remains a political issue. In the Nasserist era, the Egyptian government rethought plans for moving the Jewish cemeteries in light of the political tension between Egypt and Israel. See note from A. G. Banks to British Consulate in Cairo, 14 July 1970, FO 891/235, TNA.

75. The Egyptian national government offered land in 1879, only to rescind the offer because the Saba family owned this land as well. Correspondence from the Health Ministry to the Interior Ministry, 12 July 1881, documents 15/4–16/4, box 4, Al-tawa'if wa-l-jaliat al-ajnabiyya, Majlis al-Wuzara', DWQ.

76. Booklet by the Ministry of Finance, 28 August 1883, documents 38/4–44/4, 45/4–51/4, box 4, Al-tawa'if wa-l-jaliat al-ajnabiyya, Majilis al-Wuzara', DWQ.

77. "Règlement sur les Cimetières, Inhumations, Exhumations et Transport de Cadavres."

78. Correspondence from Minister of Interior to the President of the Council of Ministers, 23 Safar 1301/23 December 1883, document 78/4; report from the Minister of the Interior to the Council of Ministers, 22 Dhul-Hijjah 1301/12 October 1884, document 79/4; and letter from the Minister of Interior to the President of the Council of Ministers, 13 October 1884, document 80/4; all in box 4, Al-tawa'if wa-l-jaliat al-ajnabiyya, Majilis al-Wuzara', DWQ.

79. Report from the Minister of the Interior to the Council of Ministers, 22 Dhul-Hijjah 1301/12 October 1884, document 79/4; letter from the Minister of Interior to the President of the Council of Ministers, 13 October 1884, document 80/4; both in box 4, Al-tawa'if wa-l-jaliat al-ajnabiyya, Majilis al-Wuzara', DWQ.

80. The Jewish community of Alexandria split between those aligned with the Austrian Consulate and those aligned with the "local" government in the late nineteenth century, before reuniting under Austrian protection. Krämer, *Jews in Modern Egypt*, 75–77; Haag, *Alexandria*, 139–140; and Hassoun, "The Jews," 44.

81. Copies of a letter to the President of the Council of Ministers from the Minister of Public Works, 26 Rabiʿ 'Awal 1301/24 January 1884, documents 60/4 and 64/4, box 4, Al-tawa'if wa-l-jaliat al-ajnabiyya, Majilis al-Wuzara', DWQ.

82. Report from the Minister of the Interior to the Council of Ministers, 22 Dhul-Hijjah 1301/12 October 1884, document 79/4; letter from the Minister of Interior to the President of the Council of Ministers, 13 October, 1884, document 80/4; both in box 4, Al-tawa'if wa-l-jaliat al-ajnabiyya, Majilis al-Wuzara', DWQ.

83. In addition to the Maronites, Armenian Catholics utilized the Latin Catholic cemetery for burials. An 1897 request by the patriarch of the Armenian Catholics asked for land so that the community could stop burying its dead in "foreign" graves. The Egyptian government acted quickly and found space for the Armenian Catholics within a year. Finance Minister to the Council of Ministers, 8 February 1898, documents 125/4–128/4, box 4, Al-tawa'if wa-l-jaliat al-ajnabiyya, Majilis al-Wuzara', DWQ.

84. Meinardus, *Christians in Egypt*, 85; and Philipp, *Syrians in Egypt*, 172.

85. Booklet by the Ministry of Finance, 28 August 1883, documents 38/4–44/4, 45/4–51/4, box 4, Al-tawa'if wa-l-jaliat al-ajnabiyya, Majilis al-Wuzara', DWQ.

86. Correspondence from the Minister of Public Works to the President of the Council of Ministers, 26 September 1884, documents 52/4, 55/4, 56/4; correspondence from Minister of Interior to the President of the Council of Ministers, 21 Safar 1301/21 December 1883, document 78/4; both in box 4, Al-tawa'if wa-l-jaliat al-ajnabiyya, Majilis al-Wuzara', DWQ.

87. Minister of Public Works to the President of the Council of Ministers, 24 January 1884, documents 60/4 and 66/4, box 4, Al-tawa'if wa-l-jaliat al-ajnabiyya, Majilis al-Wuzara', DWQ.

88. For the situation in Syria, see Arsan, "There Is, in the Heart of Asia"; Hakim, *Lebanese National Idea*; and Makdisi, *Culture of Sectarianism*.

89. Booklet by the Finance Ministry, 28 August 1883, documents 38/4–44/4, 45/4–51/4, box 4, Al-tawa'if wa-l-jaliat al-ajnabiyya, Majilis al-Wuzara', DWQ. Later maps of the Shatbi area put the Maronite cemetery at the opposite end of the complex from the Jewish cemeteries. See 1911 map, FO 925/41172, TNA; and 1928 map of Alexandria's foreign cemeteries, FO 141/454, TNA.

90. The Egyptian government was a resource for negotiations both between and within the communities. In 1911, the Greek community of Cairo turned to the Egyptian government to help when the Greek patriarch began digging up bones after three years and reburying them in a communal vault. Letter from La Corporation de l'Union Populaire du Caire on behalf of the Greek Orthodox community to the President of the Council of Ministers, 10 August 1911, documents 65/4–66/4, box 4, Al-tawa'if wa-l-jaliat al-ajnabiyya, Majilis al-Wuzara', DWQ.

91. See 1911 map, FO 925/41172, TNA.

92. Forster, *Alexandria*, 135.

93. See also Haag, *Alexandria*, 330; Ilbert, "Citizenship," 21; and Yannakakis, "Farewell Alexandria," 111.

CHAPTER 4

1. Acte de Naissance de Borivent, Pauline Françoise Elisabeth (1908), #118, Register 58, 6EC, Alexandrie, Etat Civil, CADN.

2. Hussein Omar argues that obituary writing during this same time period proved to be central in the emerging national imagination of elite Muslim Egyptians. While I do not focus on obituaries here, I am indebted to Hussein's work for helping me crystallize ideas about connections between writing the dead and classifying the living. Omar, "Snatched by Destiny's Hand."

3. See, e.g., Schreier, *Arabs of the Jewish Faith*, esp. chap. 5.

4. Fisher, "Natives of India."

5. Stein, "Protected Persons?," 85.

6. Todd, "Transnational Projects"; and Wilder, *French Imperial Nation-State*.

7. See, e.g., Hanley, "Cosmopolitan Cursing"; Hanley, *Identifying with Nationality*; and Khuri-Makdisi, *Global Radicalism*.

8. See 353 PO/2_438, Le Caire, Ambassade, CADN, which contains extensive documentation of diplomatic maneuvering within the French Consulates, embassy in Cairo, and government in Paris to determine how the French would collate and submit data to the Egyptian government.

9. The consulates had been sharing birth information with the Egyptian government from as early as 1885. Representatives of the French and Egyptian governments negotiated an agreement for the French Consulate to send both birth and death information weekly following the June 1891 Khedival Decree mandating Egyptian state collection of personal-status records. Ibid.

10. For citizen registers, see 6EC, Alexandrie, Etat Civil, CADN. For protégés and others, see 20PO/2009041, Alexandrie, Consulat, Supplement, CADN.

11. The archive 6EC, Alexandrie, Etat Civil, CADN, begins in the early nineteenth century and continues through 1908. In 20PO/2009041, Alexandrie, Consulat, Supplement, CADN, registers 1–3 are marked as religious authorities, shipping communities, and consular agencies; 5–11 are Algerians and protégés through 1915; register 4 is a compilation of all names found within the registries, far beyond the 1915 end date of this study. Will Hanley suggests that the eliding of various types of subjects into one category and the interchangeable usage of *administré*, *protégé*, and *sujet* in the French consular records suggests a "lack of attention to the second class as a whole, as well as a tendency to lump it together." Hanley, *Identifying with Nationality*, 179. While this is true in the title of the registers, specific details of nationality are recorded in death entries.

12. European consulates emerged in Port Said after the opening of the Suez Canal. Huber, *Channelling Mobilities*, 90.

13. Décès de Lelubois (Louis Edouard) (1871), #267, register 15, 6EC, Alexandrie, Etat Civil, CADN.

14. Décès de Erlanger (Michael) (1886), 20PO/2009041_1, Alexandrie, Consulat, Supplement, CADN.

15. De Clercq and De Vallat, *Guide Pratique des Consulats*, 365–367.

16. Hanley writes: "If death brought a responsibility [for the consulates] that could not be dodged, the appeals of living impoverished Europeans to the consulate often fell on deaf ears." Hanley, *Identifying with Nationalism*, 161.

17. The citizen registries frequently contained updates on citizens who moved to other countries in the margins of the register.

18. The British civil-status registers are most likely to be found in the archives of the British Consulate that were donated to the Centre d'Etudes Alexandrines in Alexandria after completion of the research for this book.

19. Nissel, *People Count*, chap. 2.

20. I did not find the French inquests; neither have other historians. Hanley, "Foreignness," 172.

21. De Clercq and De Vallat, *Guide Pratique des Consulats*; E. Hertslet, *A Complete Collection of Treaties*, vol. 14; and FO 141/1, TNA.

22. N. Brown, "Precarious Life and Slow Death"; and Hanley, *Identifying with Nationality*.

23. K. Fahmy, "Anatomy of Justice."

24. Draft of June 1891 Khedival Decree, 353 PO/1_438, Le Caire, Ambassade, CADN.

25. E. Hertslet, *A Complete Collection of Treaties*, 14:579–580. These orders codified the processes of inquests and autopsies that were already in practice.

26. K. Fahmy, "Anatomy of Justice."

27. The use of the Foreign Jurisdiction Act to define consular rights and respon-

sibilities in 1890 suggests that Egypt was still considered "outside Her Majesty's domains" despite the "veiled" British occupation.

28. Files before 1880 were lost in the Alexandria fires and bombardment in 1882.

29. G. Hertslet, *A Complete Collection of Treaties*, 26:994.

30. This is particularly interesting in comparison with the French registers that cover sea deaths. See, e.g., 20PO/2009041_1, 2, 3, Alexandria, Consulat, Supplement, CADN.

31. Jackson, "Suspicious Infant Deaths." The first "investigative postmortem" took place in England in 1635 and in colonial America in 1639. Brock and Crawford, "Forensic Medicine," 27.

32. De Clercq and De Vallat, *Guide Pratique des Consulats*, 361–364, 367–369.

33. Ibid., 388.

34. June 1891 Khedival Decree, 353 PO/2_438, Le Caire, Ambassade, CADN.

35. Ibid., Article 28. While the version available in the French archives is a draft, subsequent correspondence after the publication of the decree makes it evident that these key components related to collection of foreign national data remained the same.

36. See, e.g., copy of correspondence, unsigned, to Alexandre Ribot of the Interior Ministry in France, 12 September 1891, 353 PO/2_438, Le Caire, Ambassade, CADN.

37. Letter from French consular employee (signature unintelligible) to Alexandre Ribot of the Interior Ministry in France, 26 September 1891, 353 PO/2_438, Le Caire, Ambassade, CADN.

38. June 1891 Khedival Decree, 353 PO/2_438, Le Caire, Ambassade, CADN. The copy of this decree saved in the French archives has several alterations on it, noting that these have already been approved. Additional correspondence between French consular employees and ministers in the French government in 1890 and 1891 confirms that France attempted to influence the language of the decree.

39. Letter to the Chargé d'Affaires from the Foreign Minister in Cairo, 8 August 1885, 353 PO/2_438, Le Caire, Ambassade, CADN.

40. Letter from French Consul of Alexandria, Amaury Lacretelle, to Minister Cogordan, Ministre Plenipotentiaire, Chargé de l'Agence et Consulat Général de France en Egypte, 23 March 1897, 353 PO/2_438, Le Caire, Ambassade, CADN.

41. Letter from French Consul of Alexandria Georges Biard d'Aunet to Monsieur le Marquis de Reverseaux, Ministre de France au Caire, 8 February 1892, 353 PO/2_438, Le Caire, Ambassade, CADN.

42. "Règlement sur les Cimetières, Inhumations, Exhumations et Transport de Cadavres."

43. Ibid.

44. Burton, "History of the Autopsy."

45. Ibid., 282; and Clark and Crawford, *Legal Medicine in History*.

46. Sim and Ward, "Magistrate of the Poor?"

47. K. Fahmy, "Anatomy of Justice." The first autopsy is a central trope in scholar-

ship on the history of medicine in Egypt. Abugideiri, *Gender and the Making of Modern Medicine*; Kuhnke, *Lives at Risk*; and Sonbol, *Creation of a Medical Profession*.

48. Kellehear, *A Social History of Dying*, 125–146.

49. Loveman, "Modern State and the Primitive Accumulation" and "Blinded like a State."

50. This is still a problem today. Szreter, "Children with a (Local) State."

51. Cuno and Reimer, "Census Registers." That extraterritoriality allowed European states the power to protect their citizens, subjects, and protégés at a high price to both the local state and the legal flexibility of its inhabitants is the key point of Marglin, *Across Legal Lines*, esp. 144–170. See also Schreier, *The Merchants of Oran*.

52. Eldem, "French *Nation*," 132–133.

53. Ibid., 134, emphasis in original.

54. In addition to Marglin, *Across Legal Lines*; Mazza, *Jerusalem*; and Schreier, *Arabs of the Jewish Faith*, questions of legal governance and empire are key to dozens of studies of the Middle East. A few that I have found particularly productive in thinking through the French and British in Egypt include Arsan, "There Is, in the Heart of Asia"; Clancy-Smith, *Mediterraneans*; Lewis, *Divided Rule*; Stein, *Saharan Jews*; and B. White, *Emergence of Minorities*.

55. Lewis, *Divided Rule*.

56. Baring, *Modern Egypt*, vols. 1 and 2.

57. Ibid., 2:246.

58. Ibid., 247–248. Cromer discounts the French in spite of acknowledging that the "French colony" contained subjects "from the most Gallic Gaul to the ultra-Levantinised Levantine" (248).

59. Ibid., 252.

60. Ibid., 245–259.

61. Ibid., 246–250.

62. Inquest on Luigi Mifsud, 1903, case 24, FO 847/44, TNA.

63. Re: The Death of Antonio Felice, 1880, case 33, FO 847/1, TNA.

64. Inquest of Jean Carlo Caruana, 1895, case 3, FO 847/25, TNA; and estate of Giuseppe Bellante, 1892, case 14, FO 847/21, TNA.

65. Inquest into the body of Giuseppe Mamo, 1880, case 30, FO 847/1, TNA.

66. Inquest on the body of Joseph Falconer, 1894, case 36, FO 847/24, TNA.

67. Inquest on the body of Serafino Buhagi, 1901, case 18, FO 847/31, TNA.

68. Alessandro Ataliotti, 1896, case 5, FO 847/25, TNA.

69. Inquest of Lilian Irlam, 1903, case 22, FO 847/22, TNA.

70. Birth, marriage, and death registries found in 20 PO/2009041, Alexandrie, Consulat, Supplement, CADN; and 6EC Alexandrie, Etat Civil, CADN.

71. Décès de Rizzoni (César) (1886), #41, 20PO/2009041_6, Alexandrie, Consulat, Supplement, CADN; décès de Autofage (Laurent Louis) (1890), #36, register 41, 6EC, Alexandrie, Etat Civil, CADN.

72. Décès de Négrier (Fernand) (1893), #6; and décès de Martin (Louis) (1884), #11; both in 20PO/2009041_1, Alexandrie, Consulat Supplement, CADN.

73. Décès de Prodanus (Alcibiade) (1877), #16; and décès de Ghebali (Eliaho) (1890), #35; both in 20 PO/2009041_7, Alexandrie, Consulat Supplement, CADN.

74. Naissance de Agier (Claudine) (1890), #70, and naissance de Agier (Maria) (1890), #71, register 14; décès de Agier (Maria) (1891), #2, and décès de Agier (Claudine) (1891), #9, register 15; all in 6EC, Alexandrie, Etat Civil, CADN.

75. Naissance de Wacil (Mohamed Aly) (1890), #69, register 41, 6EC Alexandrie, Etat Civil, CADN.

76. Décès de Wacil (Mohamed Aly) (1902), #3, 20PO/2009041_9, Alexandrie, Consulat Supplement, CADN.

77. Ibid.

78. Protection could be lost with the death of a father who was a naturalized citizen.

79. Reconnaissance d'un enfant naturel Rocheman (Henri Paul), #41; mariage de Rocheman (Alfred Paul Ibrahim) et dlle Adam (Irmine), #48; and décès de Rocheman (Irmine) née Adam (all from 1875), #49; all in register 20, 6EC, Alexandrie, Etat Civil, CADN.

80. See also the Cauros, who married in April 1903 in a church but registered the marriage with the French Consulate in February 1906, two weeks before the birth of their son on March 2. Tragically, their son died the very next day. Transcription de la acte de marriage de Cauro (Arthur, Etienne, André, Napoleon) et Gemma (Carmel), #18; naissance de Cauro (Oswald, Raphael, Pompee, Carmel), 2 Mars 1906; and décès de Cauro (Oswald, Raphael, Pompee, Carmel), 3 Mars 1906 (all 1906), #21; all in register 57, 6EC, Alexandrie, Etat Civil, CADN.

81. See, e.g., décès de Wingfield (Madeleine) en religion Soeur Marie Louise de Sion (1889), #15; and décès de Sieur Zundel (Alphonse) en religion Frère Roch Alphonse (1892), #24; both in 20PO/2009041_7, Alexandrie, Consulat Supplement, CADN.

82. See, e.g., décès de Soulfour, Michelle (1875), #6, register 20; and décès du Père Kiste Barthez (1895), #80, register 46; both in 6EC Alexandrie, Etat Civil CADN.

83. I am inspired by and borrowing here from Gary Wilder, who writes: "France's parliamentary republic was articulated with its administrative empire to compose an expanded and disjointed political formation." Wilder, *French Imperial Nation-State*, 3.

84. This is a well-researched topic. A few of the key books that have helped form my ideas and are not mentioned elsewhere in these notes include Cooper, *Citizenship between Empire and Nation*; Dubois, *A Colony of Citizens*; and E. Thompson, *Colonial Citizens*.

85. See, e.g., the entry registering the 1905 death of Yacoub Abraham Cohen. Cohen's death is marked in the protégé register, despite his being an Algerian Jewish man whose son is an Algerian Jewish French citizen. The two witnesses for his death include Elie ben Amozig, most likely a Jewish man and a peddler marked as a French constituent, and Marco Groub Cohen, the citizen son. Décès de Yacoub Abraham Cohen (1905), #1, 20PO/2009041_10, Alexandrie, Consulat Supplement, CADN.

86. Brett, "Legislating for Inequality," 455; and McDougall, *A History of Algeria*.

87. This process was neither inevitable nor without significant challenge from within the Jewish community. Schreier, *Arabs of the Jewish Faith*; Stein, *Saharan Jews*; and Stein; "Dreyfus in the Sahara."

88. Acte de décès de Rouquaia (1874), #31, 20 PO/2009041_5, Alexandrie, Consulat Supplement, CADN.

89. Décès de Colomines (Joseph, Gabriel, Vincent) (1875), #110, register 20, 6EC, Alexandrie, Etat Civil, CADN.

90. Lewis, *Divided Rule*, esp. chap. 3.

91. Cutler, "Believe in the Border."

92. Clancy-Smith, *Mediterraneans*.

93. Décès de Haim Chantob Habib (1897), #42, 20PO/2009041_8, Alexandrie, Consulat Supplement, CADN.

94. Décès de Fatouma femme de Hamida ben Khalifa (1897), #50, 20PO/2009041_8, Alexandrie, Consulat Supplement, CADN.

95. Décès de Salama (Abramins) (1897), #75, 20PO/2009041_8, Alexandrie, Consulat Supplement, CADN.

96. Clancy-Smith, *Mediterraneans*.

97. Décès de Otman ben el Tayeb el Gharbi (1892), #2, 20PO/2009041_7; décès de Said Meheni ben Dahman (1901), #47, 20PO/2009041_9, Alexandrie, Consulat Supplement, CADN.

98. Décès de Aly Mahmoud Echarafy (1902), #34, 20PO/2009041_9, Alexandrie, Consulat Supplement, CADN.

99. Décès de Daouia, veuve de Hadj Mahmoud Echarafy, nee Abdalla [Echarafy's mother] (1897), #30; and décès de Saida, fille de Mohamed el Masri, femme de Hadj Hassan Mahmoud Essahli [Echarafy's mother-in-law] (1898), #17; both in 20PO/2009041_8, Alexandrie, Consulat Supplement, CADN. For the Jewish trader, see décès de Chamoun Haim Baranes (1892), #13, 20PO/2009041_7, Alexandrie, Consulat Supplement, CADN. All others are in 20PO/2009041_7, 8, 9.

100. See, e.g., décès de Mohamed Rajab Hamouda Haddad (1901), #33, 20PO/2009041_9, Alexandrie, Consulat Supplement, CADN. All others are in 20PO/2009041_9, 10.

101. Décès de Mehanni, son of Younes ben Dahman (1900), #20; décès de Mahmoud, fils de Ahmed ben Dahman (1901), #30; and décès de Said Meheni ben Dahman (1901), #47; all found in 20PO/9002041_9, Alexandrie, Consulat Supplement, CADN.

102. For example, the register for September 1902 contains Ahmed ben Dahman, a Tunisian landlord, and Younes ben Dahman, an Algerian. Décès du Ahmed ben Dahman (1902), #70; décès de Abbas, fils de Ahmed Salah ben Temallis (1902), #77; and décès de Naamat, fille de Chehata Hassouna (1902), #78; all in 20PO/2009041_9, Alexandrie, Consulat Supplement, CADN.

103. Décès de Hamida bent Abdalla Cherkessy, femme de Hadj Salah ben Dahman (1903), #87, 20PO/2009041_9, Alexandrie, Consulat Supplement, CADN.

104. Décès de Abbas, fils de Ahmed Salah ben Temallis (1902), #77; and décès de

Naamat, fille de Chehata Hassouna (1902), #78; both in 20PO/2009041_9, Alexandrie, Consulat Supplement, CADN.

105. Décès du Ahmed ben Dahman (1902), #70, 20PO/2009041_9, Alexandrie, Consulat Supplement, CADN.

106. Clancy-Smith, *Mediterraneans*, 206.

107. Thank you to Brock Cutler for this turn of phrase.

108. Register 9, 6EC Alexandrie, Etat Civil, CADN. See all correspondence from the Health Ministry to the Interior Ministry, 12 July 1881, documents 15/4–16/4, box 4, Al-tawa'if wa-l-jaliat al-ajnabiyya, Majilis al Wuzara', DWQ.

109. See 20PO/2009041_5, Alexandrie, Consulat Supplement, CADN.

110. See 20PO/2009041_4 and 20PO/2009041_5, Alexandrie, Consulat Supplement, CADN.

111. See, e.g., "The Mecca Pilgrims and the Cholera–Dreadful Accident," 2.

112. Registers 15, 16, 6EC Alexandrie, Etat Civil, CADN.

113. Marginal notes in the subject/protégés registries are primarily corrections to the records.

114. Registers 14, 20, 6EC Alexandrie, Etat Civil, CADN.

115. Register 20, 6EC Alexandrie, Etat Civil, CADN, emphasis added.

116. See 20PO/2009041_5, Alexandrie, Consulat Supplement, CADN, emphasis added.

117. Stillborn babies were a separate category of lives/deaths. Gourdon, Rollet, and Grieve, "Stillbirths."

118. Décès de Cloux, Louis Marins (1875), #1, 20PO/2009041_5, Alexandrie, Consulat Supplement, CADN.

119. Décès de Sergierviez, Alexandre (1875), #15, 20PO/2009041_5, Alexandrie, Consulat Supplement, CADN.

120. Acte de naissance de Azar Cohen (1875), #2, 20PO/2009041_5, Alexandrie, Consulat Supplement, CADN.

121. See e.g., 20 PO/2009041_5, Alexandrie, Consulat Supplement, CADN; and register 20, 6EC, Alexandrie, Etat Civil, CADN.

122. David Todd writes of a French citizen in Cairo who was "employed by the Cairo consulate to witness acts of civil registration" in the 1870s. Todd, "Beneath Sovereignty," 106. This suggests that L'Hotelliere and others were paid for witnessing. I never found reference to payment in the archives, nor did I find evidence explaining why some registrations seemingly had paid witnesses and others did not or how the witnesses for which acts were chosen and by whom.

123. See, e.g., Décès de Dlle Emliger (Anna) (1898), #26, 20PO/2009041_8; décès de Messiqua (Clement), #41; and décès de Meggle (Clemence) (1899), #42, 20PO/2009041_9; all in Alexandrie, Consulat Supplement, CADN. See also décès de Espic (Florentin) (1900), #2, register 51, 6EC, Alexandrie, Etat Civil CADN.

124. Acte de décès de Fatma, fille de Hadj Ali ben Mohammad Essadfi (1874), #32, 20PO/2009041_5, Alexandrie, Consulat Supplement, CADN; décès de Petit (Jules François) (1871), #138, register 15, 6EC Alexandrie, Etat Civil, CADN; and décès de

Prodanus (Alcibiade) (1877), #16, 20PO/2009041_6; acte de décès de Campagnano, Luna (1876), #9, 20PO/2009041_5; acte de décès de Fatma, fille de Hadj Ali ben Mohammad Essadfi (1874), #32, 20PO/2009041_5; décès de Calamaro (Isaac) (1887), #42, 20PO/2009041_7; décès de Springer (Théophile) (1877), #14, 20PO/2009041_6; décès de Lambert Bey (Demetrius) (1880), #19, 20PO/2009041_6; décès de Vella (Maria veuve Besson (1888), #83, 20PO/2009041_7; and décès de Lucaci (Antoinette Pauline) (1887), #64, 20PO/2009041_7; all in Alexandrie, Consulat Supplement, CADN.

125. Décès du Père Illario de Ponzone Missionaire Apostolique (1880), #33, 20PO/2009041_6, Alexandrie, Consulat Supplement, CADN. Although the French buried Bonfigli, his death is not registered in their civil-status registers.

126. Décès de Siouffi (Gustave, Armand, Charles) (1871), #158, register 15, 6EC Alexandrie, Etat Civil, CADN.

127. Décès de Monnard (Edmond) (1887), #3; and décès de Bastoria (Pietro) (1887), #16, 20PO/2009041_7; both in Alexandrie, Consulat Supplement, CADN; and décès de Petit (Jules Françoise) (1871), #138, register 15, Alexandrie, Etat Civil, CADN.

128. De Clercq and De Vallat, *Guide Pratique des Consulats*, 388.

129. Décès de Nordio (Marie Anne) femme de Siouffi (1885), #39, register 39, 6EC, Alexandrie, Etat Civil, CADN.

130. Décès de Guérin (1875), #131, register 20, 6EC, Alexandrie, Etat Civil, CADN.

131. De Clercq and De Vallat, *Guide Pratique des Consulats*, 365–367.

132. Register 58, Alexandrie, Etat Civil 6EC, CADN.

133. Re: the death of Paolo Callus, 1880, case 31, FO 847/1, TNA.

134. Correspondence from Dr. Mackie to Charles Cookson, 1 February 1880, re: the death of Paolo Callus, 1880, case 31, FO 847/1, TNA.

135. Ibid.

136. Records before 1880 were lost in the 1882 bombardment of Alexandria.

137. Re: the death of Vincenzo Debono, 1880, case 25, FO 847/1, TNA.

138. More than 5,000 men and around 3,250 women registered as British subjects in Alexandria in 1897. Mak, *The British in Egypt*, 127.

139. Re: death of S. Walker, 1887, case 40, FO 847/15, TNA. I first wrote about this case in "Documenting Death," 44. A British soldier bought S. Walker what both thought was Epsom salt from a pharmacist. With no common language, the pharmacist understood the soldier to need brass cleaner. While I first assumed (and wrote) that Walker bathed in the Epsom salt/brass cleanser, subsequent rereading of the case proved me wrong. Walker drank it and died.

140. Inquest upon the body of Lilian Irlam, 1903, case 22, FO 847/33, TNA; and re: death of S. Walker, 1887, case 40, FO 847/15, TNA.

141. Upon the drowning death of Oliver Steele, the consul general warned that parts of the coast were so dangerous that if the British allowed their soldiers to bathe (swim) there, they would have to accept that some would die. Inquest on the body of Oliver Steele, 1915, case 53, FO 847/55, TNA.

142. Inquest on the body of T. H. Macfarlane, 1915, case 67, FO 847/55, TNA.

143. Inquest on the body of George Caruana, 1909, case 34, FO 847/42, TNA.

144. Re: the murder of Angelo Galea, 1885, case 43, FO 847/10, TNA; re: death of Ruggiero Desain 1885, case 39, FO 847/10, TNA; and inquest on Giovanni Bugeia, 1904, case 23, FO 847/34, TNA.

145. Regina v. Carmelo Buckingham, 1880, case 36, FO 847/1, TNA.

146. I have long argued that soldiers should be counted among the British population of Alexandria. Minkin, "Documenting Death." In his recent book, Will Hanley reverses his previous exclusion of them. See Hanley, "Foreignness," 175–176, and *Identifying with Nationality*, 26–30. Lanver Mak does not focus on the British military in his history of Britons in Egypt, although he mentions them in brief. Mak, *The British in Egypt*, 118–121.

147. See, e.g., Extract from Standing Orders for the British Force in Egypt in Inquest on the body of Private F. Blasby of the 1st Suffolk Reg who died about 11:30am on the 21st of August 1911 at Mustapha Pacha Barrack, case 33, FO 847/46, TNA.

148. Inquest on the body of Thomas Maher, Fireman of the SS *Marathon*, 1894, case 38, FO 847/24, TNA.

149. Inquest on the body of Maurice Hammond, Fireman of the SS *Kittie*, 1906, case 14, FO 847/36, TNA.

150. Inquest on the body of Michael Swiney, 1883, case 4, FO 847/5, TNA.

151. Inquest on the body of Daniel Bell, SS *Diadem*, 1892, case 15, FO 847/21, TNA.

152. Lord Cromer writes: "The discipline and good conduct of the British army in all its ranks are recognised by the most bitter Anglophobes. The worst that can be said of the soldiers is that some of them disgrace themselves by getting drunk." Baring, *Modern Egypt*, 2:253.

153. Inquest on the body of Lance Corporal H. Phillips, 1913, case 31, FO 847/50, TNA.

154. Inquest on the body of Thomas Dixon Sapper in the Royal Engineers, 1906, case 10, FO 847/36, TNA.

155. Inquest on the body of Jessie Brown who died on the 22nd day of April 1906, case 3, FO 847/36, TNA.

156. See, e.g., Inquest on the body of Jessie Brown who died on the 22nd day of April 1906, case 3, FO 847/36, TNA; re: the death of Vincenzo Debono, 1880, case 25, FO 847/1, TNA.

157. Inquest on the body of Pietro Montano, 1909, case 46, FO 847/42, TNA.

158. Tunisian local authorities also regularly identified Maltese as generic Europeans. Clancy-Smith, *Mediterraneans*, 169.

CONCLUSION

1. Al-Sayyid-Marsot, *Egypt's Liberal Experiment*.

2. See, e.g., Beinin, *Dispersion of Egyptian Jewry*; and Reynolds, *A City Consumed*.

3. The sale of the 'Abd al-Mun'im land took several decades, and the British Protestant Cemetery Committee fought both a group of Egyptian men claiming ownership of the land and the Armenian Church next door. Documents can be found in (but are not limited to) the following TNA files: FO 369/4478; FO 847/102, case 48; FO

891/60; FO 891/102; FO 891/137; FO 891/146; FO 891/147; FO 891/148; FO 891/173; and FO 891/191.

4. Report of Cemetery sub-Committee, 2 June 1930, FO 891/137, TNA.

5. See, e.g., the letter from British Consul General H. M. Eyres to the Chief Administrative Officer of the Imperial War Graves Commission in Egypt, 1 April 1953, FO 891/205, TNA. See also FO 891/235, TNA. This was not limited to Alexandria; in 1972 the British embassy objected to Egyptian governmental attempts to take over the Protestant cemetery in Cairo to build a school. FO 141/1516, TNA.

6. See FO 369/5798; FO 891/233; FO 891/235; and FO 141/1516, TNA.

7. The British Protestant cemetery is beautifully maintained and open to the public, but I had to beg my way into the rundown, locked Jewish cemetery on a 2010 visit to Alexandria.

8. Andrew Prescott Keating makes a similar point in regard to Tehran and elsewhere in "Empire of the Dead."

9. Letter from British Consulate General, Alexandria, to Her Majesty's Principal Secretary of State for Foreign Affairs, 17 April 1950, FO 369/4478, TNA.

10. The British Consulate beseeched relatives of the Alexandrian dead for money to maintain burial grounds in the late 1960s. See FO 891/233, TNA.

11. Minkin, "History from Six-Feet Below."

12. "Liste de Notoriété Médicale à Alexandrie," La France en Egypte, Consulat Générale de France à Alexandrie, last modified 10 March 2016, https://eg.ambafrance .org/Liste-de-notoriete-medicale-a-Alexandrie.

13. Minkin, "Simone's Funeral."

14. "Death of a British Citizen Abroad," British-Consulate, accessed 23 November 2018, https://www.british-consulate.net/Death-Abroad.php.

15. Letter from E. K. Green to Consul General Banks, 17 October 1967, FO 891/ 241, TNA.

BIBLIOGRAPHY

ARCHIVAL SOURCES

Egypt
Dar al-Watha'iq al-Qawmiyya (DWQ), Egyptian National Archives, Cairo
Abdeen
Majilis al-Wuzara', Al-tawa'if wa-l-jaliat al-ajnabiyya

France
Centre des Archives Diplomatiques de Nantes (CADN), Center of the Diplomatic Archives in Nantes
Alexandrie, Consulat
Alexandrie, Consulat Supplement
Alexandrie, Etat Civil
Le Caire, Ambassade

United Kingdom
The National Archives (TNA), Kew Gardens, London
Foreign Office (FO)

PUBLISHED PRIMARY SOURCES

"The Consular Service." Foreign and Commonwealth Office Collection, 1858.
De Clercq, Alexandre Jehan Henry, and C. De Vallat, *Guide Pratique des Consulats.* 5th ed. Vol. 1. Paris: A. Pedone, 1898.
Deloncle, François. "France and Egypt." Foreign and Commonwealth Office Collection, 1896.
Hertslet, Edward. *Hertslet's Commercial Treaties: A Complete Collection of Treaties and Conventions between Great Britain and Foreign Powers and of the Laws, Decrees, Orders in Council, &c., concerning the Same, So Far as They Relate to Commerce and Navigation, Slavery, Extradition, Nationality, Copyright, Postal Matters, &c., and to the Privileges and Interests of the Subjects of the High Contracting Parties.* Volume 14. London: Butterworths, 1880.
Hertslet, Godfrey E. P. *Hertslet's Commercial Treaties: A Complete Collection of Treaties and Conventions between Great Britain and Foreign Powers and of the Laws,*

Decrees, Orders in Council, &c., concerning the Same, So Far as They Relate to Commerce and Navigation, Slavery, Extradition, Nationality, Copyright, Postal Matters, &c., and to the Privileges and Interests of the Subjects of the High Contracting Parties. Volume 26. London: H. M. Stationary Office, 1913.

Hertslet, Lewis. *Hertslet's Commercial Treaties: A Complete Collection of Treaties and Conventions between Great Britain and Foreign Powers and of the Laws, Decrees, Orders in Council, &c., concerning the Same, So Far as They Relate to Commerce and Navigation, Slavery, Extradition, Nationality, Copyright, Postal Matters, &c., and to the Privileges and Interests of the Subjects of the High Contracting Parties.* Volume 11. London: Butterworths, 1864.

"The Mecca Pilgrims and the Cholera—Dreadful Accident." *New York Times*, December 23, 1871, p. 2.

Newspaper Press Directory 60, no. 1 (January 1905).

Nizarat al-maliyya, Maslahat 'umum al-ihsa'. *Ihsa' al-jam'iyat al-khairiyyin wa-l-mustashfayat at-tabi'a laha.* Cairo: Al-mitba'a al-amiriyya bi-l-Qahira, 1913.

Oakes, Augustus H., and Willoughby Maycock, comps. and eds. *British and Foreign State Papers: 1898–1899.* Vol. 91. London: Harrison and Sons, 1902.

"Règlement sur les Cimetières, Inhumations, Exhumations et Transport de Cadavres à l'Etranger, Approuve par la Console Internationale Sanitaire d'Egypte dans Ses Séances des 15 Septembre 1876, 26 Mars et 30 Octobre 1877." In *Lois, Décrets, Arrêtés et Règlements Intéressant La Municipalité d'Alexandrie 1890–1920.* Alexandria: Société de Publications Egyptiennes, 1920.

"Terrible Explosion at Alexandria: Many Killed and Wounded." *Egyptian Daily Post*, July 17, 1909.

WEB PAGES

British Consulate. "Death of a British Citizen Abroad." Accessed November 23, 2018. https://www.british-consulate.net/Death-Abroad.php.

Cavafy Archive. Accessed November 23, 2018. http://www.cavafy.com.

La France en Egypte. "Consulat Général de France à Alexandrie." Accessed November 23, 2018. https://eg.ambafrance.org/Liste-de-notoriete-medicale-a-Alexandrie.

SECONDARY SOURCES

PhD Dissertations

Carmanati, Lucia. "Bur Sa'id/Port Said, 1859–1922: Migration, Urbanization, and Empire." PhD diss., University of Arizona, 2018.

Genell, Amie. "Empire by Law: Ottoman Sovereignty and the British Occupation of Egypt, 1882–1923." PhD diss., Columbia University, 2013.

Glavanis, Pandelis Michalis. "Aspects of the Economic and Social History of the Greek Community in Alexandria during the Nineteenth Century." PhD diss., University of Hull, 1989.

Hanley, Will. "Foreignness and Localness in Alexandria." PhD diss., Princeton University, 2007.

Jakes, Aaron. "State of the Field: Agrarian Transformation, Colonial Rule, and the Politics of Material Wealth in Egypt, 1882–1914." PhD diss., New York University, 2015.

Keating, Andrew Prescott. "The Empire of the Dead: British Burial Abroad and the Formation of National Identity." PhD diss., University of California, Berkeley, 2011.

Published Secondary Sources

Abugideiri, Hibba. *Gender and the Making of Modern Medicine in Colonial Egypt.* Surrey, UK: Ashgate, 2010.

Abul-Magd, Zeinab. *Imagined Empires: A History of Revolt in Egypt.* Berkeley: University of California Press, 2013.

Aciman, André. "Alexandria: The Capital of Memory." In *False Papers: Essays on Exile and Memory*, by André Aciman, 3–21. New York: Farrar, Straus and Giroux, 2000.

———. *Out of Egypt: A Memoir.* New York: Riverhead Trade, 1996.

Amster, Ellen. *Medicine and the Saints: Science, Islam, and the Colonial Encounter in Morocco, 1877–1956.* Austin: University of Texas Press, 2013.

Anderson, Benedict. *Spectre of Comparisons: Nationalism, Southeast Asia, and the World.* London: Verso Books, 1998.

Ariès, Philippe. *The Hour of Our Death.* Translated by Helen Weaver. 2nd ed. New York: Vintage Books, 2008.

Arnold, David. *Colonizing the Body: State Medicine and Epidemic Disease in Nineteenth-Century India.* Berkeley: University of California Press, 1993.

Arsan, Andrew. "'There Is, in the Heart of Asia, . . . an Entirely French Population': France, Mount Lebanon, and the Workings of Affective Empire in the Mediterranean, 1830–1920." In *French Mediterraneans: Transnational and Imperial Histories*, edited by Patricia Lorcin and Todd Shepard, 76–100. Lincoln: University of Nebraska Press, 2016.

'Ashmawi, Sa'id. *Al-Yunaniyyun fi Misr: Dirasa tarikhiyya fi al-dur al-iqtisadia al-siyasi, 1805–1956.* Cairo: 'Ayn li-l-dirasa al-ijtima'iyya wa-l-insaniyya.

———. "Perceptions of the Greek Money-Lender in Egyptian Collective Memory at the Turn of the Twentieth Century." In *Money, Land and Trade: An Economic History of the Muslim Mediterranean*, edited by Nelly Hanna, 244–277. London: I. B. Tauris, 2002.

Bacqué-Grammont, Jean-Louis, and Aksel Tibet, eds. *Cimetières et Traditions Funeraires dans le Monde Islamique.* Vol. 2. Ankara: Turk Tarih Kurumu Basimevi, 1996.

Baldwin, M. Page. "Subject to Empire: Married Women and the British Nationality and Status of Aliens Act." *Journal of British Studies* 40, no. 4 (2001): 522–556.

Barak, On. *On Time: Technology and Temporality in Egypt.* Berkeley: University of California Press, 2013.

Baring, Evelyn, Earl of Cromer. *Modern Egypt.* 2 vols. London: Elibron Classics, 2005.

Baron, Beth. *The Women's Awakening in Egypt: Culture, Society, and the Press*. New Haven, CT: Yale University Press, 1997.

Bashkin, Orit. "My Sister Esther: Reflections on Judaism, Ottomanism and Empire in the Works of Farah Antun." In *The Long 1890s in Egypt: Colonial Quiescence and Subterranean Resistance*, edited by Marilyn Booth and Anthony Gorman, 315–341. Edinburgh: Edinburgh University Press, 2014.

Beinin, Joel. *The Dispersion of Egyptian Jewry: Culture, Politics, and the Formation of Modern Diaspora*. Berkeley: University of California Press, 1998.

Beinin, Joel, and Zachary Lockman. *Workers on the Nile: Nationalism, Communism, Islam, and the Egyptian Working Class, 1882–1914*. Princeton, NJ: Princeton University Press, 1987.

Ben-Amos, Avner. *Funerals, Politics and Memory in Modern France 1789–1996*. Oxford: Oxford University Press, 2000.

Boyle, Stephanie Anne. "Cholera, Colonialism, and Pilgrimage: Exploring Global/Local Exchange in the Central Egyptian Delta, 1848–1907." *Journal of World History* 26, no. 3 (2015): 581–604.

Brett, Michael. "Legislating for Inequality in Algeria: The Senatus-Consulte of 14 July 1865." *Bulletin of the School of Oriental and African Studies, University of London* 51, no. 3 (1988): 440–461.

Brock, Helene, and Catherine Crawford. "Forensic Medicine in Early Colonial Maryland, 1633–1683." In *Legal Medicine in History*, edited by Michael Clark and Catherine Crawford, 25–44. Cambridge: Cambridge University Press, 1994.

Brophy, Thomas J. "On Church Grounds: Political Funerals and the Contest to Lead Catholic Ireland." *Catholic Historical Review* 95, no. 3 (2009): 491–514.

Brown, Michael. "Medicine, Reform, and the 'End' of Charity in Early Nineteenth-Century England." *English Historical Review* 124, no. 511 (2009): 1353–1388.

Brown, Nathan. "The Precarious Life and Slow Death of the Mixed Courts of Egypt." *International Journal of Middle East Studies* 25, no. 1 (1993): 33–52.

Brown, Vincent. *The Reaper's Garden: Death and Power in the World of Atlantic Slavery*. Cambridge, MA: Harvard University Press, 2008.

Bullock, Steven, and Sheila McIntyre. "The Handsome Tokens of a Funeral: Glove-Giving and the Large Funeral in Eighteenth-Century New England." *William and Mary Quarterly* 69, no. 2 (2012): 305–346.

Burbank Jane, and Fred Cooper. *Empires in World History: Power and the Politics of Difference*. Princeton, NJ: Princeton University Press, 2010.

Burton, Julian L. "A Bite into the History of the Autopsy from Ancient Roots to Modern Decay." *Forensic Science, Medicine and Pathology* 1, no. 4 (2005): 277–284.

Campos, Michelle. *Ottoman Brothers: Muslims, Christians, and Jews in Early 20th-Century Palestine*. Stanford, CA: Stanford University Press, 2010.

Can, Lale. "The Protection Question: Central Asians and Extraterritoriality in the Late Ottoman Empire." *International Journal for Middle East Studies* 48, no. 4 (2016): 679–699.

Carmanati, Lucia. "Alexandria 1898: Nodes, Networks, and Scales in Nineteenth-

Century Egypt and the Mediterranean." *Comparative Studies in Society and History* 59 (January 2017): 127–153.

Chalcraft, John. *The Striking Cabbies of Cairo and Other Stories: Crafts and Guilds in Egypt, 1863–1914.* Albany: State University of New York Press, 2005.

Chaparro, Martina Will de, and Miruna Achim, eds. *Death and Dying in Colonial Spanish America.* Tucson: University of Arizona Press, 2011.

Cherry, S. "The Hospitals and Population Growth: The Voluntary General Hospitals, Mortality and Local Populations in the English Provinces in the Eighteenth and Nineteenth Centuries, Part I." *Population Studies* 34, no. 1 (1980): 59–75.

———. "The Hospitals and Population Growth: The Voluntary General Hospitals, Mortality and Local Populations in the English Provinces in the Eighteenth and Nineteenth Centuries, Part II." *Population Studies* 34, no. 2 (1980): 251–265.

Chesson, Meredith. "Social Memory, Identity and Death: An Introduction." In "Social Memory, Identity and Death: Anthropological Perspectives on Mortuary Rituals," special issue, *Archaeological Papers of the American Anthropological Society* 10, no. 1 (2001): 1–10.

Chopra, Preeti. *A Joint Enterprise: Indian Elites and the Making of British Bombay.* Minneapolis: University of Minnesota Press, 2011.

Clancy-Smith, Julia. *Mediterraneans: North Africa and Europe in an Age of Migration c. 1800–1900.* Berkeley: University of California Press, 2011.

Clark, Michael, and Catherine Crawford, eds. *Legal Medicine in History.* Cambridge: Cambridge University Press, 1994.

Cole, Juan. *Colonialism and Revolution in the Middle East: Social and Cultural Origins of Egypt's 'Urabi Movement.* Cairo: American University in Cairo Press, 1999.

Cooper, Fred. *Citizenship between Empire and Nation: Remaking France and French Africa, 1945–1960.* Princeton, NJ: Princeton University Press, 2014.

———. *Colonialism in Question: Theory, Knowledge, History.* Berkeley: University of California Press, 2005.

Cooper, Fred, and Ann Laura Stoler, eds. *Tensions of Empire: Colonial Culture in a Bourgeois World.* Berkeley: University of California Press, 1997.

Cooter, Roger, Mark Harrison, and Steve Sturdy, eds. *Medicine and Modern Warfare.* Amsterdam: Rodopi, 1999.

Cuno, Kenneth. *The Pasha's Peasants: Land, Society, and Economy in Lower Egypt, 1740–1858.* Cambridge: Cambridge University Press, 1992.

Cuno, Kenneth, and Michael Reimer. "The Census Registers of Nineteenth-Century Egypt: A New Source for Social Historians." *British Journal of Middle Eastern Studies* 24, no. 2 (1997): 193–216.

Curl, James Stevens. *The Victorian Celebration of Death.* Stroud, UK: Sutton Publishing, 2004.

Curtis, Sarah. "Charity Begins Abroad: The Filles de la Charite in the Ottoman Empire." In *In God's Empire: French Missionaries and the Modern World*, edited by Owen White and J. P. Daughton, 89–108. Oxford: Oxford University Press, 2012.

Cutler, Brock. "Believe in the Border, or How to Make Modernity in the Nineteenth-

Century Maghrib." *Journal for the Economic and Social History of the Orient* 60, no. 1–2 (2017): 83–114.

Daughton, J. P. *An Empire Divided: Religion, Republicanism, and the Making of French Colonialism, 1880–1914*. Oxford: Oxford University Press, 2006.

de Dreuzy, Agnes. *The Holy See and the Emergence of the Modern Middle East: Benedict XV's Diplomacy in Greater Syria (1914–1922)*. Washington, DC: Catholic University of America Press, 2016.

Derr, Jennifer. "Labor-Time: Ecological Bodies and Agricultural Labor in 19th- and early 20th-Century Egypt." *International Journal of Middle East Studies* 50, no. 2 (2018): 195–212.

DiGirolama, Vincent. "Newsboy Funerals: Tales of Sorrow and Solidarity in Urban America." *Journal of Social History* 36, no. 1 (2002): 5–30.

Driessen, Henk. "Mediterranean Port Cities: Cosmopolitanism Reconsidered." *History and Anthropology* 16, no. 1 (2005): 129–141.

Dubisch, Jill. "Death and Social Change in Greece." *Anthropological Quarterly* 62, no. 4 (1989): 189–200.

Dubois, Laurent. *A Colony of Citizens: Revolution and Slave Emancipation in the French Caribbean, 1787–1804*. Chapel Hill: University of North Carolina Press, 2004.

Durrell, Lawrence. *The Alexandria Quartet*. New York: Dutton, 1962.

Eldem, Edhem. "The French *Nation* of Constantinople in the Eighteenth Century as Reflected in the Saints Peter and Paul Paris Records, 1740–1800." In *French Mediterraneans: Transnational and Imperial Histories*, edited by Patricia Lorcin and Todd Shepard, 131–167. Lincoln: University of Nebraska Press, 2016.

Ellis, Matthew. "Anomalous Egypt? Rethinking Egyptian Sovereignty at the Western Periphery." In *The Long 1890s in Egypt: Colonial Quiescence and Subterranean Resistance*, edited by Marilyn Booth and Anthony Gorman, 169–194. Edinburgh: Edinburgh University Press, 2014.

———. *Desert Borderland: The Making of Modern Egypt and Libya*. Stanford, CA: Stanford University Press, 2018.

Ener, Mine. *Managing Egypt's Poor and the Politics of Benevolence, 1800–1952*. Princeton, NJ: Princeton University Press, 2003.

Fahmy, Khaled. *All the Pasha's Men*. Cambridge: Cambridge University Press, 1998.

———. "The Anatomy of Justice: Forensic Medicine and Criminal Law in Nineteenth-Century Egypt." *Islamic Law and Society* 6, no. 2 (1999): 224–271.

———. "The Essence of Alexandria Part I." *Manifesta Journal* 14 (January 2012): 64–72.

———. "The Essence of Alexandria Part II." *Manifesta Journal* 16 (December 2012): 22–27.

———. "For Cavafy with Love and Squalor: Some Critical Notes on the History and Historiography of Modern Alexandria." In *Alexandria, Real and Imagined*, edited by Anthony Hirst and Michael Silk, 263–280. London: Ashgate, 2004.

———. "Medicine and Power: Towards a Social History of Medicine in Nineteenth-Century Egypt." *Cairo Papers in Social Science* 23, no. 2 (2000): 15–62.

———. "Towards a Social History of Modern Alexandria." In *Alexandria, Real and Imagined*, edited by Anthony Hirst and Michael Silk, 281–306. London: Ashgate, 2004.

———. "Women, Medicine and Power in Nineteenth-Century Egypt." In *Remaking Women: Feminism and Modernity in the Middle East*, edited by Lila Abu-Lughod, 35–72. Princeton, NJ: Princeton University Press, 1998.

Fahmy, Ziad. "Jurisdictional Borderlands: Extraterritoriality and 'Legal Chameleons' in Pre-colonial Alexandria, 1840–1870." *Comparative Studies in Society and History* 55 (April 2013): 305–329.

———. *Ordinary Egyptians: Creating the Modern Nation through Popular Culture.* Stanford, CA: Stanford University Press, 2011.

Faust, Drew Gilpin. *The Republic of Suffering: Death and the American Civil War.* New York: Alfred A. Knopf, 2008.

Fenton, Tom. "The Day They Buried the Ayatollah." *Iranian Studies* 41, no. 2 (2008): 241–246.

Fisher, Michael H. "Excluding and Including 'Natives of India,' Early Nineteenth-Century British-Indian Race Relations in India." *Comparative Studies of South Asia and the Middle East* 27, no. 2 (2007): 303–314.

Flaks, James. "The Death of the Monarch as Colonial Sacrament." In *Death and Dying in Colonial Spanish America*, edited by Martina Will de Chaparro and Miruna Achim, 100–120. Tucson: University of Arizona Press, 2011.

Forster, E. M. *Alexandria: A History and a Guide; and Pharos and Pharillon.* Edited by Miriam Allot. Cairo: American University in Cairo Press, 2004.

Foster, Elizabeth. *Faith in Empire: Religion, Politics, and Colonial Rule in French Senegal, 1880–1940.* Stanford, CA: Stanford University Press, 2013.

Foucault, Michel. "Of Other Spaces." Translated by Jay Miskowiec. *Diacritics* 16, no. 1 (1986): 22–27.

Fox, Richard Wightman. *Lincoln's Body: A Cultural History.* New York: W. W. Norton, 2015.

Freundschuh, Aaron. *The Courtesan and the Gigolo: The Murders in Rue Montaigne and the Dark Side of Empire in Nineteenth-Century Paris.* Stanford, CA: Stanford University Press, 2017.

Fuhrmann, Malte. "Cosmopolitan Imperialists and the Ottoman Port Cities: Conflicting Logics in the Urban Social Fabric." *Cahiers de la Méditerranée* 67 (December 2003): 149–163.

Gasper, Michael. *The Power of Representation: Publics, Peasants, and Islam in Egypt.* Stanford, CA: Stanford University Press, 2009.

Gewald, Jan-Bart. "Flags, Funerals and Fanfares: Herero and Missionary Contestations of the Acceptable, 1900–1940." *Journal of African Cultural Studies* 15, no. 1 (2002): 105–117.

Gitre, Carmen. *Acting Egyptian: Theater and Identity in Cairo, 1869–1930.* Austin: University of Texas Press, 2019.

Goldschmidt, Arthur, Jr., and Robert Johnston. *Historical Dictionary of Egypt.* Rev. ed. Cairo: American University in Cairo Press, 2004.

Gorman, Anthony. "Internationalist Thought, Local Practice: Life and Death in the Anarchist Movement in 1890s Egypt." In *The Long 1890s in Egypt: Colonial Quiescence, Subterranean Resistance*, edited by Marilyn Booth and Anthony Gorman, 222–252. Edinburgh: University of Edinburgh Press, 2014.

———. "The Italians of Egypt: Return to Diaspora." In *Diasporas of the Middle East: Contextualizing Community*, edited by Anthony Gorman and Sossie Kasbarian, 138–170. Edinburgh: Edinburgh University Press, 2015.

Gorsky, Martin, and Sally Sheard, eds. *Financing Medicine: The British Experience since 1750*. New York: Routledge, 2006.

Gott, Suzanne. "'Onetouch' Quality and 'Marriage Silver Cup': Performative Display, Cosmopolitanism, and Marital Poatwa in Kumasi Funerals." *Africa Today* 54, no. 2, (2007): 79–106.

Gourdon, Vincent, Catherine Rollet, and Madeleine Grieve. "Stillbirths in Nineteenth-Century Paris: Social, Legal, and Medical Implications of a Statistical Category." *Population* (English ed.) 64, no. 4 (2009): 601–634.

Haag, Michael. *Alexandria: City of Memory*. Cairo: American University in Cairo Press, 2004.

Hakim, Carol. *The Origins of the Lebanese National Idea 1840–1920*. Berkeley: University of California Press, 2013.

Halevi, Leor. *Muhammad's Grave: Death Rites and the Making of Islamic Society*. New York: Columbia University Press, 2007.

Halim, Hala. *Alexandrian Cosmopolitanism: An Archive*. New York: Fordham University Press, 2013.

Hammad, Hanan. "Regulating Sexuality: The Colonial-National Struggle over Prostitution after the British Invasion of Egypt." In *The Long 1890s in Egypt: Colonial Quiescence and Subterranean Resistance*, edited by Marilyn Booth and Anthony Gorman, 195–221. Edinburgh: Edinburgh University Press, 2014.

Hanley, Will. "Cosmopolitan Cursing in Late Nineteenth-Century Alexandria." In *Cosmopolitanisms in Muslim Contexts: Perspectives from the Past*, edited by Derryl MacLean and Sikeena Karmali Ahmed, 92–104. Edinburgh: University of Edinburgh Press, 2012.

———. "Grieving Cosmopolitanism in Middle East Studies." *History Compass* 6, no. 5 (2008): 1346–1367.

———. *Identifying with Nationality: Europeans, Ottomans, and Egyptians in Alexandria*. New York: Columbia University Press, 2017.

Harrison, Mark, Margaret Jones, and Helen Sweet, eds. *From Western Medicine to Global Medicine: The Hospital beyond the West*. New Delhi, India: Orient Blackswan, 2009.

Harvey, David. *Justice, Nature and the Geography of Difference*. Manchester, UK: Blackwell Publishing, 1996.

Hassoun, Jacques. "The Jews, a Community of Contrasts." In *Alexandria 1860–1960: The Brief Life of a Cosmopolitan Community*, edited by Robert Ilbert and Ilios Yannakakis, translated by Colin Clement, 36–52. Alexandria: Harpocrates Publishing, 1997.

Hawas, May. "How Not to Write about Cosmopolitan Alexandria." *Politics/Letters* 13 (May 2018). http://politicsslashletters.org/not-write-cosmopolitan-alexandria/#_edn2.

Ho, Engseng. *The Graves of Tarim: Genealogy and Mobility across the Indian Ocean.* Berkeley: University of California Press, 2006.

Hodes, Martha. *Mourning Lincoln.* New Haven, CT: Yale University Press, 2015.

Hourani, Albert. *Minorities in the Arab World.* London: Oxford University Press, 1947.

Huber, Valeska. *Channelling Mobilities: Migration and Globalisation in the Suez Canal Region and Beyond, 1869–1914.* Cambridge: Cambridge University Press, 2013.

Ibrahim, Vivian. "Legitimising Lay and State Authority: Challenging the Coptic Church in Late Nineteenth-Century Egypt." In *The Long 1890s in Egypt: Colonial Quiescence and Subterranean Resistance,* edited by Marilyn Booth and Anthony Gorman, 117–140. Edinburgh: Edinburgh University Press, 2014.

Ilbert, Robert. *Alexandrie 1830–1930: Histoire d'une Communauté Citadine.* 2 vols. Cairo: Institut Français d'Archéologie Orientale, 1996.

———. "A Certain Sense of Citizenship." In *Alexandria 1860–1960: The Brief Life of a Cosmopolitan Community,* edited by Robert Ilbert and Ilios Yannakakis, translated by Colin Clement, 18–34. Alexandria: Harpocrates Publishing, 1997.

Ilbert, Robert, and Ilios Yannakakis, eds. *Alexandria 1860–1960: The Brief Life of a Cosmopolitan Community.* Translated by Colin Clement. Alexandria: Harpocrates Publishing, 1997.

Imhof, Arthur. "The Hospital in the 18th Century: For Whom? The Charite Hospital in Berlin, the Navy Hospital in Copenhagen, the Kongsberg Hospital in Norway." *Journal of Social History* 10, no. 4 (1977): 448–470.

Iseminger, Gordon. "The Old Turkish Hands: The British Levantine Consuls, 1856–1876." *Middle East Journal* 22, no. 3 (1968): 297–316.

Jackson, Mark. "Suspicious Infant Deaths: The Statute of 1624 and Medical Evidence at Coroners' Inquests." In *Legal Medicine in History,* edited by Michael Clark and Catherine Crawford, 64–86. Cambridge: Cambridge University Press, 1994.

Jagailloux, Serge. *La Medecine Moderne en Egypte de Bonaparte au XXeme Siecle 1798–1988.* Alexandria: Centre d'Etudes d'Alexandrie (Foundation Gaston Zananiri), 1989.

Jakes, Aaron. *Colonial Economism: Financialization, British Rule, and the Crisis of Capitalism in Egypt 1882–1922.* Stanford, CA: Stanford University Press, forthcoming.

———. "The Scales of Public Utility: Agricultural Roads and State Space in the Era of the British Occupation." In *The Long 1890s in Egypt: Colonial Quiescence and Subterranean Resistance,* edited by Marilyn Booth and Anthony Gorman, 57–86. Edinburgh: Edinburgh University Press, 2014.

Jalland, Pat. *Death in the Victorian Family.* New York: Oxford University Press, 1996.

Jasanoff, Maya. "Cosmopolitan: A Tale of Identity from Ottoman Alexandria. *Common Knowledge* 11, no. 3 (2005): 393–409.

Jindra, Michael, and Joël Noret, eds. *Funerals in Africa: Explorations of a Social Phenomenon.* New York: Berghan Books, 2013.

Johnson, Ryan, and Amna Khalid, eds. *Public Health in the British Empire: Intermedi-*

aries, Subordinates, and the Practice of Public Health, 1850–1960. New York: Routledge, 2012.

Jones, Colin. *The Charitable Imperative: Hospitals and Nursing in Ancien Regime and Revolutionary France*. New York: Routledge, 1989.

Kalmbach, Hilary. "Training Teachers How to Teach: Transnational Exchange and the Introduction of Social-Scientific Pedagogy in 1890s Egypt." In *The Long 1890s in Egypt: Colonial Quiescence and Subterranean Resistance*, edited by Marilyn Booth and Anthony Gorman, 87–116. Edinburgh: Edinburgh University Press, 2014.

Kaminsky, Uwe. "German 'Home Mission' Abroad: The *Orientarbeit* of the Deaconess Institution Kaiserwerth in the Ottoman Empire." In *New Faith in Ancient Lands: Western Missions in the Middle East in the Nineteenth and Early Twentieth Centuries*, edited by Heleen Murre-Van Den Berg, 191–209. Boston: Brill Academic Publishers, 2006.

Karus-Friedberg, Chana. "Across the Pacific: Transnational Context in the Japanese Plantation Workers' Cemetery in Pahala, Hawai'i." *International Journal of Historical Archaeology* 15, no. 3 (2011): 381–408.

Kazamias, Alexander. "Cromer's Assault on 'Internationalism': British Colonialism and the Greeks of Egypt, 1882–1907." In *The Long 1890s in Egypt: Colonial Quiescence and Subterranean Resistance*, edited by Marilyn Booth and Anthony Gorman, 253–284. Edinburgh: Edinburgh University Press, 2014.

Kedourie, Elie. "The Death of Adib Ishaq." *Middle Eastern Studies* 9, no. 1 (1973): 95–109.

Kellehear, Allan. *A Social History of Dying*. Cambridge: Cambridge University Press, 2007.

Keller, Richard. *Colonial Madness: Psychiatry in French North Africa*. Chicago: University of Chicago Press, 2007.

Kelly, Catherine. *War and the Militarization of British Army Medicine, 1793–1830*. London: Pickering and Chatto, 2011.

Khuri-Makdisi, Ilham. *The Eastern Mediterranean and the Making of Global Radicalism, 1860–1914*. Berkeley: University of California Press, 2013.

Kiest, Karen S. "Czech Cemeteries in Nebraska from 1868: Cultural Imprints on the Prairie." In *Ethnicity and the American Cemetery*, edited by Richard Meyer, 77–103. Bowling Green, OH: Bowling Green State University Popular Press, 1993.

Kitroeff, Alexander. *The Greeks in Egypt 1919–1937: Ethnicity and Class*. St. Antony's Middle East Monographs No. 20. Oxford: Ithaca Press, 1989.

Kozma, Liat. *Policing Egyptian Women: Sex, Law, and Medicine in Khedival Egypt*. Syracuse, NY: Syracuse University Press, 2011.

Krämer, Gudrun. *The Jews in Modern Egypt, 1914–1952*. Seattle: University of Washington Press, 1989.

Kreiger, Martin. "Dutch Cemeteries in South India." In *Mediating Netherlandish Art and Material Culture in Asia*, edited by Thomas DaCosta Kaufmann and Michael North, 83–94. Amsterdam: Amsterdam University Press, 2014.

Kselman, Thomas A. *Death and the Afterlife in Modern France*. Princeton, NJ: Princeton University Press, 1993.

Kuhnke, LaVerne. *Lives at Risk: Public Health in Nineteenth-Century Egypt*. Berkeley: University of California, 1990.

Lambert, David, and Alan Lester. *Colonial Lives across the British Empire: Imperial Careering in the Long Nineteenth Century*. Cambridge: Cambridge University Press, 2006.

Landau, Jacob. "Prolegomena to a Study of Secret Societies in Modern Egypt." *Middle Eastern Studies* 1, no. 2 (1965): 135–186.

Lane, Edward William. *An Account of the Manners and Customs of the Modern Egyptians*. London: J. M. Dent and Sons, 1908.

Laqueur, Thomas. *The Work of the Dead: A Cultural History of Mortal Remains*. Princeton, NJ: Princeton University Press, 2016.

Lazarev, Anouchka. "Italians, Italianity, and Fascism." In *Alexandria 1860–1960: The Brief Life of a Cosmopolitan Community*, edited by Robert Ilbert and Ilios Yannakakis, translated by Colin Clement, 72–84. Alexandria: Harpocrates Publishing, 1997.

Lefebvre, Henri. *The Production of Space*. Translated by Donald Nicholson Smith. Oxford: Blackwell, 1991.

Lessersohn, Nora. "'Provincial Cosmopolitanism' in Late Ottoman Anatolia: An Armenian Shoemaker's Memoir." *Comparative Studies in Society and History* 57, no. 2 (2015): 528–556.

Lester, Alan. "Imperial Circuits and Networks." *History Compass* 4, no. 1 (2006): 124–141.

Lewis, Mary Dewhurst. *Divided Rule: Sovereignty and Empire in French Tunisia 1881–1938*. Berkeley: University of California Press, 2014.

Lim, Patricia. *Forgotten Souls: A Social History of the Hong Kong Cemetery*. Hong Kong: Hong Kong University Press, 2011.

Lorcin, Patricia, and Todd Shepard, eds. *French Mediterraneans: Transnational and Imperial Histories*. Lincoln: University of Nebraska Press, 2016.

Loveman, Mara. "Blinded like a State: The Revolt against Civil Registration in Nineteenth-Century Brazil." *Studies in Society and History* 49, no. 1 (2007): 5–39.

———. "The Modern State and the Primitive Accumulation of Symbolic Power." *American Journal of Sociology* 110, no. 6 (2005): 1651–1683.

Mabro, Robert. "Alexandria 1860–1960: The Cosmopolitan Identity." In *Alexandria, Real and Imagined*, edited by Anthony Hirst and Michael Silk, 247–262. London: Ashgate, 2004.

Máire, Byrne, and Larkin Rita. "Churchyard and Cemetery Sculpture." In *Art and Architecture of Ireland*, vol. 3, *Sculpture 1600–2000*, edited by Andrew Carpenter and Murphy Paula, 401–406. Dublin: Royal Irish Academy, 2015.

Mak, Lanver. *The British in Egypt: Community, Crime and Crisis 1882–1922*. London: I. B. Tauris, 2012.

Makdisi, Ussama. *The Culture of Sectarianism: Community, History, and Violence in*

Nineteenth-Century Ottoman Lebanon. Berkeley: University of California Press, 2000.

Malone, Hannah. "New Life in the Modern Cultural History of Death." *The Historical Journal* (2018): 1–20. doi:10.1017/S0018246X18000444.

Mansel, Phillip. *Levant: Splendour and Catastrophe on the Mediterranean.* New Haven, CT: Yale University Press, 2010.

Marcus, Abraham. *The Middle East on the Eve of Modernity: Aleppo in the Eighteenth Century.* New York: Columbia University Press, 1989.

Marglin, Jessica. *Across Legal Lines: Jews and Muslims in Modern Morocco.* New Haven, CT: Yale University Press, 2016.

Marsot, Afaf Lufti al-Sayyid. *Egypt's Liberal Experiment 1922–1936.* Berkeley: University of California Press, 1977.

Martinez-Fernandez, Luis. "'Don't Die Here': The Death and Burial of Protestants in the Hispanic Caribbean, 1840–1885." *The Americas* 49, no. 1 (1992): 23–47.

Mazower, Mark. *Salonica, City of Ghosts: Christians, Muslims, and Jews, 1430–1950.* New York: Vintage Books, 2004.

Mazza, Roberto. *Jerusalem: From the Ottomans to the British.* London: I. B. Tauris, 2009.

McCoan, J. C. *Egypt.* New York: P. F. Collier and Son, 1902.

McDougall, James. *A History of Algeria.* Cambridge: Cambridge University Press, 2017.

Meinardus, Otto F. A. *Christians in Egypt: Orthodox, Catholic, and Protestant Communities Past and Present.* Cairo: American University in Cairo Press, 2006.

Meyer, Richard, ed. *Ethnicity and the American Cemetery.* Bowling Green, OH: Bowling Green State University Press, 1993.

Minkin, Shane. "Documenting Death: Inquests, Governance and Belonging in 1890s Alexandria." In *The Long 1890s in Egypt: Colonial Quiescence and Subterranean Resistance*, edited by Marilyn Booth and Anthony Gorman, 31–56. Edinburgh: Edinburgh University Press, 2014.

———. "History from Six-Feet Below: Death Studies and the Field of Modern Middle East History." *History Compass* 11, no. 8 (2013): 632–646.

———. "Simone's Funeral: Egyptian Lives, Jewish Deaths in Twenty-First-Century Cairo." *Rethinking History: The Journal of Theory and Practice* 16, no. 1 (2012): 71–89.

Mitchell, Timothy. *Colonising Egypt.* Berkeley: University of California Press, 1988.

Mubarak, 'Ali. *Al-Khitat al-Tawfiqiyya al-Jadida.* Vol. 7, *Midinat Iskandariyya.* Cairo: Dar al-kutub wa-l-watha'iq al-qawmiyya, 2005.

al-Muwaylihi, Muhammad. *Hadith 'Isa ibn Hisham* [The story of 'Isa ibn Hisham]. Translated by Roger Allen. In *A Period of Time: A Study and Translation of Hadith 'Isa ibn Hisham Muhammad al Muwaylihi*, by Roger Allen. Oxford: St. Antony's College Middle East Centre, 1992.

Necipoglu, Gulru. "Dynastic Imprints on the Cityscape: The Collective Message of Imperial Funerary Complexes in Istanbul." In *Cimetières et Traditions Funeraires dans le Monde Islamique*, edited by Jean-Louis Bacqué-Grammont and Aksel Tibet, 2:23–36. Ankara: Turk Tarih Kurumu Basimevi, 1996.

Nelson, Sioban. *Say Little, Do Much: Nursing, Nuns, and Hospitals in the Nineteenth Century*. Philadelphia: University of Pennsylvania Press, 2001.

Nirenberg, David. *Communities of Violence: Persecution of Minorities in the Middle Ages*. Princeton, NJ: Princeton University Press, 1996.

Nissel, Muriel. *People Count: A History of the General Register Office*. London: Office of Population Censuses and Surveys, Her Majesty's Stationery Office, 1987.

Noorani, Yaseen. "A Nation Born in Mourning: The Neoclassical Funeral Elegy in Egypt." *Journal of Arabic Literature* 28, no. 1 (1997): 38–67.

Olwig, Karen Fog. "A Proper Funeral: Contextualizing Community among Caribbean Migrants." *Journal of the Royal Anthropological Institute* 15, no. 3 (2009): 520–537.

Omar, Hussein. "'And I Saw No Reason to Chronicle My Life': Tensions of Nationalist Modernity in the Memoirs of Fathallah Pasha Barakat." In *The Long 1890s in Egypt: Colonial Quiescence and Subterranean Resistance*, edited by Marilyn Booth and Anthony Gorman, 287–314. Edinburgh: Edinburgh University Press, 2014.

———. "'Snatched by Destiny's Hand': Obituaries and the Making of Class in Modern Egypt." *History Compass* 15, no. 6 (2017). https://onlinelibrary.wiley.com/doi/abs/10.1111/hic3.12380.

Owen, Roger. *Cotton and the Egyptian Economy: A Study in Trade and Development*. Oxford: Clarendon Press, 1969.

———. *Lord Cromer: Victorian Imperialist, Edwardian Proconsul*. Oxford: Oxford University Press, 2004.

———. *The Middle East in the World Economy 1800–1914*. London: I. B. Tauris, 2002.

Pamuk, Orhan. *Istanbul: Memories and the City*. Translated by Maureen Freely. New York: Alfred A. Knopf, 2005.

Peckham, Robert, and David Pomfret, eds. *Imperial Contagions: Medicine, Hygiene, and Cultures of Planning in Asia*. Hong Kong: Hong Kong University Press, 2013.

Philipp, Thomas. *The Syrians in Egypt 1725–1975*. Stuttgart: Franz Steiner Verlag Wiesbaden GMBH, 1985.

Platt, D. C. M. *The Cinderella Service: British Consuls since 1825*. London: Longman Group, 1971.

Podoler, Guy. "Death as a Nationalist Text: Reading the National Cemetery of South Korea." In *Death, Mourning, and the Afterlife in Korea: Ancient to Contemporary Times*, edited by Charlotte Horlyck and Michael Pettid, 112–133. Honolulu: University of Hawai'i Press, 2014.

Pollard, Lisa. "Egyptian by Association: Charitable States and Service Societies, circa 1850–1945." *International Journal of Middle East Studies* 46, no. 2 (2014): 239–257.

———. *Nurturing the Nation: The Family Politics of Modernizing, Colonizing, and Liberating Egypt, 1805–1923*. Berkeley: University of California Press, 2005.

Puente, Julius. "The Nature of the Consular Establishment." *University of Pennsylvania Law Review and American Law Register* 78, no. 3 (1930): 321–345.

Raafat, Samir. "A Snapshot of Egypt's Postal History." *Egyptian Mail*, December 3, 1994.

Ranger, Terrence. "A Decent Death: Changes in Funerary Rites in Bulawayo." In *Funerals in Africa: Explorations of a Social Phenomenon*, edited by Michael Jindra and Joël Noret, 41–68. New York: Berghan Books, 2013.

Rastegar, Kamran. *Literary Modernity between the Middle East and Europe: Textual Transactions in Arabic, English, and Persian Literature*. New York: Routledge, 2007.

Reimer, Michael. *Colonial Bridgehead: Government and Society in Alexandria 1807–1882*. Cairo: American University in Cairo Press, 1997.

Reynolds, Nancy. *A City Consumed: Urban Commerce, the Cairo Fire, and the Politics of Decolonization in Egypt*. Stanford, CA: Stanford University Press, 2012.

Rifaʿat al-Imam, Muhammad. *Al-Arman fi Misr: Al-qarn at-tasiʿ ʿashar*. Cairo: Nubar l-il-tibaʿa, 1995.

———. *Al-Arman fi Misr: 1896–1961*. Cairo: Nubar l-il-tibaʿa, 2003.

———. *Tarikh al-Jalia al-ʿArmaniyya fi Misr*. Cairo: Al-amiyya al-Misriyya al-ʿamma li-l-kitab, 1999.

Roberts, Nicholas. *Islam under the Palestine Mandate: Colonialism and the Supreme Muslim Council*. London: I. B. Tauris, 2016.

Robertson, J. M. *A History of Free Thought in the Nineteenth Century*. Vol. 2. New York: G. M. Putnam's Sons, 1930.

Robinson, Ronald, and John Gallagher, with Alice Denny. *Africa and the Victorians*. London: Macmillan, 1981.

Rosenberg, Charles. "And Heal the Sick: The Hospital and the Patient in Nineteenth-Century America." *Journal of Social History* 10, no. 4 (1977): 428–447.

———. *The Care of Strangers: The Rise of America's Hospital System*. Baltimore: Johns Hopkins University Press, 1993.

Rosenow, Michael. *Death and Dying in the Working Class, 1865–1920*. Urbana: University of Illinois Press, 2015.

Rothman, E. Nathalie. *Brokering Empire: Trans-imperial Subjects between Venice and Istanbul*. Ithaca, NY: Cornell University Press, 2012.

Rugg, Julie. *Churchyard and Cemetery: Tradition and Modernity in Rural North Yorkshire*. Manchester, UK: Manchester University Press, 2013.

Russell, Mona. *Creating the New Egyptian Woman: Consumerism, Education, and National Identity 1863–1922*. New York: Palgrave Macmillan, 2004.

Said, Edward. *Orientalism*. New York: Pantheon Books, 1978.

Saul, Samir. *La France et L'Egypte de 1882 à 1914: Intérêts Économiques et Implications Politiques*. Paris: Ministère de l'Économie, des Finances et de l'Industrie, 1997.

Schlöch, Alexander. *Egypt for the Egyptians! The Socio-political Crisis in Egypt, 1878–1882*. Oxford: Ithaca Press, 1981.

Schreier, Joshua. *Arabs of the Jewish Faith: The Civilizing Mission in Colonial Algeria*. New Brunswick, NJ: Rutgers University Press, 2010.

————. *The Merchants of Oran: A Jewish Port at the Dawn of Empire.* Stanford, CA: Stanford University Press, 2017.

Shalabi, Hilmi Ahmad. *Al-'aqaliyat al-'irqiyyah fi Misr fi al-qarn at-tasi' 'ashar.* Cairo: Maktabat an-nahda al-Misriyya, 1992.

Shields, Sarah. *Fezzes in the River: Identity Politics and European Diplomacy in the Middle East on the Eve of World War II.* Oxford: Oxford University Press, 2011.

Sim, Joe, and Anthony Ward. "The Magistrate of the Poor? Coroners and Deaths in Custody in Nineteenth-Century England." In *Legal Medicine in History,* edited by Michael Clark and Catherine Crawford, 245–267. Cambridge: Cambridge University Press, 1994.

Sonbol, Amira. *The Creation of a Medical Profession in Egypt, 1800–1922.* Syracuse, NY: Syracuse University Press, 1991.

Starr, Deborah. *Remembering Cosmopolitan Egypt: Literature, Culture, and Empire.* New York: Routledge, 2009.

Stein, Sarah Abrevaya. "Dreyfus in the Sahara: Jews, Trans-Saharan Commerce, and Southern Algeria under French Colonial Rule." In *French Mediterraneans: Transnational and Imperial Histories,* edited by Patricia Lorcin and Todd Shepard, 265–292. Lincoln: University of Nebraska Press, 2016.

————. "Protected Persons? The Baghdadi Jewish Diaspora, the British State, and the Persistence of Empire." *American Historical Review* 116, no. 1 (2011): 80–108.

————. *Saharan Jews and the Fate of French Algeria.* Chicago: University of Chicago Press, 2014.

Sulayman, Muhammad. *Al-ajanib fi Misr, 1922–1952: Dirasa fi tarikh Misr al-ijtima'i.* Cairo: 'Ayn li-l-dirasa al-ijtima'iyya wa-l-insaniyya, 1996.

Szreter, Simon. "Children with a (Local) State: Identity Registration at Birth in English History since 1538." In *Children without a State: A Global Human Rights Challenge,* edited by Jacqueline Bhabha, 331–351. Boston: MIT Press, 2011.

Thomas, Martin, and Richard Toye. *Arguing about Empire: Imperial Rhetoric in Britain and France, 1882–1956.* Oxford: Oxford University Press, 2017.

Thomas, Nicholas. *Colonialism's Culture: Anthropology, Travel, and Government.* Princeton, NJ: Princeton University Press, 1994.

Thompson, Elizabeth. *Colonial Citizens: Republic Rights, Paternal Privilege, and Gender in French Syria and Lebanon.* New York: Columbia University Press, 1999.

Thompson, Jason. "Edward Lane in Egypt." *Journal of the American Research Center in Egypt* 34 (1997): 243–261.

Tignor, Robert. *Modernization and the British Colonial State.* Princeton, NJ: Princeton University Press, 1966.

Todd, David. "Beneath Sovereignty: Extraterritoriality and Imperial Internationalism in Nineteenth-Century Egypt." *Law and History Review* 36, no. 1 (2018): 105–137.

————. "Transnational Projects of Empire in France c. 1815–1870." *Modern Intellectual History* 12, no. 2 (2015): 265–293.

Tombs, Robert, and Isabelle Tombs. *That Sweet Enemy, Britain and France: The History of a Love-Hate Relationship.* New York: Vintage Books, 2008.

Trice, Tom. "Rites of Protest: Populist Funerals in Imperial St. Petersburg, 1876–1878." *Slavic Review* 60, no. 1 (2001): 50–74.

Troutt Powell, Eve. *A Different Shade of Colonialism: Egypt, Great Britain, and the Mastery of the Sudan*. Berkeley: University of California Press, 2003.

Tzortzopoulou-Gregory, Lita. "Remembering and Forgetting: The Relationship between Memory and the Abandonment of Graves in Nineteenth- and Twentieth-Century Greek Cemeteries." *International Journal of Historical Archaeology* 14, no. 2 (2010): 285–301.

Vatikiotis, P. J. *The Modern History of Egypt*. New York: Frederick A. Praeger, 1969.

Verdery, Katherine. *The Political Lives of Dead Bodies: Reburial and Postsocialist Change*. New York: Columbia University Press, 1999.

Vitalis, Robert. *When Capitalists Collide: Business Conflict and the End of Empire in Egypt*. Berkeley: University of California Press, 1995.

Warren, Adam. "Medicine and the Dead: Conflicts over Burial Reform and Piety in Lima, 1808–1850." In *Death and Dying in Colonial Spanish America*, edited by Martina Will de Chaparro and Miruna Achim, 170–202. Tucson: University of Arizona Press, 2011.

Wein, Peter. "The Long and Intricate Funeral of Yasin al-Hashimi: Pan-Arabism, Civil Religion, and Popular Nationalism in Damascus, 1937." *International Journal of Middle Eastern Studies* 43, no. 2 (2011): 271–292.

Whidden, Jamie. *Egypt: British Colony and Imperial Capital*. Manchester, UK: Manchester University Press, 2017.

White, Benjamin. *The Emergence of Minorities in the Middle East: The Politics of Community in French Mandate Syria*. Edinburgh: Edinburgh University Press, 2011.

White, Henry. "Consular Reforms." *North American Review* 159, no. 457 (1894): 711–721.

White, Owen, and J. P. Daughton. *In God's Empire: French Missionaries and the Modern World*. Oxford: Oxford University Press, 2012.

Wilder, Gary. *The French Imperial Nation-State: Negritude and Colonial Humanism between the Two World Wars*. Chicago: University of Chicago Press, 2005.

Willis, John. "Governing the Living and the Dead: Mecca and the Emergence of the Saudi Biopolitical State." *American Historical Review* 122, no. 2 (2017): 346–370.

Wilson, Christopher. "Representing National Identity and Memory in the Mausoleum of Mustafa Kemal Ataturk." *Journal of the Society of Architectural Historians* 68, no. 2 (2009): 224–253.

Wissa, Karim. "Freemasonry in Egypt 1798–1921: A Study in Cultural and Political Encounters." *Bulletin (British Society for Middle Eastern Studies)* 16, no. 2 (1989): 143–161.

Yannakakis, Ilios. "Farewell Alexandria." In *Alexandria 1860–1960: The Brief Life of a Cosmopolitan Community*, edited by Robert Ilbert and Ilios Yannakakis, translated by Colin Clement, 106–122. Alexandria: Harpocrates Publishing, 1997.

Zubaida, Sami. "Cosmopolitanism and the Middle East." In *Cosmopolitanism, Identity and Authenticity in the Middle East*, edited by Roel Meijer, 15–34. New York: Routledge, 2013.

INDEX